D1564585

Muslim
National Communism
in the
Soviet Union

**Publications of the Center for
Middle Eastern Studies, Number 11**
Richard L. Chambers, General Editor

Alexandre A.
Bennigsen
S. Enders Wimbush

Muslim National Communism in the Soviet Union

A Revolutionary Strategy for the Colonial World

Товарищи Мусульмане! Под зеленым знаменем Пророка шли вы завоевывать ваши степи, ваши аулы. Враги народа отняли у вас родные поля. Ныне под красным знаменем Рабоче-Крестьянской революции под звездой армии всех угнетенных и трудящихся собирайтесь с востока и запада, с севера и юга. В седла товарищи! Все в полки Всевобуч!

ОБРАЩАЙТЕСЬ ЗА СПРАВКАМИ
ИНСПЕКЦИЯ

Кавалерийские Формировочный Центр Упр. Всевобуч.
Всеросс. Глава Штаба.
Москва, Малый Ржевский, 3.

D. MOOR.

The University of Chicago Press
Chicago and London

50106

Alexandre A. Bennigsen is director of studies in the
social sciences at the Ecole des Hautes Etudes en
Sciences Sociales, University of Paris, and visit-
ing professor of history at the University of
Chicago. He is the author of numerous books.

S. Enders Wimbush, a social science associate of
the Rand Corporation, is the author of several
scholarly articles.

Russian revolutionary posters are taken from
Viacheslav Polonskii, ed., *Russkii revoliutsionnyi
plakat* (Moscow, 1925), and Fritz Mierau, ed.,
Links! Links! Links! (Berlin, 1970), both kindly
lent by A. L. de Saint-Rat.

The University of Chicago Press, Chicago 60637
The University of Chicago Press, Ltd., London

Library of Congress Cataloging in Publication Data

Bennigsen, Alexandre.
  Muslim national communism in the Soviet Union.

  (Publications of the Center for Middle Eastern
Studies; no. 11)
  Bibliography: p.
  Includes index.
  1. Communism—Russia—History. 2. Nation-
alism and socialism. 3. Muslims in Russia.
I. Wimbush, S. Enders, joint author. II. Title.
III. Series: Chicago. University. Center for Middle
Eastern Studies. Publications; no. 11.
HX313.B42   335.43'0947   78–8608
ISBN 0–226–04235–9

To the memory of Mir-Said Sultan Galiev and his comrades, who sought national independence in revolution but who died fighting that same revolution to preserve their freedom.

Contents

50106

**Photo section following
page 86**

Acknowledgments

This book was completed under the auspices of the Project on Nation Building and National Integration in the USSR, which was funded by the Ford Foundation and administered by the American Association for the Advancement of Slavic Studies. We wish to thank the Project for its substantial financial support. Timely financial assistance also was given by the Committee on Slavic Area Studies and the Middle East Studies Center of the University of Chicago.

Mr. Wimbush wishes to thank the Fulbright-Hays Commission and the International Research and Exchanges Board for providing him with both funding and the opportunity to complete research crucial to this study.

We found the intellectual atmosphere of the University of Chicago to be exceptionally stimulating. Jeremy Azrael was an unusually valuable critic. Vaclav Laska, Slavic bibliographer of the University of Chicago Libraries, graciously extended his services to us. Our cartographer, Christopher Muller-Wille, of the University's Department of Geography, was especially helpful and prompt. We would be remiss not to thank the students of the seminar on Nation Building and National Integration in the Soviet Union, and Khalil Jahshan in particular, for their penetrating comments on parts of the manuscript. Gloria Gibbs of the University deserves our special thanks for her editorial assistance and comments.

Azamat Altay, Turkic-Slavic bibliographer for Columbia University, provided very important supporting materials.

Finally, we wish to acknowledge and thank Jane Ann Danford Wimbush for the valuable contributions she made toward putting the manuscript into final form. Her literary abilities, sense of editorial balance, and fine sense of humor helped to make these final labors a delightful task.

A Note on
Transliteration

It is particularly difficult to reconcile transliteration styles of Russian, Turkic, Persian, and Arabic words and personal names; thus, the system adopted in this book is obviously imperfect.

For Russian or Slavic words and personal names, for words of Turkic (or other) origin which have been "naturalized" in Russian (Karamzin, Karataev—not Qaramzin or Qarataev), and for well-known geographical names (such as Azerbaidzhan), we follow the transliteration system of the Library of Congress.

For Turkic, Arabic, and Persian personal names and words which have not been so "naturalized" in Russian, we have attempted to reconcile as far as possible the transliteration of Oriental words with the Library of Congress system for Slavic languages. Thus, we distinguish the soft (h) (ه, ح) and the hard (kh) as (خ): for example, Husein and Mohammed and not Khusein and Mokhammed.

We distinguish between the hard (ق)—as in *tariqat* and *qadymist*—and the soft (ك), as in *tekke* and *Kerim*.

The Arabic and Persian (ج) and Turkish (c) is rendered by (j): Haji not Khadzhi, Jadid not Dzhadid.

The Arabic, Persian, and Turkic long (i) (ي) is rendered by (y).

The Arabic (ع) is rendered by (c) and (غ) by (gh). But in order to avoid

xv

further complication, we do not distinguish the long and short vowels of Arabic and Persian, except in some rare transliterations of Arabic titles.

Also we have observed the phonetic peculiarities of various Turkic languages. Thus in Kazan Tatar, Ibragimov and Galimjan are accurate transliterations, while in Crimean Tatar these names become Ibrahimov and Alimjan.

October Revolution in a Tatar Village

Russian Bolshevik agitator
Товарищи, давай переделаем нашу церков в конюшню.

Tatar peasants
Правульно, таварыш, правульно. . . .

Agitator
А теперь товарищи, давай из мечети сделаем клуб.

Peasants
Пошел к чорту собачий сын, совсем не правульно.

Introduction

In the first decade of the twentieth century, radical intellectual groups in major European cities awaited the triumph of a political ideology whose time had come, or so they thought. Marxism, both revolutionary and evolutionary, was in the latter stages of a long gestation, and as the imperial powers moved closer to war, it seemed to excited Marxists that the shoot which they had planted many years before now was at last about to flower. These were troubled yet stimulating times for many Europeans. One society and culture was withering away—as Marx said it must—but a new order was being fashioned to take its place.

Europe and Marxism. If this dichotomy spoke not of the inevitable, it did seem natural enough, for nowhere else in the world could one find the prepared social and economic conditions on which Marx had based his entire system. When Marxism eventually triumphed in Russia first, most European Marxists lowered their eyes in embarrassment. Had they known that these same ideas as early as 1905 had penetrated significantly beyond Russia to Muslim Asia, and that by the middle of the century's second decade Marxist ideas would be adapted to restructure societies which most Europeans believed to be even more primitive than Russia, they probably would have turned away in disbelief.

Socialist ideas, in fact, came to Muslim Russia not on the wings of a labor demonstration, as they had in Europe, but gradually, as if on the back of a quiet, interrupted steppe wind. The impact of these ideas in an alien milieu; their adoption by native elites; their metamorphosis in revolution and civil war; the synthesis of socialism, nationalism, and Islam into a new, dynamic ideology—national communism; the ascent and liquidation of the men called Muslim national communists; and the transmission of their ideas to the non-Soviet world are themes of this book. Taken together, they constitute more than a little-known episode of revolutionary history and more than a chapter in the formation of the Soviet state. In addition, Muslim national communism was a skillfully elaborated revolutionary strategy for the entire colonial or semicolonial world, and herein lies its importance both for twentieth-century history and for the future.

National communism was foremost a blueprint for national liberation. Its proponents, in fact, ignored most of the formulas of orthodox Marxism—the class struggle, the supremacy of the industrial proletariat, and internationalism—and focused instead on its essence: that the time was at hand when the oppressed nations of the world would rise up and cast off their oppressors, surround them, or subordinate them to a new revolutionary dynamic. The nation was at the heart of Muslim national communist theories, but these Muslims considered themselves to be genuine Marxists, nonetheless. To be oppressed was to be proletarian, they concluded, and their theory of "proletarian nations" underlies all else. Marxism must be rooted in individual nations for it to be meaningful, they argued, and a national revolution must precede the social revolution and class struggle. The latter, in fact, was to be postponed indefinitely. Peasants and bourgeoisie rather than the industrial proletariat were the people of the revolution; the logical environment for struggle could be the countryside, rather than the city. Finally, the Muslim national communists believed that Islamic culture and way of life and Marxism are not by definition incompatible ideologies. On the contrary, they could coexist and even complement one another.

Chapter 1 describes how socialism first came to Russia's Muslims; how it was transmitted both into and within Muslim society; the receptivity of the native milieu; the individuals or types of individual and the organizations which adopted it; and the gradual evolution of the resultant "national socialism" into "national communism." Chapter 2 analyzes the importance of the October Revolution and of the Russian Civil War in bringing about this change. The emergent doctrine of national communism is discussed in chapter 3 in most of its ideological and organizational particulars. The national communists' struggle for power with the Russian center of the new Soviet state and their ultimate liquidation are the subjects of chapter 4. Chapter 5 considers the legacy of Muslim national communism, both in the Soviet Union and abroad; and chapter 6 presents conclusions and prospects.

We have appended to the main text several important articles by Sultan Galiev, as well as the program of the ERK Party and Joseph Stalin's report at the Fourth Conference of the Central Committee of the RCP (b) for easy reference and more detailed reading than is provided in the body of the book. As this manuscript abounds with little-known individuals and political groups, we have attached glossaries to describe the most important, as well as a glossary of Russian and Oriental terms. We have also added a chronology of events which we discuss in the text and of related events which bear on the subject.

Ours is not an exhaustive analysis of the phenomenon of Muslim national communism in the Soviet Union, but rather an interpretive essay which we hope will be suggestive of the need for further research. The theories of Sultan Galiev and other Muslim leaders have relevance in other national milieus as well as in the multinational Soviet state, and we attempt to introduce some of the ideological parallels with other socialist movements outside the USSR in chapter 5. The transmission of Muslim national communist ideas to these new environments, in particular, requires much more extensive and systematic research. Indeed, this is a subject warranting its own volume. We seek only to demonstrate the variety of movements and individuals who have taken Muslim national communist ideas as their own, modified them, and then brought them to bear on political situations which resemble those of the Soviet Muslim national communists only in their barest outlines. This spectrum of possible applications is broad, and an understanding of the appeal of these ideas is essential to our understanding of politics and revolutionary movements in the Third World.

Ultimately, this book is about the unpredictable appeal of Marxism to societies which differ dramatically from the prototype society for which Marx intended his doctrine. In the broadest sense, we are considering the phenomenon of ideological adaptation and change, of the propensity of some human groups to see in Marxism the answer to their local demands and dilemmas, even though Marxism in its orthodox form would appear to shed little light on their unorthodox problems.

The Soviet Muslim communists brought their national problems to the altar of Marxism and left, claiming that Marxism's real potential—indeed, its roots—lay not in the West but in Asia. They were the first to do so, but certainly not the last, and this should make them worthy of our consideration.

The continued appeal of Marxism in the underdeveloped world suggests the strength of their vision. This vision, which gave Marxism an Asian face, has left us with more than a scattering of unrelated banterings by cranks and dreamers. On the contrary, we have been left a potent and consistent body of ideas, which is the product of men who were both deep thinkers and who were committed to action. Their ideas now have been incorporated into other strategies throughout the Third World. Their message, however, remains largely unchanged.

A. Moor. Москва

D. Moor. Moskou

One

Sultan Galiev   I was led toward socialism
by the love of my nation
which weighs so heavily on
my heart.

From National Socialism to National Communism

National communism was a clear and concise explanation of a political and social reality as well as a commitment to change. Abstract philosophizing on the nature of man or on the desirability of some far-off utopia was conspicuously absent from the writings of national communists. Their ideas from the beginning were colored by a realistic assessment of what they could accomplish within the changing political environment of the Russian Empire and of what they could attain if that empire should cease to exist. Alienated from their recent past, which had been dominated by the continual subordination of Muslim society to Russian control, Muslim national communists sought spiritual support in the legacies of the Genghisid and Timurid empires. Modern socialism offered them a theory of action and of organization.

By 1917, socialist ideas had spread throughout the Russian Empire to Russians and non-Russians, Christian and Muslim alike. While the strength of socialist organizations differed from region to region, in all areas of the empire these groups had attained a relatively high level of political sophistication. With the exception of several exclusive ethnic organizations (Jewish, Finnish, Polish, and Armenian, for example), they all were Russian-dominated and Russian-led. If a non-Russian socialist wished to participate in the work of these groups, it was necessary for him to join a Russian socialist party. A Chuvash socialist, for example, either joined a Russian socialist party or none at all, as there were no Chuvash socialist organizations.

To remedy this situation, a number of non-Russian socialists began to form their own socialist organizations, which would be divorced completely from Russian control. Where they were successful, we can identify specific conditions, or preconditions, which facilitated these attempts. These preconditions varied little between such advanced social groups as the Muslim Tatars, Christian Orthodox Georgians, and Jews; Western Christian nationalities, like the Ukrainians; and underdeveloped rural and nomadic Muslim peoples like the Uzbeks and Kazakhs. Moreover, the same factors which facilitated the formation of native national socialist parties became important again in the 1920s, when national socialist parties were replaced by national communist movements. These preconditions can be outlined as follows:

1. *The existence of a strong, consolidated "historical" nation and/or a tradition of statehood.* Socialism does not create nations. It is instead a stage in the historical evolution of an already consolidated nation, or, more seldom, of a nation in formation. A "historical" nation is one in which self-identity is highly developed and consistent. Except through outright genocide, this human unit is less susceptible to disintegrating influences, such as attacks on its cultural and social traditions or common language, than is an ethnic group in which these attributes are not so strongly assimilated. The existence of a historical territorial homeland with a tradition of statehood is also important. It is significant that before 1917, no socialist ideas had taken root in nations lacking this tradition. Georgia, the Kazakh hordes, Armenia, the Tatar sanctuaries on the Volga and in the Crimea, and, of course, Russia were penetrated; the Eastern Finns and North Caucasians were not.

2. *Long periods of national oppression and/or rule by an alien elite.* Socialist ideas found an especially fertile soil among minorities which were dominated and controlled by their more powerful "protectors," as can be seen in the cases of Russian domination of her borderland minorities, German predominance in the Austro-Hungarian Empire, or Turkish superiority in the Ottoman Empire. Mother Russia, on the other hand, was herself the workshop of a quasi-alien elite ruling from St. Petersburg. Accompanied by the persistence of a long-standing antagonism and a feeling of suspicion and distrust by the oppressed toward their overlords, these conditions were sufficient to spark a national socialist movement. Often, however, these antagonisms were held in check by a more potent reality: the oppressor was a protector in fact, and it was through his military benevolence that small mi-

norities could enjoy a national existence. In this way, for example, Russians stood between Armenians and Turks, just as they defended the Mongols from the Chinese.

3. *The evolution of a national elite who potentially enjoyed the support of the native popular masses.* The native elites among Russia's borderland minorities were not numerous, although they often had the advantage of first-class educations. Two aspects of the native elite are especially important. First, everywhere they came from nonproletarian backgrounds: small landed nobility in Georgia, rich merchants in Tatarstan, bourgeois intellectuals in the Ukraine, landed nobility or upper-class industrial bourgeoisie in Baku.

Second, the traditional elite was not replaced by a new national socialist elite from different social backgrounds in the years immediately preceding 1917, nor did a third elite group arise in the 1920s to lead national communist movements. From the beginning until the 1930s when a new generation appeared, the elite remained the same throughout. The heart of their doctrine—nationalism—remained the same as well. Only their method of presentation and organization changed: from progressive *jadid* democratism, to national socialism, to national communism, and finally, in the 1930s, to nationalism. This evolution essentially was tactical. Success at any given time depended on a timely adaptation to different political climates and ultimately of articulating an ideology which was an unreproachable, logical extension of Leninist internationalism.

Ali Khan Bukeykhanov and Ahmed Baytursun, leaders of the Kazakh Alash Orda, are typical. Beginning in 1908 as members of the Russian KD (Constitutional Democrats), they had by 1917 moved leftward to the national socialist camp. During the Civil War they joined the Bolshevik party, and in the 1920s they emerged as champions of national communism. They disappeared in the 1930s along with other national communists who opposed the Bolsheviks on purely nationalist grounds. This journey took them from being nationalists within the czarist government, to nationalists operating within the ideological framework of the new regime in Moscow, and ultimately again to nationalists unwilling to mask their true feelings.

Mass support for this elite lay in the force of its respective personalities. Seldom was this support prejudiced by matters of doctrine. In general, class consciousness among the native masses was nonexistent. Where it did exist, it often had confusing national overtones. Thus in the Ukraine the conflict was one of Ukranian peasants against Russian landlords; in Tatarstan, of Tatar workers against Russian industrialists; and in Baku, of Muslim workers against Armenian, Russian, Swedish, or Georgian oil magnates.

4. *The existence of a traditional native fighting force which was willing to fight for an indigenous national party.* Marxism calls for an organized proletariat to carry the revolutionary banner in a permanent and systematic manner. Without this force, Marxism would have remained only as an intellectual doctrine or a short-lived theory of rebellion. Theory and practice often are strange bedfellows, and so it was in the national borderlands. In short, there simply was no organized urban proletariat—with the notable exception of Baku—to lend its support to the formation of native-run national socialist organizations. National elites, therefore, sought their strength in other quarters.

Azerbaidzhani elites, of course, looked to the Baku workers with their long revolutionary tradition. Elsewhere traditional fighting forces had a less orthodox face. In the Ukraine, where urban proletarians were largely Russian proletarians, national socialists relied on the *hayduk* tradition of peasant revolts. In the Caucasus the anti-Russian *jihad* of Shamil and his *murids* was evoked. Kazakh nationalists drew on that nation's violent tradition of nomad uprisings which recently had been punctuated by the short but bloody rampage of 1916. Throughout the Muslim world the fighting heritage of the Sufi *tariqa* was renewed and revitalized. The Andizhan revolt of 1898 was a graphic reminder of *tariqa* ambitions.

By a curious paradox some brotherhoods adopted revolutionary and even socialist ideas. This was especially true of the Naqshebandi *tariqa*, which had a long and violent history of opposition to Russian power. In socialism some adepts found new arguments to buttress their traditional holy war against infidels. Perhaps the most intriguing case is that of the dissident Naqshebandi in Kazan, the Vaisi ("the Holy Regiment of Ibn Uwais"), which accepted Russian socialism as part of its political-religious creed. Naqshebandi adepts also joined radical forces in Chechen territory, in Daghestan, Ferghana, and Southern Kazakhstan.

5. *The failure of moderate democratic movements to achieve national goals.* Following Stolypin's refusal in 1908 to satisfy any national demands, the influence of liberal democratic movements in the national areas declined rapidly and the movements themselves steadily disintegrated. In the wake of the democratic movements' demonstrated inability to achieve their desired national goals, a left wing with socialist ideas began to emerge. The native democrats had agreed to cooperate with the czarist regime; as national socialists they would not. For the latter socialism offered new opportunities to win national concessions, if not, in fact, to achieve outright national independence.

National socialism after 1908 represented the radicalization of nationalism under the leadership of the same national elites.

6. *The acquisition by elites of a true revolutionary praxis.* With the esca-
   lation of events from 1905 to 1917, native elites began gradually to
   forego the luxury of abstract debating for the more immediate need of
   preparing themselves to assume leadership of a revolutionary movement should it become necessary. Socialist ideas lent novelty and a
   sense of urgency to their determination. To native elites socialism was
   a new formula for organization, and this organizational framework
   was seen as stronger and more resistant to outside pressures than the
   loose structures of the other, nonsocialist parties. Where intense social
   struggles were already in existence, this praxis came quickly. Baku
   and Kazan in the years immediately preceding 1917 were particularly
   fertile ground. However, the same pattern was or would be repeated
   outside of the Russian Empire: in Tabriz, Iran; in Saloniki, Turkey;
   and perhaps to a lesser degree in Batavia, Dutch Indonesia.

7. *The possibility for socialist ideas to penetrate the native milieu.* On
   this precondition all others rest, for without the impact of socialism on
   the native elite before 1917, national communism would not have been
   born in the Soviet Union in the 1920s. The means and methods of this
   penetration are complex. In general, we can say that the movement of
   socialist ideas into the national territories depended on three main
   conditions: first, the interest taken by Western socialists—both Russian and European—in broadening their ideological universe to
   include the national problem; second, the receptivity of the national
   elite to socialist ideas; and third, the existence of media—men, institutions, or publications—through which these revolutionary ideas could
   flow.

The Transfer of Socialist Ideas

At best, socialist leaders, both European and Russian, before the Russian
Revolution of October 1917 were indifferent to the problems of oppressed
minorities and to the "national question." At their worst, they simply were
ignorant and uncaring of anything beyond the boundaries of their urban
proletarian world. There were, of course, several exceptions to this generalization, notably the Irish struggle against English rule and the agony of the
Poles at the hands of the Russians; but these were thought of by Western
socialists as persistent European problems and susceptible to a Marxist solution because these societies possessed proletarian elements. Their eyes were

fixed on Europe, for it was here that the revolution would change the course of human history.

Of the world beyond Europe, of the East, Western socialists knew virtually nothing. In some cases, such as that of Islamic civilization, the East was treated with scorn. For the Western socialist leader, the East existed only as one factor in international politics, a potentially unsettling one at that. As such, it could affect the relations between socialist states and the capitalist world but it was itself never the target of socialist advances. Because it had no proletariat, it could have no revolution. The "national problem" was marginal, destined to die a natural death in the socialist world. With the success of the socialist revolution in industrial Europe—England, France, and Germany primarily—the national problem, like the socialist state, was destined to wither away.

With the exception of Stalin and to a lesser degree Lenin in 1920, all Bolshevik leaders, as true internationalists, remained indifferent to the national colonial question. Socialists speaking of Russia thought of St. Petersburg and Moscow, of the Don Basin, or the Urals; never of Turkestan or the Volga Tatar region. Partly this was due to an antipeasant attitude inherited from Marx. Only after the October Revolution were the peasants officially accorded a place within the revolutionary doctrine, and even then there was much behind-the-scenes grumbling by orthodox Marxists. Moreover, there was a strongly antinational faction among European socialists. The most outspoken was Rosa Luxemburg, but the same attitude can be found in the works of Russian Bolsheviks like Zinoviev, Bukharin, and especially Trotsky. (Trotsky, in fact, entirely ignored the national question, although while he was in exile in Alma-Ata the crisis was already acute in the local communist party.) With some rare exceptions which we shall consider later, there was virtually no socialist proselytism in the colonial world prior to and for some time after the October Revolution. No serious attempt was made to create socialist organizations in Asia. It was not until the Second Congress of the Komintern in 1920 that the Bolsheviks became interested in revolution in Asia.

In only one area of the Muslim world did Western and Russian socialist leaders take an active interest: Tabriz from 1908 to 1911. Nearly all socialist leaders—Lenin included—followed the progress of the Tabriz revolt. This interest stemmed largely from other motives. The Persian turmoil, far from being a revolution in its own right, was considered primarily for its potential international impact; that is, for the opportunity it afforded to fight English and Russian imperialism in Iran. Socialists completely ignored the possibility of the formation of a Persian socialist movement.

In spite of this indifference, ignorance, and unconcern, by the beginning of the twentieth century socialist ideas were seeping into the colonial and semicolonial world. They were brought in haphazardly by foreign socialists and some Western-educated native elites. This transfer was neither organized nor systematically pursued by Russian or Western socialists before 1917. Once introduced into the native milieu, moreover, socialist ideas rapidly assumed an indigenous, non-Western form. Otto Bauer's concept of extraterritoriality was particularly well received among leaders of the oppressed minorities; the ideas of the more radical Bolsheviks were not. Extraterritorial cultural autonomy was especially appealing to those nationalists who could foresee no possibility of obtaining total independence.

Before 1917 socialist groups appeared sparsely in the Third World. Saloniki in the Ottoman Empire could claim several active organizations: Jewish Federation Socialiste de Saloniki, Macedonian, Bulgarian, and even Turkish (Osmanlı Sosiyalist Partisi). In general, the prevailing influences were French and Austrian, although French socialists who claim that the influence of Jauressian ideas led to the birth of socialism in the Ottoman Empire have overstated their case. In Georgia and in Egypt (Alexandria) French influence was also important. The Armenian Dashnaktsutun and Hnchak parties were created in Switzerland under German influence, but they soon spread to Eastern Anatolia and finally to Russian Armenia. Dutch socialist ideas penetrated Java (Batavia). Armenian, Georgian, and Russian influences all were important in Tabriz. In Baku, Russian, Armenian, and Georgian socialist ideas began to take root; and in Kazan and Orenburg, Russians had the field largely to themselves.

The spread of socialist ideas was, in most cases, limited to the urban elite. The dispersion of the general population, the lack of formal institutions, and the political immaturity of the native masses all contributed to the isolation of native socialists in their urban enclaves. But if the countryside lacked exposure, a number of outlying cities provided an excellent milieu for the cultivation of socialist ideas. Socialist leaders in Baku were especially active before 1917. Tiflis, Kiev, Kazan, and Orenburg were only slightly less so.

The diffusion of these ideas depended first on contacts between the native intelligentsia and local Russian revolutionaries. In some cases, these revolutionaries probably did more to undermine the authority of the czarist regime in the borderlands than they might have done in St. Petersburg or Moscow, where they could be controlled more easily. The "Petrashevskii Circle" demonstrated this phenomenon in the nineteenth century when its members were exiled to the Kazakh steppes. In that locale, the force of their ideas was to last until 1917.

Bolsheviks, Mensheviks, Social Revolutionaries, and other carriers of socialist doctrine were no less effective. Minority radicals often served as intermediaries. Jews were especially important in the transfer of socialist ideas to Alexandria and Saloniki, Armenians worked Baku and Tabriz, and Tatars infected many areas of the Ottoman Empire, Central Asia, and Persia. It is probable that many of these ideas failed to reach outlying areas in their original form. Otto Bauer's writings, for example, probably were read in the original in Georgia and the Ukraine but not in Kazan. Nonetheless, the kernel of Bauer's ideas—the concept of extraterritorial cultural autonomy—arrived everywhere largely intact; even in a secondhand form this idea was sufficiently attractive to engage the minds and passions of native nationalists.

Formal institutions for the transfer of ideas, on the other hand, were noticeably lacking. After 1905, many native elites affiliated with Russian socialist parties, but predictably these organizations directed their message mainly to the Russian urban proletariat rather than to the natives. *Jadid* schools of the Gaspraly *usul-u jadid* (new method) variety in the Volga region and in some parts of Central Asia also functioned as conduits for socialist ideas. Other natives were exposed to socialist ideas in Western and European universities. Everywhere, students accepted socialist ideas because they appeared to be immediately relevant to their fight for national liberation. Koranic schools were not affected; they continued to stress traditional Islamic unity. The majority of nationalist leaders, in fact, were to emerge from the Russian-Tatar teachers' college in Kazan, from purely Russian educational institutions, or from schools abroad in places like Constantinople and France.

The existence of a strong native proletariat was not in itself a sufficient condition for the emergence of national socialism. The experience of Baku proletarians is instructive. At the beginning of the twentieth century Baku was probably the only place in the entire Muslim world, from Morocco to Indonesia, which could claim an authentic industrial proletariat. By 1913 there were some 100,000 Muslim workers in Baku: permanent industrial workers rather than part-time farmers who occasionally sought employment in small factories. They included Azeris and Daghestanis, North Persians (Azeri Turks or Persians), as well as a liberal mixture of Armenians, Georgians, Jews, and Russians. In theory, this would seem to have been the ideal testing ground for development of genuine class consciousness: the subordination of national loyalties to the solidarity of the industrial proletariat. In practice, however, the class struggle in Baku rapidly became a religious struggle with strong nationalist overtones. In 1918 and 1919, when the conflict between Christian Armenians and Muslim Azeris, Daghestanis, and Persians escalated to full civil war, Muslim and Armenian proletarians, like their European predecessors in 1914, totally ignored the fundamental principle of class solidarity and willingly slaughtered each other.

In other Muslim areas, as in Russia herself, the proletariat was either too dispersed or too weak. The Volga Tatars, the most developed of all Russian Muslim communities, in 1913 possessed a native proletariat of over 130,000. Their potential contribution to the class struggle was lost, however, due to their wide dispersal throughout the Russian Empire, from the Donets Basin to the Urals. Ultimately they were to play no role in the February and October revolutions.

European and Russian socialist leaders for the most part were outwardly hostile to the idea of independent or autonomous national socialist parties, even when these parties pretended that their main goal was propagation of socialist ideas in the native milieu. Lenin was no exception. National parties, however dedicated to socialist principles, were viewed by the European and Russian socialists as deviations from orthodox Marxist tenets of organization. Socialism, they argued, was a monolithic movement with an international basis; ethnic or religious distinctions were contradictory and unacceptable. Russian socialists—and particularly the Bolsheviks—were vehemently opposed to national socialist parties, as Lenin's attack on the Bund clearly illustrates. Most Russian socialist groups, of course, were attempting to consolidate their own hegemony over the socialist movement. National socialist parties, therefore, were more than ideologically impure: they were competitors for the allegiance of a sizable part of the population of the empire.

Theoretical and practical considerations notwithstanding, Russian socialists were forced to make some exceptions to the rule, mainly for tactical reasons. Armenian socialist parties were exempted because Turkish socialism was nonexistent, and because their loyalty to the Socialist International was supposed to be unquestionable. Two purely Muslim socialist organizations were tolerated, although they differed widely in their respective organization and goals. The first, Uralchylar, took its name from the Tatar publication *Ural* appearing from January to April 1907 in Orenburg. The group was composed of some twenty-five or thirty Volga Tatar intellectuals with a few token workers thrown in for true proletarian color. Its leaders, Husein Yamashev and Gafur Kulahmetov, of wealthy merchant bourgeois origin, were true Social Democrats of a Bolshevik-Internationalist trend and were hostile to all forms of nationalism. Unfortunately for the young Uralchylar (but perhaps fortunate for the Russian Bolsheviks) both Yamashev and Kulahmetov were dead by early 1918, and by 1919 nothing remained of this anomalous Muslim political party. Its only surviving leader, Ömer Teregulov, was eventually to damn the Soviet regime and emigrate to Turkey.

A second indigenous socialist party, Hümmet ("Endeavor"), was of a somewhat different complexion. Founded in Baku by local Muslim Social Democrats of Bolshevik persuasion in 1904, this party was also genuinely socialist but restricted to Muslims. As such it was a striking paradox in the history of Russian socialism. It was the first, and indeed the only, time that Russian Social Democrats agreed to the creation of a party based on national—and moreover religious—grounds, a sort of "Muslim Bund." Their reasons were an explicit acknowledgment of local conditions. The Social Democratic party in Baku was dominated by Armenians, and, as violent conflict between Armenians and Muslims intensified throughout Transcaucasia, Muslims increasingly drew a close parallel between "socialist" and "Armenian." Consequently, Social Democratic control of the Muslim proletariat was thrown into question. Lenin reluctantly agreed to the creation of the all-Muslim Hümmet in hopes that it could be retained within the Bolshevik sphere of influence. The decision to grant the Hümmet autonomy may have been taken by the local branch of the Russian Social Democrats in recognition of the successful agitation undertaken by the Muslims. That Lenin finally granted his approval is not in doubt.

The Hümmet did not live up to Lenin's expectations. It never became truly Bolshevik, blending as it did socialism with nationalism, and it never broke completely with the national movement. Nor did it ever openly attack Islam or pan-Turkic ideas. Speaking through their official publication (which was also called *Hümmet* and totaled six issues between October 1904 and January 1905), Hümmet leaders painted themselves as far more nationalist than Marxist. Their strongest attacks were reserved for czarist despotism. Islam itself was tolerated, and when the Muslim clergy came under fire it was for their subservience to Moscow. Hümmet's socialist appeals struck a resonant chord in the native milieu because their slogans against autocracy and capitalism were interpreted as attacks on the infidels: Armenians and Russians.

Even after 1917, Hümmet leaders rejected the idea of merging with the Russian Social Democratic party. Instead, they opted for Muslim separatism because of "the psychology of the Muslim masses and the fact that Hümmet had its own history." The Hümmet remained deeply involved in Muslim and Turkic affairs until 1920 when it finally was absorbed by the Russian party, a move which was suggested in 1906 by a little-known executive of the Caucasian Committee of the Russian Social Democratic Workers party (Bolshevik), Joseph Visarionovich Djugashvili, alias Stalin.

These two small Muslim socialist parties, the Uralchylar and the Hümmet, were the only two such organizations on which the Bolsheviks would confer ideological sanction. Elsewhere before 1917, Muslim groups which called themselves "socialist"—Berek, Tangchylar, and so on—were simply radical nationalist parties which had formed in the wake of powerful national liberal movements. Often they were inspired by, but not organically attached to, Russian Socialist Revolutionary groups. In most cases, they made up the extreme left wing of their respective nationalist organizations; they did not behave as independent organizations vis-à-vis the Socialist International. Most, even after the February Revolution, refused to break with their parent nationalist organizations. Their socialism was always suspect, and they were largely oblivious to the source of their inspiration, whether SR or SD.

The Relevance of Socialism to Nationalist Elites

We have stressed that native elites in most cases considered socialism to be a plan for organization and action and not a comprehensive body of doctrine promising to restructure their national society along proletarian internationalist lines. Several aspects of socialism were especially appealing.

1. As a technique for underground work. By 1917, socialist movements had already proved their efficiency. Patterned mainly on the SR model, local socialist organizations, even when they pretended to be Social Democrats, emphasized the value of conspiracy and direct action. Minority national socialists, however, seldom achieved the kind of iron, centralized discipline so characteristic of the Bolsheviks. Their organizations remained loose bodies with no clear hierarchy and little discipline. In addition, their leaders, out of practical necessity or confusion, continually moved from one camp to another, from the national organization to the socialist organization and vice versa. Nonetheless, no other model of political organization could hold out the same model of efficiency as the socialist. A tightly knit and centrally controlled socialist organization was in a better position to fight for nationalist demands. Therefore, it should have come as no surprise to anyone that after the outbreak of the October Revolution most of the prerevolutionary Muslim socialist leaders joined the anti-Soviet camp as the fiction of the Bolsheviks' internationalism became clear. It was in this way that the anti-Bolshevik movements enlisted the support of such prominent national socialists as Emin Rasul Zade, Ayaz Iskhaki, and Fuad Tuktar.

2. As a technique for mass action. The great majority of native national socialist leaders belonged to the traditional elite. Contact with their own native masses was severely limited. Socialism, or more accurately socialist organization, with its emphasis on mass action, agitation, strikes, and even

terrorism (inspired by the SR's and condemned by the SD's), was in essence an ersatz populism: a means by which the enormous gap between elites and masses could be bridged. The reward would be a unified nationalist movement. The national elite thus were prepared to adopt socialist tactics as their own. Significantly, in the long tradition of Muslim radicalism—including the Qarmatians, the Ismailis, and the fighting *tariqa* of the eighteenth and nineteenth centuries—Muslim leaders of the early twentieth century could find many romantic examples of direct action, terrorism, and sacrifice, but nowhere a model for mass organization. While socialist ideas were abstract and often ill fitting, the socialist model of mass organization was precisely what the Muslim national leaders required, and they rapidly adapted it to their own needs.

3. The promise of outside support. In spite of the limited interest shown by European and Russian socialists in the problems of ethnic minorities, socialism at least suggested to the national socialists the *possibility* of obtaining Western support. Armenian socialist parties in particular made strong overtures to the West for assistance (and obtained it), as did the Young Turks (from the French Socialists in 1908) and the Tabriz revolutionaries, who received the sympathy of virtually all foreign socialists. More broadly, all revolutionaries who were fighting European or Russian imperialism could count on the moral support of European socialists. Although these sympathies from abroad seldom translated into direct financial or military assistance, nonetheless they had a positive influence on natives who were in the process of organizing into socialist parties, or who were pursuing more active roles in the revolutionary struggle.

4. The possibility for equality, if not outright independence. Of all ideologies floating loose around the Russian Empire before 1917, socialism more than any other practical ideology stressed the principles of brotherhood and equality among peoples. If Bolshevik "internationalism" was vague in its particulars, Otto Bauer's principle of extraterritorial cultural autonomy was not. Socialism, in this "right-wing" form, made a solution to the "national problem"—and hence independence or equality in a federation—conceivable.

Non-Russians of the empire before 1917 were faced with essentially the same clear-cut decision which the Algerians, Syrians, Lebanese, and Indonesians were to face in the 1920s: either to join the main socialist organizations of the dominant ethnic group in their multinational societies or create national organizations of their own. For many reasons, most opted for the latter. The most powerful incentive for non-Russians certainly was an inbred mistrust of the Russians. The Bundist argument also was influential: that a national socialist organization is better equipped and better placed to represent the interests of the native. Spokesmen for Hümmet, Uralchylar, and later the Yevsektsiia argued that the national socialist organization was more efficient for spreading socialism to the native masses, largely because native socialists enjoyed the distinct advantage of being able to speak the language of the people.[1] National communists were to adopt both of these arguments in the 1920s.

Conclusion

National movements were declining everywhere in the period from 1905 to 1911. Socialism, on the other hand, appeared as a conquering doctrine; the future belonged to it. It was a justification for radicalism and even violence (once the SR model was adopted). Socialism required that the recent past be viewed with a certain iconoclasm, a view which most Muslim national socialists were eager to take. In this, they contrasted with their democratic-liberal predecessors, who sought only to reform the recent past and not to reject it. Moreover, socialism provided these elites with an organizational scheme through which they could express their dissent. Socialism, for them, was not only a passkey to the future, but also a window on the distant past—the Golden Age of Islamic civilization, the independent Ukraine of Hmelnitskii, the Georgian kingdom of Queen Tamar. It was a means of ridding themselves of Russians and of those native elements which had compromised with the czarist regime. From these national socialist elites, from the new techniques of political organization, and from long years of suppressed frustration at Russian rule would emerge national communism.

This, then, is the general picture of Russia's minorities on the eve of the revolution. Their national socialist programs, where they did exist, were interesting attempts to reconcile the conflicting and often contradictory ideological trends of their environment—bolshevism, menshevism, anarchism—with their radical nationalism. Into this cauldron they added a substantial potion of radical pan-Islam, culled from the writings of men like Jemaleddin al-Afghani and Abdurrashid Ibragimov. Importantly, not one of the Muslim socialist groups had as yet asked the fundamental question: Are Islam and Marxism compatible? For these groups, socialism, before 1917, was a means and not an end, and therefore the question was superfluous. Yet by the very nature of their national goals, they were already challenging the famous Stalinist formula which they had not yet heard: the new sociopolitical order would be "socialist in content and national in form." If anything, they knew, it would be just the opposite.

In 1917, there probably were no more than one of two dozen Muslim Bolshevik militants in the Russian Empire. One year later there would be thousands of non-Russian communists and the first tentative discussions of a national communism would take place. Where did these new communists come from? What brought them to the Russian Communist party? We shall consider these questions in the following chapter.

Two

Napoleon   Les gros bataillons ont
toujours raison.

The Impact of
Revolution
and Civil War

The Bolshevik Revolution, we are instructed from an early age, was one of the foremost, perhaps *the* foremost, political event of our century if not of all time. It disrupted (or sabotaged) a righteous cause in the Great War; it injected a new ideological irritant backed by power into an already confused galaxy of confused political ideas; and, ultimately, it was the harbinger of a world divided into hostile camps based on their mutual understanding of the improbability and undesirability of coexistence. In the opinion of one enthusiastic fellow-traveler, these were the "ten days which shook the world."

For reason of our own Eurocentrism, this myth from the time of John Reed's first writing has gone virtually unchallenged. Some of the world was shaken, of course. Petrograd rocked violently, and there certainly was some under-the-breath swearing in political caucus rooms from Washington to Paris. But in Russia's own backyard, in the non-Russian ethnic borderlands of the empire, the October Revolution went practically unnoticed: not for ten days, not even for nearly six months, was the ominousness of Bolshevik power felt. The first indications of Bolshevik strength and intentions were known in these areas only after February 1918; and it was not until 1920 in some cases that this strength was sufficient to reintegrate most of the former Russian Empire under Soviet rule.

Especially in the Muslim areas of the empire the October Revolution failed to precipitate any immediate or dramatic changes. There native administration with its embryonic civil and military organs continued to function with only minor conflicts alongside the new Soviet administration. For their part, the Bolsheviks simply lacked the power to subordinate non-Russian parties to their own organizations, despite their well-publicized successes in Petrograd and Moscow. In general, the Bolshevik organizations were composed of Russians and other "Europeans" (Poles, Letts, Ukranians, and Jews); the native organizations of local bourgeois liberals. The contest for power was three-sided: the provisional governments which had been established in February 1917, the Bolshevik-dominated soviets, and the local nationalist forces. In Kazan, Simferopol, Baku, and Kokand, provisional governments were ushered out with a minimum of force, and the local native administrations took over through March 1918. In Georgia, Mensheviks who already dominated the local soviets were the leading nationalist force as well. In the Middle Volga, the Urals, the Crimea, Turkestan, and Transcaucasia, the Bolshevik offensive was postponed until spring of 1918.

Socialist ideas, as we mentioned in the last chapter, had penetrated substantially into these borderland areas by the time of the February Revolution, although the reason for their popularity was largely tactical and not ideological. Nowhere did the fledgling socialist factions succeed in disengaging themselves from the existent liberal nationalist movements, and nowhere did they articulate a nationalist-socialist doctrine distinct from Russian Marxism. Everywhere, the socialist factions acted as a left wing to the liberal nationalist movements, contesting their bourgeois, moderate leadership but not openly opposing it.

Despite increasing factionalism, until October 1917 and in some Muslim territories until the spring of 1918, the idea of Muslim *Umma* remained in force. The great Pan-Russian Congress of Muslims in May 1917, which was attended by representatives of all Muslim organizations from the extreme Right to the extreme Left, dramatized the solidarity of Muslims of the empire as a whole. There was some dialogue over the nature of the political relationship of Muslims to Russians in any future Russian state (federalists finally defeated the centralists by a vote of 446 to 271), but the ideals of pan-Turkism and pan-Islamism were affirmed. Significantly, the delegates expressed nearunanimity on the fundamental concern of all factions—that the destiny of Muslim peoples must be made separate and distinct from that of the Russians. The new and more revolutionary leadership which was elected at this congress came from the same traditional elite as their forerunners. They were wealthy merchants, industrial bourgeoisie, and, occasionally, as in the Kazakh steppes and Azerbaidzhan, nomadic and landed aristocracy. This unity, the unity of the *Umma*, disintegrated into pro-Soviet and anti-Soviet factions only after the October Revolution and especially at the beginning of the Civil War.

   Between the February and October revolutions, however, various individuals and entire Muslim organizations embarked on a paradoxical evolution *within* the confines of *Umma*. Native socialists gradually adopted a more nationalistic line, due mostly to the behavior of the Russian moderate-liberal and right-wing socialist parties (Constitutional Democrats, Mensheviks, and Socialist Revolutionaries) which had assumed power in Petrograd after the February Revolution. In spite of the lip service these "liberals" paid to the notion of minority rights and for the restitution of historical native grievances, they quickly showed themselves to be not altogether different from their czarist predecessors. Once in power they often behaved like true colonialists and occasionally adopted antinative attitudes which were even more harsh than those of czarist authorities. For Muslim socialists, the framework of compromise with Russian power to which they had adapted from the beginning was no longer plausible. The fabric of accommodation had been permanently rent, first by Stolypin in 1908, now by the behavior of their fraternal Russian socialist compatriots. In theory, only the Bolsheviks remained favorably disposed toward the minorities after February 1917, but they, too, were Russians. And, as we shall see, they, too, were to provide yet another disillusionment to the native intelligentsia in 1923–24, when they would present irrefutable evidence that they had willingly inherited the Great-Russian chauvinism and the imperial outlook of those Russian state builders who had passed before them. Finally, for many non-Russians and particularly for the Muslims in Russia's periphery, the February Revolution was seen as the first stage of the disintegration of the old empire. National independence, a wild dream in 1914, suddenly gained new currency. In 1917 it was not only conceivable but possible as well.

   These influences caused many individuals and groups who before February considered themselves to be "socialists" or "internationalists" to swing to the Right, toward the hard-line nationalists. The Kazan Tatar socialist Tangchylar was one such group. Both of its central figures, Ayaz Iskhaki and Fuad Tuktar, had been members of the Russian Social Revolutionary party. Soon after the events of February 1917 they became leaders of the Muslim national movement, and by 1918, both had become leading opponents of the Soviet government. Similarly, Mehmed Emin Rasul Zade, former leader of the Hümmet and a pro-Bolshevik, returned to the Azerbaidzhani national movement from the ranks of the Social Democrats. Eventually he became president of the national Musavat party and of the independent Azerbaidzahn Republic in 1920, and a violent anti-Bolshevik.

Radical nationalists, on the other hand, began their own paradoxical evolution, and in this movement we find some truth in Dimanshtein's overstated claim: "Even the most hardened clericals and reactionaries were transformed into socialists."[1] In fact, within the *Umma* on the extreme Left a number of new Muslim "socialist committees" were born between February and April 1917. The best known of these committees, the Muslim Socialist Committee of Kazan, was typical, listing among its members those of Menshevik, Bolshevik, Socialist Revolutionary, and even anarchist revolutionary views. They were not tied, however, to Russian socialist parties of the same name. Like most members of the *Umma*, the leaders of these committees sought to establish a clear demarcation between Muslims and Russians. These leaders were nearly all former radical nationalists, but they recognized in socialist organization a superior means of mobilization and a commitment to action. Their Marxism was vague, if not unlearned. Their aims were twofold: reformist vis-à-vis traditional Islam, and nationalist vis-à-vis the creation of independent Muslim polities free from Russian domination. They took a more hostile attitude toward the Muslim clergy than the general rank-and-file socialists and toward the upper strata of the bourgeoisie and the landed nobility. Among Muslim elites, they championed a more advanced labor strategy and a bolder program of land reform. Like most Muslims at this time, land reform meant to them the expulsion of Russians from lands which they had seized from natives over the course of two centuries. Two prominent leaders of the Kazan committee, Mir-Said Sultan Galiev and Mulla-Nur Vahitov, would become important leaders and articulators of Muslim national communism in the 1920s. For them, as with so many other native elites, the Muslim committees were a training ground for synthesizing seemingly contradictory doctrines.

The Kazan socialist committee and similar revolutionary political groups throughout the territories from Crimea to Turkestan were viewed by the Bolsheviks—or at least by Lenin and Stalin, the only two Bolsheviks with more than a superficial interest in the national question—as useful organizations for the spread of Bolshevik influence. They believed that these groups, regardless of their current associations and ideological blemishes, would "bolshevize" the fellow-travelers and temporary allies, that they were genuine schools of Marxism. In fact, the committees achieved just the opposite effect, inculcating even their most radical members with nationalist ideas.

In the winter and spring of 1918, the local Bolsheviks, frustrated and disgruntled over having to share authority in the borderlands with the natives after the October Revolution, systematically undertook to erase all traces of this uneasy duality. In January, Russian workers' militias were successful in subduing the Kazakh Alash Orda. The steppe cities of Akmolinsk, Kustanay, Aktübinsk, Orenburg, Turgaisk, and Semipalatinsk fell in rapid succession. In that same month Simferopol, the capital of the Crimean Tatars, met a similar fate. Kokand was razed in February and the population massacred. Kazan, Vernyi (Alma-Ata), and Baku were subdued in March. By the end of spring 1918, all national Muslim organizations, whether inclined toward neutrality or openly hostile, had been dispersed, subdued, or liquidated. Central Muslim organizations, like the Milli Shura ("National Council") in Petrograd and the Harbi Shura ("Military Council") in Kazan, were disbanded.

Political failures, however, offset these early military successes. At the beginning of the Civil War in spring 1918, the Bolsheviks found themselves in a precarious position in the borderlands. Their first forays were heavy-handed and brutal, and, consequently, they evoked only opposition from the native masses. This was the period of the "cavalry raids," an expression employed in Soviet literature to describe the spontaneous assaults by city proletarians on villagers and peasants. These "raids" usually were inspired by strong antireligious prejudice, and they were launched against Muslim and Christian alike. Soviet historians place the blame for this reaction against Soviet rule on the local soviets, which were dominated by Russians who lived in these areas. After the October Revolution, in fact, the already marginal relations between local Russians and natives deteriorated rapidly. The revolution, these Russians believed, was a purely Russian affair which should affect not only Petrograd and Moscow, but also reassert Russian hegemony in the rest of the empire. On this basis, non-Russians had been systematically excluded from Party positions of influence and authority. "It is impossible to admit Muslims to the supreme organs of the Communist party," explained Kolesov, chairman of the Tashkent Congress of Soviets, " . . . because they do not possess any proletarian organization."[2]

As a result of these factors, early in 1918 native Muslim elites joined the White counterrevolutionary forces in considerable numbers. In its first phase the counterrevolution was guided by leftist and liberal elements from older Russian coalitions, usually Mensheviks and right-wing Socialist Revolutionaries. Their attitude toward the non-Russian nationalities, while not actually liberal, was at least realistic. They understood that any anti-Bolshevik movement required non-Russian support if it were to succeed, and they set about helping to establish in the provinces native organizations which would cooperate with them. In part they succeeded. The right-wing SR-dominated Committee of the Constituent Assembly (Komuch) in Samara (now Kuibyshev), for example, in early 1918 secured and directed the anti-Bolshevik efforts of the well-trained Bashkir detachments under the leadership of Zeki Validov. The Komuch at this time became the coordinator of all non-Russian anti-Soviet factions, including the Ural and Orenburg cossacks, the Tatar Millet Medzhlisi, the Kazakh Alash Orda, and the Bashkir National Committee.

It is doubtful, however, that native groups wholeheartedly supported the counterrevolutionary forces—whether the Komuch or the Czech legionnaires. On the contrary, most would have preferred to remain neutral, for they shared with the Russian colonists the belief that the revolution was first and foremost a Russian problem. From their standpoint, Reds and Whites were equally offensive because they were equally Russian. Neither of these Russian groups advocated a pronative policy, but neither was there a sufficiently powerful or unified native force to challenge Russian supremacy. Little by little, the ebb and flow of the Civil War in the East drew individual native groups into the contest for their own territories. While they harbored few illusions about the concern or good will of either Russian faction for the Muslim community, native elites knew that they had to make a choice between the two, and that this choice ultimately would determine any future political relationship between Moscow and the borderlands. "Whether you want to or not," wrote Sultan Galiev in 1921, "you must take part in it, and consciously or unconsciously become either White or Red." [3]

White or Red? This was the dilemma shared alike by all Muslims of Russia and by most other non-Russians of the empire. Ahmed Baytursun describes the unpleasant choice facing the Kazakh-Kirghiz, but these sentiments were shared nearly everywhere:

> The [Kazakh-Kirghiz] received the first revolution with joy and the
> second with consternation and terror. It is easy to understand why. The
> first revolution had liberated them from the oppression of the czarist re-
> gime and reinforced their perennial eternal dream of autonomy. . . . The
> second revolution was accompanied in the borderlands by violence, plun-
> dering, exactions and by the establishment of a dictatorial regime . . .
> in short, it was a period of sheer anarchy. In the past, a small group of czar-
> ist bureaucrats oppressed the [Kazakh-Kirghiz]; today the same group
> of people, or others, who cloak themselves in the name of Bolsheviks per-
> petuate in the borderlands the same regime . . . . Only the politics of Kol-
> chak which promised the return to the czarist regime forced Alash Orda
> to turn itself toward the Soviet regime, even though, judging by the local
> Bolsheviks, it did not appear to be a very attractive alternative. [4]

Because the Civil War raged the length and breadth of the Eastern territories, it stimulated the local intelligentsia to mobilize for battle in pursuit of
their own goals. Significantly, the Red Army was for the non-Russian, non-

proletarian peoples their first school of political action (see Appendix B). It was to prove to be a much more practical period of instruction than the esoteric prerevolutionary debates of the small socialist organizations. Twenty years before Mao Tse-tung would describe his own military organization as a fundamental tool in the political struggle, this idea was understood and articulated by a number of native elites. For them, the psychological impact of this army in motion was overwhelming. Massive numbers of them rushed to join its ranks and, subsequently, the ranks of the Russian Communist party. This phenomenon of the socialist army as political machine deserves closer attention, inasmuch as it has clear analogues in our own time.

Between May 1918 and the end of the Civil War in the summer of 1920, a dramatic change occurred which saw tens of thousands of non-Russians, and especially Muslims, desert the Whites and join the Red Army. Some enlisted individually, but the majority went over en masse with their parent nationalist organizations. Of these, only the Azerbaidzhani Hümmet was officially recognized by the Bolsheviks as a genuine socialist party. Not surprisingly, in 1920 the Hümmet became the nucleus of the Communist party of Azerbaidzhan.

Other radical nationalist organizations, although lacking official ideological standing in the eyes of the Bolsheviks, followed suit. The Bashkirs, under the leadership of Ahmed Zeki Validov, joined the Soviet forces in February 1919 in protest against Kolchak's disbanding of Bashkir national regiments previously in his service. The Kazakh Alash Orda, a nationalist liberal organization with moderate socialist tendencies, agreed to recognize Soviet power in June 1919, under prodding of Lenin's personal representative Jangildin and the Kazakh commander, Ahmed Baytursun. The Crimean Tatar Milli Firqa, because of the extreme antinative attitude of Denikin, abandoned the Whites in June 1919, carrying their fight underground in an implicit statement of support for the Bolsheviks. They surfaced again in October 1920 when the Red Army penetrated the Crimea. By then, the Milli Firqa was firmly in the Bolshevik camp, despite Wrangel's last-minute concessions to Tatar nationalists. Denikin's anti-Muslim policies also offended the mountain peoples of the North Caucasus, many of whom fought with the religiously inspired forces of Sheikh Uzun Haji and Imam Najmuddin of Gotzo (Gotzinski). The anti-Russian passion of these diverse peoples knew no bounds. When the Red Army finally drove the Whites from Daghestan, they, too, were set on by the mountainmen with a fervor reserved for the true infidel.

In Azerbaidzhan, the underground struggles of the Hümmet (composed entirely of Azeri Turks) and of the Adalat (composed mostly of Persian Azerbaidzhanis) against threats from the British and from the Turks precipitated a closer union between the two parties. In April 1920 when the Red Army finally conquered Azerbaidzhan they found a strong Muslim communist organization already in place. And in Central Asia, some native nationalist forces, like the Young Bukharians, conferred their full support on the Bolsheviks only after the Red Army had curbed what was ostensibly its own ally, the Tashkent soviet. The unabashed colonialist behavior of this soviet, nonetheless, by this time had provoked a potent popular uprising—the Basmachi—which was to harass Soviet power in most of Central Asia until 1928 and in some regions until as late as 1936. By 1920, however, the Bolsheviks had secured the support or neutrality of most radical nationalist elites in the Muslim East, and these elites soon became important figures in the Turkestan Communist party.

The importance of these defections (or in some cases the abandonment of neutrality) should not be minimized. The volte-face of the Bashkirs under Zeki Validov, for example, weighed heavily on the final military outcome in that region. His regiments in 1919 numbered some two thousand experienced fighters, a large force for the Eastern (Ural) front, which had the distinct advantage of fighting on its own terrain. As a pro-Soviet force it contributed importantly to Kolchak's final defeat. The same can be said for the war in the North Caucasus. The Caucasian mountaineers engaged a number of Denikin's units, which were needed for his march on Moscow in the fall of 1919, in a guerrilla-style war for several months.

Four factors were responsible for the gravitation of many native Muslim elites to the Bolshevik camp and for the creation of a large corps of fellow-travelers. The first was the ineptitude of the White leadership and its inability to comprehend the national sentiment of the natives in whose midst they were fighting. It is generally accepted that White generals were hopeless blunderers, Russian chauvinists, devoid of any sense of political reality, and imbued with simplistic notions of the nature of the world in general and the future of Russia in particular. Surely, this was true for some. Admiral Kolchak sought the restoration of the Romanovs: a highly unrealistic inclination given all that had transpired in the years of revolution and civil war.

Others like Denikin and Alexeev, however, were distinguished and clever general staff officers not altogether lacking in political education and common sense. Ultimately, their aims evince a sophisticated and realistic appraisal of what was required of Russia and of themselves if Russia were to survive as a great power. They fought for the reunification of the empire—with or without the monarchy. Only in this way, they believed, could Russia regain her prominent position in the world. From their vantage point the Bolsheviks were less evil for their political and social doctrines—although these, too, were abhorrent—than for their apparent willingness to destroy the empire.

Native nationalist forces which were demanding autonomy and/or independence, whether in direct collaboration with the Bolsheviks or not, were considered by these White leaders to be part of this same iconoclasm. The Whites, who often maintained headquarters in or at the borders of non-Russian territories, were reminded daily of the destructive potential of native separatism. For some of them, nationalist Kazakhs, Azerbaidzhanis, Armenians, Georgians, Bashkirs, Ukrainians, and others posed an even more odious threat to the future of the empire than the deepening shadow cast by the Bolsheviks themselves. Thus almost from the beginning of the Civil War, counterrevolutionary Whites and native nationalist forces were by definition out of step. Local practices by individual White commanders exaggerated these political distinctions and thereby transformed them into religious, cultural, and racial distinctions as well. Rapprochement was inconceivable, if not impossible.

The second factor responsible for shifting some national minority support to the side of the Bolsheviks was the personal acuity of Stalin, who, more than any other Bolshevik, understood that to win the allegiance or neutrality of the non-Russians was to take a giant step toward winning the Civil War. Stalin himself made the decision to entice minority nationalist leaders into the Bolshevik party, despite the strong opposition this move engendered from other prominent Bolsheviks. A Georgian, Stalin knew from personal experience that support for the Bolshevik cause could be enlisted successfully in non-Russian areas of the empire only by native leaders. By this decision, moreover, Stalin was already showing himself to be the measure of the more visible Trotsky, the commissar of war. Trotsky's use of former czarist officers to staff the Red Army commands was by its nature a limited tactical maneuver.

Imperial trappings from czarist times, of which the officer corps was a conspicuous reminder, were destined to the dustbin of history. Russia's minorities, on the other hand, were a permanent fact of life. By deciding to enlist their leaders, Stalin was establishing, in effect, that nationality would be an important political criterion in future state consolidation. Minority national leaders, he recognized, were important and useful pieces in any move to aggrandize power at the center, and he was determined that these pieces should stand in his back row.

The Commissariat of Nationality Affairs, or Narkomnats (*Narodnyi komissariat po delam natsional' nostei*), was created in November 1917 to serve as a mediator between disputing nationalities and as an advisory body to other branches of the Soviet government. Stalin was appointed chairman; under his stewardship Narkomnats rapidly assumed control of nearly every activity touching the non-Russian populations: press, agriculture, administration, education, propaganda, culture, and military affairs, to name some of the most important. By late 1922, Stalin had transformed this organization into an embryonic federal government with administrative and representational functions which paralleled those of the larger Soviet structure. In a sense, Narkomnats became a government within a government.

Narkomnats, however, was not simply a creature of Stalin's lust for power. At its inception, it was a symbolic gesture to Russia's minorities that they would now be granted a greater voice in the management of their national affairs, on one hand, and, on the other, a real attempt on the part of Lenin and Stalin to come to grips with an increasingly evident problem to which few Bolsheviks had given much thought. However opportunistic its original goals, however callously Stalin subsequently rejected demands for ethnic autonomy—liquidating national leaders in the process—Narkomnats as a specific institution was unprecedented in Russian history. As such, it initially attracted the attention of leaders from nearly all of the contested national areas and the active support of many. Subsumed by Narkomnats were small commissariats for dealing with the affairs of particular ethnic groups: Jewish, Ukrainian, Georgian, Armenian, Latvian, Chuvash, Polish, Buryat, Lithuanian, Estonian, and others.

One of the most important sections of Narkomnats was the Central Muslim Commissariat, or Muskom. As in the other sections of the parent organization Stalin succeeded in securing the participation of a number of prominent Muslim leaders. Typically, they were former nationalists who viewed this new Soviet institution as a stage on which they could act out their national demands. Typically, too, they were of nonproletarian origins. Muskom was directed by a Bashkir and two Tatar intellectuals. Sherif Manatov, the Bashkir, was a former right-wing nationalist, who, after 1918, became a full-fledged and extremely loyal Bolshevik, thus bearing out the promise of Narkomnats. Perhaps because of this loyalty, he was to enjoy the luxury of dying peacefully in his bed. The two Tatars, Mulla-Nur Vahitov and Galimjan Ibragimov, were former left-wing radical nationalists. Theirs was a different fate: Vahitov was shot by the Czechs in May 1918 and Ibragimov was liquidated by Stalin somewhat later. This, in fact, was to become the pattern for disposing of radical nationalists as Stalin consolidated his hold on the Communist party and the Soviet state.

It is difficult to evaluate the symbolic and/or actual impact which Stalin's policies and Narkomnats had on those non-Russians who ''traveled'' with the Bolsheviks. The nonproletarian, non-European Muslims in general were despised by the Bolshevik leadership, and hence their contribution to the Soviet cause from the onset has been discounted. Moreover, those radical nationalist leaders who did join the Party almost never reached the highest echelons of the Party or state machinery. Their public visibility—and hence acknowledgment for their achievements—remained severely restricted. Their exploits were and still are practically unnoticed by Western observers and historians, their role in the Civil War largely ignored. In general, they are studied only within the historical confines of Narkomnats and "the national problem." That Muslim soldiers and officers together comprised almost fifty percent of the Sixth Red Army which held the Siberian front against Kolchak—the main front of the war—is often forgotten or ignored, even though without this support the Bolshevik victory would have been problematic.

Third, a number of nationalists joined the Bolsheviks because they believed that the counterrevolutionaries were simply Russian chauvinists. "Suppose that the Constituent Assembly and a bourgeois republic win in Russia," argued Hanafi Muzaffar, a prominent Volga Tatar radical intellectual. "The Assembly will be dominated by the Great-Russians who will never liberate themselves from their narrow nationalistic chauvinism; on the contrary, their chauvinism will grow steadily. . . ."[5] Despite their considerable excesses, the Bolsheviks were still an unknown quantity to many Muslim nationalists. The goals of most of the White leaders, on the other hand, were known and understood. With the empire in turmoil, these nationalists were determined that it should not be reconstituted as it formerly had been. Some of them sincerely accepted the Bolsheviks' professions of internationalism and national equality. But for the majority of those who "fellow-traveled," any change was preferable to no change, and it was change which the Bolsheviks appeared to offer if they offered anything at all.

Finally, a considerable number of Muslims viewed the revolution in Russia—and hence the Bolshevik cause—as the first step to the liberation of Islam from European and Russian encroachment. One observer noted,

> The essential point for us is the survival of our nation and even more broadly, the survival of all Muslim peoples and all colonial peoples who are oppressed and threatened by European imperialism. But as long as Europe can use its might to maintain its imperialistic policy [in the East] our situation will remain hopeless. However, in Europe herself new forces are growing which are becoming more threatening every day for imperialism. . . . It would be a great mistake for us peoples oppressed by Europe to fail to recognize that Marxism is fighting imperialism. As the Communist party is fighting this same imperialism in Russia and abroad, we must accept Soviet power. We must not fear the antireligious character of the dictatorship of the proletariat because the alliance between the Russian proletariat and the Muslims could deal a death blow to Europe.[6]

In this declaration we can see the roots of native support for the Soviet cause. Marxism should be accepted and the forces that espouse it should be encouraged because Marxism alone is an anti-imperialist doctrine. Soviet power draws its strength from Marxism, and, therefore, the Russian proletariat, in theory, is potentially an anti-imperialist force. It is doubtful, of course, that many radical nationalists reached this conclusion from reading Marx; in fact, it is unlikely that more than a handful of them had ever read him. Furthermore, few native leaders were prepared to trust the Russian proletariat very far. Instead, native elites accepted Marxism and the equation of anti-imperialism and Soviet power only in a superficial sense. Of the rather diffuse, vague, but omnipresent socialist ideas which were floating about Europe and Russia at this time, Marxism appeared to be the most viable because it apparently had touched off a revolution in the Russian capital and because it ostensibly was the guiding ideological force of the powerful Bolshevik army which was then in the field. These tangible manifestations of power and success reinforced in the minds of native radical nationalists the belief that Marxism was action as well as ideas. All other ideologies appeared to be bankrupt in comparison.

Despite firsthand evidence of "the antireligious character of the dictatorship of the proletariat," native national socialists rationalized that an alliance with the Russian proletariat was possible because the communism of the latter in fact was compatible with Islam. "Muslim people will unite themselves to communism," predicted Hanafi Muzaffar. "Like communism, Islam rejects narrow nationalism. Islam is international and recognizes only the brotherhood and the unity of all nations under the banner of Islam."[7] Ahmed Baytursun, speaking for his own people, noted that the Kazakhs "will accept communism even before all other peoples, because its traditional way of life is already close to communism."[8] The relative ambiguity of the Bolshevik position on nationalities at this time prevented Hanafi Muzaffar, Baytursun, and others like them from realizing that the banner of Islam hardly would share a flagstaff with the banner of Lenin, if it were allowed to fly at all. Nonetheless, the feeling that communism and Islam were of a similar piece and complementary was shared widely among Muslim leaders. They were encouraged in this belief by some important religious leaders. Musa Jarullah Bigi, for example, then the greatest living leader of Russian Islam, not only lauded this potential alliance but envisaged communism as a springboard for a deeper penetration of Islam in Asia. "A great revolution has triumphed in Russia, giving birth to a regime of justice and equality instead of the former tyrannic regime," he extolled. "There Muslims enjoy equality, unity, and peace. . . . We must take advantage of this situation to promote the Koranic Unity of Believers. . . ."[9]

Typologies of the New
Bolsheviks

Whether for the ineptitude of the White leadership, Stalin's personal ingenuity, anti-Russianism, or because they felt that socialism and Islam were natural partners, a significant number of Muslim leaders did lend their support to the revolutionary forces during the Civil War. Few continued to oppose the Bolsheviks; the vast majority remained neutral or at least disinclined to make the seemingly academic choice between Bolsheviks and Whites. The following typologies suggest the complexity of the political spectrum by mid-1918. The various groups are described in terms of their political, social, and psychological/motivational backgrounds. The categories range from the most staunchly anti-Bolshevik individuals to those who eventually joined the Russian Communist party.

Counterrevolutionaries
and Those Who Joined
the Whites

Few in number, many of them were monarchists or former czarist officers; but this group also included several former socialists like Ayaz Iskhaki and Fuad Tuktar. Socially they came from the upper levels of their society: wealthy bourgeoisie, rich landlords, and, in the Caucasus, petty noblemen. In addition, this group included a number of conservative clerics. Except for the former socialists, they were interested in modern ideologies only inasmuch as the ideologies posed a threat to their own established social and economic perquisites. A strong sense of loyalty and service to the old regime motivated the nonsocialists, as did their abhorrence of the Bolsheviks' atheism and the latter's successful destabilization of established social and economic relationships.

Those Who Remained
Neutral, Passive, or Who
Emigrated

This was by far the largest category: the nonpolitical and those for whom the current disruptions were simply an unpleasant time to be lived through. On the other hand, this group included some militant pan-Turkists and pan-Islamists, like Abdurashid Ibragimov, who believed that the fight for Islam in the Russian Empire, while important, was secondary to its preservation in the Dar ul-Islam abroad. Consequently, many ardent Muslims—including a number of Muslim clerics—emigrated to other Muslim countries, especially to Turkey and Iran.

Those who remained were drawn largely from the Tatarstan middle-class bourgeoisie and landed nobility; with some exceptions, from the peasantry; and from the urban poor. They fought for no one, believing that neither side was an acceptable alternative, or, conversely, because their political consciousness was too undeveloped to suggest a choice. Except for the pan-Islamists, this was the inert mass which quietly or skeptically watches most revolutionary events, letting history unfold around them while playing virtually no active part.

Fellow-Travelers

The distinction between one who fellow-travels and one who remains neutral is difficult to make, as it begs the question of support. Used here, the term *fellow-traveler* designates those identifiable individuals who at some time subjectively decided to support the Bolsheviks, including, in most cases, physical support. Also in this category are some nonpoliticals who essentially were order followers, those who probably would follow any leader if his authority were sufficiently pronounced. By and large, however, this group was comprised of active supporters who saw real benefits flowing from a Bolshevik victory, but who stopped short of joining the Russian Communist party. Radical religious sects, like the Vaisi; moderate religious leaders, like Abdullah Bubi, Musa Jarullah Bigi, and Rizaeddin Fahreddinov; and moderate *jadids* were typical. They came from the middle class, bourgeoisie nobility, and clerical professions, but they also included some mountaineers and nomads. Some Sufi brotherhoods often tended toward radicalism; the nomads and mountaineers—on whose land there had been a steady Russian encroachment—toward xenophobia. The *jadids* and moderate clerics viewed the Bolsheviks as the lesser evil, and, in some cases, as genuine internationalists. Moreover, they considered themselves to be the natural and more progressive leaders of Muslim society. Like Zeki Validov in his early incarnation, they were reluctant to abandon their masses to an unknown fate. Many expected a Bolshevik victory, and their fellow-traveling afforded them a good opportunity to position themselves for the imminent postwar political struggle.

Those Who Joined the Russian Communist Party

Ironically, few of those who consummated their relationship with the Bolsheviks by joining the RCP were former socialists, with the exception of several former SR's, such as Galimjan Ibragimov. Instead, radicals from across the entire political universe ultimately became full members: radical left-wing *jadids* like Sultan Galiev; radical right-wingers like Sherif Manatov; slightly more moderate reformers like the Young Bukharians; professional army officers, and especially former officers from national units; and Okhrana agents, among others. With the exception of the Baku contingent and an occasional Tatar, there were few workers in the ranks of the Muslim new Bolsheviks from Kazakhstan, Azerbaidzhan, and Daghestan, who came mostly from the feudal nobility or the wealthy bourgeoisie. In other places, entire nomadic clans enlisted, such as the Kypchak tribe in Kazakhstan. The middle and petty bourgeoisie also were heavily represented, as were some reformist clerics. These new volunteers could claim more than their share of adventurers, idiots, traitors, and other social misfits, but they could likewise claim some of the most gifted natural leaders. In fact, of the four general types described here, only the first group—those who openly opposed the Bolsheviks—could boast a cadre with such a highly developed traditional sense of leadership and service. At the time of their recruitment into the RCP most of those natives who joined were imbued with a strong intuition of the final Bolshevik victory. Hence, their decision to join the Bolsheviks had a pragmatic side. It was also an idealistic decision: Internationalism, they believed, would elevate them to equality with the Russians; the realization of socialism was a prelude to the realization of national liberation.

Importantly, while most members of the latter group shared with the Bolsheviks a commitment to radical change, they were not true Marxists but radical nationalists. For them, the revolution was opportune because it lent new movement to the dialogue between the Russian center and the non-Russian periphery, a relationship which over the last half-century had become stagnant and one-sided. Yet, from the beginning of their gravitation toward the Bolsheviks, they culled from Leninism especially those tenets which could sustain their national demands. With the consolidation of the revolution and victory in the Civil War, however, the Russian communists soon demonstrated that internationalism had many strings attached, and the non-Russian nationalists within the RCP soon discovered that the real struggle for equality and national liberation had just begun. Their synthesis of nationalism and socialism into national communism and the problems which arose from these nationalists' articulation and support of this new concept within an alien and hostile political-institutional environment are discussed in chapter 3.

Muslim territories of the Soviet Union.

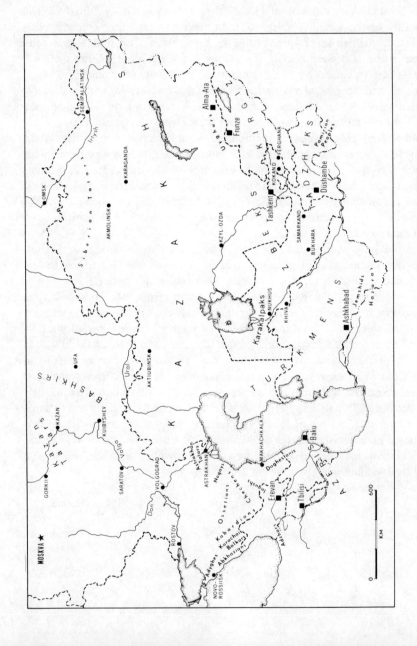

Three

Old Russian Proverb   С волками жить, по
                       волчьи выть.

Solzhenitsyn   Contrary to the expectations
                       of Marxism, the 20th cen-
                       tury has demonstrated the
                       inexhaustible strength and
                       vitality of national feeling.

National
Communism

Submerged in revolution and civil war, the Russian Empire cum Soviet experienced the unleashing of forces which had been suppressed and repressed for many decades. It was as if Dostoevsky had created his Grand Inquisitor and his most famous dictum for this one Russian apocalypse which he could not foretell: "God is dead; all things are permissible." The Bolsheviks, who controlled the Russian center, fought other Russians and natives for the non-Russian periphery. Beyond the immediate task of establishing their authority in newly conquered territories, the Bolsheviks seemed unsure of the direction which their rule should take among the non-Russians: In what ways would the new Marxist state differ from the old imperial one? Should non-Russians be cut loose from the empire? Should they be held forcibly, and, if so, was Soviet power sufficient to hold them? What were the normative characteristics of Marxist rule, and how were they to be implemented? The enormous size of the empire, the diversity and questionable allegiance of its population, the isolated pockets of Bolshevik power, and the inadequacy of communications with the center proscribed any quick-answer solutions.

Non-Russian Bolsheviks, on the other hand, contemplated an entirely different set of questions. For most of them, the revolution and imminent Bolshevik victory in the Civil War were liberating, inasmuch as they spelled an end not only to the Russian czars but also to the czar's surrogates in these revolutionary times, the Whites. The Bolshevik attitude toward non-Russian nationalities was unclear, to be sure, but they claimed to be Marxists, and one of the main tenets of Marxism, at least as the non-Russian Bolsheviks chose to interpret it, was social, and consequently, national liberation. The national communists were, therefore, among the first to fall into the ideological trap described by Maxime Rodinson: "Classical Marxism, for once faithful to Marx himself, postulates that a Socialist state cannot be imperialist. But no proof is provided to support this thesis...."[1] In fact, their contacts with Moscow Bolsheviks during the Civil War had convinced many national communists that Marxism was an ideology which could be adapted to meet their own national demands, an ideology with many faces. Those Russian Bolsheviks who were charged with winning the natives to the Bolshevik cause at that time undoubtedly did little to contradict this impression. It is certain that they were disinclined to refer to the nation as an expendable, transitory phenomenon leading to an antinational communism which by definition would exclude underdeveloped peoples in favor of the united proletariat.

Hindsight grants us the luxury of understanding that it is precisely those liberal-democratic and national tenets of Marxism which are among the first to be jettisoned with the consolidation of a communist revolution. It is not surprising, therefore, that non-Russian Communists who lacked this advantage were inclined to see Marxism as a universal creed promising freedom and equality to all men through the restructuring of socioeconomic relationships. They had no precedents by which to evaluate the potential of Marxist revolution. Thus, any social or economic reordering would be different from that which they had known.

The imponderables of Marxism under these conditions were not a threat but a promise of better things. The Russian Bolsheviks were the purveyors of this ideology and, consequently, they were deserving of support. Lenin personally radiated a certain charisma which earned him the confidence of many non-Russians. Stalin, being a Caucasian, was considered to have a better understanding, if not a deep sympathy, for his fellow-borderlanders in the East. Ultimately, however, it was not to the Russians that they lent their support, but to the Communist party. This organization, although Russian-dominated, was perceived to be the energizer behind the ideology, and while the animosity of non-Russians toward Russians remained as before, nonetheless it was hoped that the Party, acting within the ideological confines of Marxism, would remain true to its creed by equalizing the social and political distance between them.

These new non-Russian Communists approached the Marxist-Leninist victory with a program in their heads, a program of national liberation. Unlike the fellow-travelers, who viewed the socialist way as only one alternative for winning national autonomy, they were prepared to acknowledge no possibility of national liberation outside the socialist system. The liberal national-democratic struggle which preceded the revolution had left them bitterly disappointed, and they concluded that the national movement must now be subordinated to a new set of political variables. The time for bourgeois liberal reformers was past; their historical role was played out. Henceforth, they ceased to be a "progressive" class. On the contrary, they now had become a potential ally of Russian or European imperialism and its agent in their midst, native capitalism. This was the basic premise of national communism: that only a socialist regime could destroy with one blow and in one generation imperial domination by alien forces and thereby lay the foundations for true liberation.

The national communists—as those non-Russian Bolshevik elites who accepted this premise hereafter shall be called—were rigidly dedicated to working within the framework of Marxism-Leninism as they understood it. They sought to adapt its tenets to their specific *national* conditions. At first, they perceived no conflict with the Russian leadership which dominated the Communist party. They accepted the Marxist-Leninist lexicon literally: "national autonomy," "imperialism," and "internationalism" were taken not as a license to pursue their own national road, but as an obligation to do so. As early as 1920 they began to debate and manipulate its abstract formulas in a way which they believed would best fulfill their requirements. For its part, the Russian leadership indulged them, as the theoretical writings of Sultan Galiev and others in the important Soviet journal on nationality affairs, *Zhizn' Natsional' nostei*, make clear. It did so for several reasons: a desire to avoid alienating the minorities before Bolshevik power was completely solidified; an underestimation of the strength of this mutated Marxism or the dynamism of the national communists; an uncertainty over the proper relationship between the Russian center and the borderlands; and the absence of a personality strong enough to control centrifugal nationalism by controlling or eliminating its spokesmen, as Stalin eventually would do. Nor had the Bolsheviks yet given up the idea of a world revolution ignited by their own. In this larger conflagration the native communists, although considered by the Russians to be not entirely trustworthy, were potential allies.

Not all non-Russian Bolsheviks were true national communists. A minority, although they had once been active in the national struggles in their respective areas, chose as early as 1920–21 to remain in the Party and to adhere unconditionally to the official line as it was elaborated and evolved under Stalin, even when it became clear that Stalin's policies not only failed to provide solutions to national problems, but were plainly antiminority as well. Some of these collaborators were genuine proletarians or russified natives of a purely "internationalist" persuasion. Others were former opponents of the Soviet regime, liberal nationalists, and even conservatives who became staunch loyalists in order to survive.[2] During the crucial years of War Communism and the early NEP (1918–23) they were prominent in the "Left factions" of local communist parties. They were despised as "traitors" by the national communists for their servility to the Russians, but also mistrusted by their Russian comrades because their intolerance of their own peoples was widening the gap between the Communist authorities and the native masses. Their role in the development of communism and of national communist ideas was minimal.

Another minority of nationalists who earlier had supported the Bolsheviks against the Whites, in some cases joining the Russian Communist party, concluded by 1920 that it was impossible to cooperate with the Soviet regime. These men chose armed rebellion.[3] Their motives were mixed. Some simply despaired of working with the Bolsheviks. Others, like Enver Pasha, were romantic optimists who believed that armed resistance could succeed. It is possible that some, even at this early date, had fathomed Stalin's true nature and understood that the only possible solution was to fight the Bolsheviks before all possibility of victory had vanished.

Those native communists who collaborated wholeheartedly with the Russian communists and those who adopted armed resistance were relatively few; they can be placed at either end of a spectrum representing native communist reaction. The great majority rejected these two extremes, choosing instead to remain, in pursuit of their own national goals, within the mainstream of Party activity. Within the local communist parties they constituted an intellectual and dynamic "right wing." They could be found in nearly all new Soviet republics, especially in all Muslim territories, the Ukraine, Georgia, and among the widely scattered Jews. Their pre-1917 political backgrounds were as diverse as their ethnic identities: former radical nationalists who joined the Party only in 1917 or during the Civil War, as was the case with nearly all Muslims; some left-wing Socialist Revolutionaries, like the Tatar Galimjan Ibragimov; Old Bolsheviks, like the Ukrainian Mykola Skrypnik and the Georgians Filip Makharazdze and Budu Mdivani; a few from pre-1917 non-Russian socialist parties, for example the Ukrainian Borotbists and Nariman Narimanov, a former member of the Azeri Hümmet; and others. In almost every instance they came from nonproletarian, middle-class and upper-middle-class intelligentsia social backgrounds. Although good theoreticians, their common debt to radical nationalism instilled in them a sense of the primacy of action over theory: an urgency to devise theories that explained real conditions and which could serve as a nonabstract, practical guide to social change.

The Ideological Basis

National communism did not present a united front; there was no common doctrine. We shall concentrate mainly on the theories of the most daring and, ultimately, the most influential national communist: the Volga Tatar Mir-Said Sultan Galiev. Yet we intend to show that national communism can be characterized by a certain underlying ideological unity, especially in its Muslim, Georgian, Ukranian, and Jewish variants. This ideological unity was based on the notion of "proletarian nations" and the understanding that socialism had failed to solve the national problem.

Proletarian Nations

Faced with the distinct but not dissociated problems of carrying out a Marxist revolution in societies sorely deficient of proletarian elements and of operating within revolutionary organizations which were overwhelmingly Russian-dominated, the national communists set about adapting the new ideology to their specific programs. Two central ideas can be found in nearly all of their revisions, although they were articulated first among the Muslim national communists in the East and specifically by Sultan Galiev. These two theoretical reformulations of Marxism-Leninism form the backbone of what we know as national communism.

The first idea can be summarized as follows: Nonproletarian nations can bypass the capitalist stage of development and leap directly from feudalism or precapitalism to socialism. The strongest proponents of the possibility of this jump from feudalism to socialism portrayed it as a logical extension of Lenin's theory of the genesis of revolution in underdeveloped, noncapitalist societies. Marxism-Leninism draws much of its potency from its apparent applicability to concrete problems. Muslim national communists who were looking for a way to apply it to their own situation saw in Lenin's *Imperialism: The Highest Stage of Capitalism* a thesis which came close to explaining their dilemmas. In his famous answer to Edward Bernstein, Lenin argued that capitalist competition for colonial markets and resources would transpose the class struggle to the international arena, creating in the process a world divided into "haves" and "have-nots," or those who exploit and those who are exploited. Backwardness, therefore, once seen as a stumbling block for socialist revolution, now became an asset. The capitalist chain would break at its weakest link, where exploitation was the most aggressive and local misery the most advanced.

In March 1918, Sultan Galiev seized on this dichotomy and molded it to his own purposes. The world, he argued, was divided into oppressors and oppressed. This subtle alteration of Lenin's original categories allowed Sultan Galiev to shift the focus of the doctrine of imperialism away from economically exploited classes of people—such as the proletariat within a nation—to the nation in its entirety. Unwilling to jettison the concept of the revolutionary proletariat so basic to Marxism, he redefined it to include the oppressed nations of the East:

> All Muslim colonized peoples are proletarian peoples and as almost all classes in Muslim society have been oppressed by the colonialists, all classes have the right to be called "proletarians." . . . Muslim peoples are proletarian peoples. From an economic standpoint there is an enormous difference between the English or French proletarians and the Afghan or Moroccan proletarians. Therefore, it is legitimate to say that the national liberation movement in Muslim countries has the character of a Socialist revolution.[4]

Thus, there are proletarian nations and nonproletarian nations which correspond to those nations which are oppressed and to those which oppress them. The fight for socialism, logically, is between these different classes of nations, rather than between the different classes of individuals who inhabit them. "A middle-level Russian or German peasant is richer than the richest of the Tatar Kulaks," argued Faskhuddinov in support of his compatriot, Sultan Galiev. "Therefore we must stop discussing the oppression of the Tatar peasants by Tatar Kulaks, and, instead, talk of the general backwardness of the Tatar peasantry as a whole."[5] Explicit to this argument is the rejection of the orthodox Marxist dogma that the socialist revolution would destroy nations through the consolidation of socioeconomic classes. To the contrary, the result would be not a classless society but a world of "classless"—that is, equal—nations. By definition, the socialist revolution would weld the allegiance of populations to their nations, for only in this way could they become true "proletarians." Both Lenin and the Muslim national communists sought to internationalize the class struggle, but they differed on the nature of the classes themselves.

Lenin, who had fashioned his "weakest-link" metaphor to legitimize his own revolutionary activity in rural-agricultural Russia, undoubtedly believed that he was justified in standing orthodox Marxism on its head because of his personal commitment to the primacy of revolution over theory. But here, too, the Muslim national communists were prepared to draw seemingly logical conclusions for their own societies from theoretical Leninism, much as Lenin had done with Marxism. If the chain will break at its weakest link—that is, where oppression is the greatest—they concluded, then those peoples who constitute the broken link are necessarily *more revolutionary* than where the chain remains intact. "The Tatars," declared another of Sultan Galiev's companions, Veli Iskhakov, "objectively are more revolutionary than the Russians, because they have been more heavily oppressed by czarism than the Russians."[6] Russian Bolsheviks summarily rejected this claim, partially from jealous pride at having touched off the first Marxist revolution, partially because once in power they were prepared to stress again the orthodox road to socialism, partially because they sought to avert any further revolutions—which would surely take an anti-Russian form—in areas which they were trying to control, and partially because they were ill disposed toward the idea of "proletarian nations," a concept which was at once inherently anti-Russian and potentially infectious.

Obviously, the orthodox Marxist concept of internal class struggle and the Muslim national communist idea of "proletarian nations" could not exist side by side as they were of a different piece, if not contradictory. The national communists decided that the internal class struggle would not have to be foregone entirely, but that it must be delayed indefinitely. They recognized that there were some class distinctions in native society; these distinctions, they concluded, were not sufficiently apparent to prevent all classes from acting together as a unified "proletarian nation." Those few wealthy landlords and other *compradors*—native "agents" of Russian capitalism—could be dealt with summarily and eliminated from Muslim society. Beyond this the class struggle would not go. "The Soviet regime, representing the dictatorship of the working class, is justifiable in Central Russia where industrial capitalism has already attained its full development," argued the Crimean Tatar Ahmed Özenbashly,

> . . . but this same regime applied to the nomadic Muslim masses or to groups which have just entered the era of merchant capitalism could never survive. . . . We need to be helped to pass naturally through various stages of economic development, and not to skip over them in order to reach directly a form of government which we could neither understand nor assimilate. In Turkestan, Kirghizia, Bashkiria, the Caucasus, Tatarstan, and the Crimea, we must adopt the principle of *national* and not *class* power.[7]

This preference for national over class solidarity had a practical basis, according to most Muslim national communists. "Muslim peoples are not yet divided into antagonistic classes," maintained Sultan Galiev in 1918. "They do not possess an industrial proletariat. Therefore a proletarian revolution is impossible in Muslim society, at least for the time being. We must limit ourselves to a 'soviet' revolution without class struggle."[8] Another Tatar communist and comrade of Sultan Galiev, Ganeev, was more explicit:

> With the exception of some nonqualified workers who are not very different from peasants, there are no Tatar workers. We are invited [by Moscow] to rely on our local proletariat. This would be possible if there were at least 3,000 qualified Tatar workers, but we are very far from that number.[9]

Others were less concerned with the requirements of orthodox Marxism, admitting in some cases to the existence of classes within native society but discounting these distinctions in favor of national unity. "We take the same position as the socialists in terms of the worker and peasant question," declared Galimjan Ibragimov in 1918.

> Two banners exist, and one of them is red. If we unite under that banner then we can resolve the national question anew. Not all of us belong to socialist parties. We have class differences. That which unites us is national feeling, however. This feeling stands above class feeling. Forgetting transitory class feelings, we must unite on a national basis.[10]

These sentiments were echoed in the program of the clandestine ERK party. "Independent Turkestan is the ideal goal of our entire downtrodden nation; therefore a temporary conjunction and fighting solidarity of *all* classes of this downtrodden nation is normal and logical."[11] With few dissenting voices, nearly all national communists concluded that, at least in the first stage of the revolution, the internal class struggle must be postponed. Even among the communist leaders of more advanced Soviet nations with highly stratified social classes—in Georgia, for example—this view received strong support.

   In general, they buttressed their arguments by pointing to the dual nature of revolutions in underdeveloped nations: social and economic conditions could not sustain the simultaneous waging of both a social revolution against indigenous oppressors and a revolution for national liberation. The former, consequently, must give way to the latter, as the national revolution was deemed more in the immediate best interests of the native population. Their reasoning was strictly practical and defensive. Because there was no native proletariat, or a tiny one at best, there was no reservoir from which to draw political cadres for the new socialist regime. Long experience and a finely honed sense of their real geopolitical situation rightly had taught these national communists that most key posts in the new regime would fall to Russian proletarians. By putting off the social revolution supported by Russian Bolsheviks they believed that this unpropitious development could be delayed, or, if they were successful at consolidating national support, avoided altogether. In the meantime, traditional native leaders, in most cases nonproletarian intellectuals, would remain in place. Only the Jewish Poale Zion argued (in 1922) for the primacy of the social revolution over the national one, but the proportion of genuine proletarians among the Jews was significantly higher than among the other non-Russian minorities. Even the Jews, however, believed that "the new order will solve their national and economic problems."[12]

Russian Communists began to answer these unorthodox arguments almost from the beginning. Their response usually was double-edged: that a native proletariat which was capable of assuming power indeed did exist, but that in most cases it was "too weak and morally too unstable to become the leading class."[13] For the first ten to fifteen years of Soviet rule this debate over the existence or nonexistence of a native proletariat would seesaw back and forth between the national communists and those organs of the central Soviet government responsible for minority problems. As these organs and the policies which were articulated through them fell increasingly under Stalin's influence, the tide turned perceptibly against the national communists. Not surprisingly, as the dialogue slowly evolved into a monologue directed from the center, the Russian Bolshevik leaders did precisely what it was feared they might do: They invited the Russian proletariat to assume power in the non-Russian territories, proclaiming that this proletariat alone possessed sufficient proletarian consciousness to promote a dictatorship in its name.

The Failure of Socialism to Solve the National Question

This second main theoretical starting point for national communism stood in stark contrast to the orthodox Marxist-Leninist tenet that developing socialism would end for all times the national question. National oppression, this argument runs, is the product of capitalist imperialism. With the demise of the bourgeois-capitalist regimes and the ascendency of socialists and socialism, the basis for this oppression is removed. National communists, on the other hand, rejected this thesis, based on their long experience with Russian domination—first because they doubted that the revolution in fact had changed what they considered to be the naturally aggressive nature of the imperialist, any more than the leopard could change his spots; and second because the national basis of social organization was to them preferable to any other. They appealed to the revolution not to dilute their national identity but to enhance it. In their skepticism, the national communists resembled their predecessors of the Jewish Bund, who warned continually that a victorious Russian proletariat was perfectly capable of betraying the rights of national minorities. In their commitment to the nation, they were closer to the Austrian Marxists Karl Renner and Otto Bauer, who considered that nations will survive under socialism.

The changing nature of the Russian Bolshevik party as well as the reprehensible behavior by the Russian Red Guards during the first years of revolution and civil war heightened the natives' distrust. In order to solidify its hold on its political and territorial gains, the Party in 1920 admitted a massive number of new Russian members. These new recruits were hardened Civil War heroes, tough, primitive Russian peasants, and violent, dynamic, and aggressive workers: a different breed than the intellectually sophisticated, westernized Old Bolsheviks of the earlier revolutionary period. The new elements looked on the natives much as the natives looked on them—as hostile chauvinists who should be put in their place. The Bolshevik party, the national communists concluded, was rapidly acquiring a menacing Great-Russian face; and they began to employ more frequently expressions such as "communist Bonapartism," "Russianism," "pan-Russianism," "Great-Russian chauvinism," and "imperial chauvinism" to counter this threat.

As early as 1918, Sultan Galiev began to incorporate his distrust of the Russians and his skepticism of the ultimate effect of the Socialist revolution on the Russian state into his national communism. "Let us consider the case of the British proletariat, the most developed of them all," he hypothesized, leaving little doubt about the true object of his concern.

> If a revolution succeeds in England, the proletariat will continue oppressing the colonies and pursuing the policy of the existing bourgeois government; for it is interested in the exploitation of these colonies. In order to prevent the oppression of the toiler of the East we must unite the Muslim masses in a communist movement that will be our own and autonomous.[14]

He astutely assessed the rightward drift of the revolution and the gradual substitution of Great-Russian ethnic priorities for the socialist ones which initially had dominated its litany. In early 1920, Sultan Galiev concluded that the socialist experiment in Russia was doomed to failure, leaving only two possible outcomes:

1. The gradual transformation of the Communist party of the Soviet Union into a state capitalist system and into a bourgeois democracy;

2. The destruction of Soviet power as a consequence of an armed struggle with the Western European bourgeoisie. In the event of the transformation of

Soviet power into a state capitalist system, right-wing Great-Russian elements, who at the present time are hostile to the general line of the Communist party, will assume power and put an end to the revolutionary experience.[15]

The leaders of the ERK party, too, were pessimistic. At approximately the same time that Sultan Galiev was protesting the encroachment of Russians on native affairs, they forcefully condemned the "neocolonialism" of the Russian Bolsheviks. Like Sultan Galiev and the Bund before him, the ERK leaders adopted in their party program a specific acknowledgment of the potential for imperialism of a proletarian dictatorship:

> [The proletariat of an imperialist nation] knows that in order to obtain raw materials from and to sell its metropolitan merchandise in the colonies it must retain the old system of oppression. In this respect, the metropolitan proletarians who have inherited power from the bourgeoisie are not distinguishable from the the latter, notwithstanding their official recognition of the rights of colonized peoples. . . . Hence the opinion prevails among native toilers that the socialists of the metropolis are worse hypocrites and oppressors than the bourgeoisie itself. . . . The Russian Revolution has also demonstrated that when socialism is victorious in only *one* country, socialists of the metropolis have confidence only in the worse centralizing elements of the imperialist nation and mistrust the native proletariat because it represents a decentralizing element.[16]

This continued and even expanded colonial exploitation after the socialist revolution, argued Sultan Galiev, was an inherent and unchangeable characteristic of all colonial nations whether they were dominated by capitalist or socialist forces. Neither the necessity for nor the attractiveness of imperialist gains would be lost under a dictatorship of the proletariat. To eliminate the problem of continued Russian exploitation of the Muslim borderlands, he called for a complete inversion of their present relationship. Russia was to be economically unfrocked and politically emasculated:

> Old Russia, still alive under the new mask of the Union of Soviet Socialist Republics, cannot last forever. Soviet Russia is a transitory phenomenon. The hegemony of the Russian people over other nations necessarily must be replaced by the dictatorship of these same nations over the Russians.[17]

This two-part theoretical innovation—that socialism does not stem the tide of colonialism and that because of this the oppressed should now mandate the affairs of the oppressors, regardless of what they call themselves—was destined to change completely the ideological justification for communist revolutions in nonindustrial countries. In Communist China, as we shall see, this idea was adopted by the ruling group, who called for the encirclement of industrial nations by the underdeveloped nations of the world.

These two revisions left little meat on the bones of European Marxism. With the exception of those provisions for national liberation, virtually every crucial ideological prescription was stripped away or thrown into suspicion by Sultan Galiev and his fellow Muslim national communists. Significantly, the concept of a socialist movement was preserved, but the meaning of Marxism as it was known in Russia and the West was redefined dramatically. Socialism to the national communists, was not a program for the entire world but only for oppressed nations; it was first and foremost a minority doctrine. By rejecting the class struggle as an essential element, they implied that the industrial proletariat—and hence industrial nations—were not the natural leaders nor the logical focus of socialist activity. By denying that socialism in its European or Russian form could put an end to colonialism, they rejected the notion that socialism was a humanizing doctrine in and of itself. Instead, they implied, socialism assumes the character of the nation which advocates it. If that nation was a capitalist oppressor before the revolution, it will remain a socialist oppressor after it. Therefore, socialism is progressive only when it is adopted by the oppressed. It was through these revisions—and in full knowledge of what these revisions implied—that the Muslim national communists were able to push into the background the latent irony of their doctrine: if the socialist revolution enhances the national identity of oppressed nations, could it not in fact do the same for oppressors?

A "Muslim Way" to Communism

"Everybody knows," declared Narbutabekov, a delegate from Turkestan to the Congress of the Peoples of the East at Baku in September 1920, "that the East is different from the West and that its interests are quite different. Therefore, any attempt to introduce Communist principles directly will encounter strong resistance inevitably. If we want millions of Muslims to accept the Soviet regime, we must adapt it to their conditions."[18] East is not West, Muslims are not Russians. These feelings led to the first searchings for a "national road" to communism among the national communist elites of the Soviet East, but also among other non-Muslim Soviet nationalities like the Georgians and Ukranians, several decades before it was picked up by the Yugoslavs, the Chinese, the Albanians, and others. In general, national communists sought to distinguish clearly between the "Russian way" and their own road by stressing the desirability of adapting socialism to their own economic, historical, and social conditions. These initial efforts should not be confused, however, with more contemporary efforts by modern states to give socialism a "human face"—as in the case of the Czechoslovaks—or with the attempts of modern-day Italian communists to devise a "humanistic, Mediterranean communism" in juxtaposition to the prototypical Russian variety. Soviet national communists sought to give communism a "national face." No attempt was made to liberalize or democratize Soviet experience; instead, national communists sought to bring communism into accord with particularities of national life. Importantly, none of the national communists, at least in the 1920s when an opportunity for dissent still existed, condemned Leninism on moral grounds.

Like their modernist reformer Muslim predecessors, who insisted on *ijtihad*—their right to interpret the Koran in their own way—and who rejected *taqlid*, or blind submission to traditional authority, the Muslim national communists claimed for themselves the right to interpret Marx in light of their own national conditions. By refusing to relinquish this right to European and particularly to Russian Marxists, they set a precedent of ideological independence which has plagued the communist movement to this day. To do this, they attempted to identify communism as an organic stage in the evolution of their own societies, thereby denying that it was an end product only of Western industrial, capitalist experience. "Tatar Communists," wrote Tobolev, one of the Russian leaders of the Tatar Obkom and an adversary of Sultan Galiev, "pretend that dialectical materialism, which they refer to as 'energetic materialism,' is not a product of European Marxist thought, but that it had been formulated for the first time many centuries ago in the East, by the [Genghisid] Mongols, and that it is therefore part of the traditional patrimony of the Turko-Mongols."[19] In the Ukraine, national communist leaders adopted a similar approach, tracing the roots of communism in their society to the tradition of the Zaporozhian cossacks.

The importance of the national communists' efforts to "reroot" communism in their own pasts should not be minimized. It was more than an effort to give communism a "national face"—that is, to establish that it is the nation which activates Marxism and is its prime mover. In addition, national communists attempted to show that the nation was the parent of communism, that it was its life giver as well as its energizer. On this basis, they could reject logically outside interference without renouncing Marxism or its revolutionary tradition and influence from other communist organizations as they were of different parents. By their attempts to demonstrate that socialism was a logical stage in their historical development, Muslim national communists insisted that this was not simply a cosmetic improvement which would make their societies fashionable in a world of rapidly changing political forms, but that socialism in fact was carried in the genes of their nations' historical bloodlines. This artery stretched back beyond the recent past to the Golden Age of Muslim civilization, to the empires of Genghis Khan and Timur. Unlike the early Bolsheviks, who argued that the past must be obliterated entirely so that the new order would not be polluted from the beginning, Muslim national communists sought only to obliterate the recent past, the years following the Russian conquest of their peoples. This period, they suggested by implication, had retarded their normal organic development, but at the same time it had strengthened in almost Darwinistic fashion the gene of which they were the eventual incarnation. In many respects, their efforts to resuscitate the past were not particularly original, especially when they attempted to establish prerevolutionary reformist *jadidism* as a direct antecedent to communism. The actual examples they chose to prove the purely Asiatic origins of communism, however, were not as important as the act of relocating its genesis. By so doing they emphasized once again the applicability of socialism only to historical nations with a strong tradition of statehood. This belief, moreover, strengthened their commitment to reinterpret Marxism in terms of their own national experience. Socialism transplanted in a nonhistorical milieu, they believed, could only be an imitation of something foreign, something from outside. European or Russian socialism, therefore, was ersatz socialism which could do nothing to solve the problems of nonproletarian, non-Russian peoples.

The common thread stretching from the Golden Age of Muslim civilization to the birth of national communism was Islam. Sultan Galiev and his Muslim comrades recognized intuitively that if they were to be successful at promoting Marxism in their societies they necessarily must integrate its teachings with those of Islam, for any head-to-head confrontation would surely spell disaster for the former. Later, Sultan Galiev and his followers would be accused by Soviet authors of being true Muslim believers and therefore unacceptable socialists. This is questionable. There can be little doubt that Sultan Galiev and other Muslim national communists were sincere Marxists and probably true atheists, hostile to all religions, including Islam. Their interest was in the preservation of Islamic society and culture and not of the Islamic religion, a distinction which is not difficult to make for the Muslim secularizer. Islam is a "way of life" doctrine in which virtually all aspects of life—including religion—intermingle and are mutually reinforcing. A frontal assault on Islam—advocated by Russian Bolsheviks and even tried during the period of the "cavalry raids"—the Muslim national communists realized was self-defeating.

Sultan Galiev suggested a different approach in his pamphlet *Metody an-tireligioznoi propagandy sredi Musulman* (1921).[20] The relationship of the Communist party to Islam, he argued, should be one of opposing fanaticism and obscurantism in particular quarters of the Islamic community, a campaign originally undertaken by the *jadid* reformers at the end of the nineteenth century. Muslim reformers Musa Jarullah Bigi, Ziya Kemali, and Abdullah Bubi were particularly effective, Sultan Galiev noted, and their work should serve as a model for subsequent propagandizing. The gist of his arguments was that Islam should not be destroyed but secularized, with complete laiciza-tion as the ultimate goal. In this way the community of believers, the *Umma*, could be preserved while its most objectionable reactionary elements gradually could be purged. This liberal treatment of Islam contrasted sharply with the prevailing Communist party line on religion which was expressed by bitter and sustained attacks by Russian Bolsheviks on all religions, whether Christianity, Judaism, or Islam.

Comrades of Sultan Galiev who controlled the government of the Tatar Republic in 1922 attempted to institutionalize this moderate line through the creation within the Commissariat of Justice of a special Shariy'at commission. This commission was entrusted with the task of reconciling and coordinating Soviet and Koranic law. This same government in 1923 organized a solemn commemoration of the thousand-year conversion of the khanate of Bulghar to Islam; but this celebration was aborted with the arrest of Sultan Galiev. This event notwithstanding, systematic attacks on Islam did not begin until 1928. Even then, they were conducted by Russians and other "Europeans" from the center, not by the Muslims themselves.

The Eastern Strategy

The theories of the Muslim national communists in the 1920s were always tempered by hard realism. The theoreticians were both intellectuals and men of action. Above all, they understood that the Great-Russian imperial tradition was ongoing: that once a territory fell under Russian control it remained for all times a part of the imperium. Logically, their relationship with Russian communists was tempered by their natural suspicion that the new masters of the empire might attempt to perpetuate the imperial policies of their predecessors. Theory and practice served the same purpose—to neutralize Great-Russian imperialism at its source, or, if that failed, to defeat it by forming new alliances and new coalitions.

Like all coalition builders, the Muslim national communists hoped to in-crease their following in order to offset the overwhelming numerical superiority of the Great-Russians. Unable to foretell the native population explosion of the 1950–70s, a phenomenon which at the present time is the source of great concern among the Soviet Russian leadership, these men charted a theoretical course which, if successful in practice, would guarantee them supremacy not only over the Russians, but over the entire industrial world. What emerged was an "Eastern strategy."

The thrust of this new strategy was this: that the revolution should be exported beyond the borders of the former czarist empire, incorporating into the national communist universe millions of oppressed peoples—mostly Asian Muslims. This was feasible, Sultan Galiev and other prominent Muslims argued, for two reasons. First, the revolution in Europe was dead and showed no signs of revival. Second, Asia was a powder keg which would explode when exposed to the palest flicker of revolutionary flame.

According to Rubinstein, the Sultangalievists considered Europe to be "a cold revolutionary hearth" which no longer warranted the attention of serious revolutionaries. Successful national liberation movements in the colonies, on the other hand, could "sound the death knell of Western capitalism." The national communists, he concluded,

> acted as standard-bearers not only of Tatar nationalism but also of pan-Islamic democracy, and they pretended that the Russian Revolution had no better an ally than Muslim nationalism. And this movement was supposed to become a permanent ally, and not simply a temporary one as the Komintern wished, because it could achieve what the Western proletariat could not achieve.[21]

Rubinstein, who wrote in 1930 and whose explicit purpose was to condemn national communism and its protagonists, has left us an accurate characterization of Sultan Galiev's ideas. These ideas were developed by the Tatar leader in a series of three articles (a fourth was scheduled but never appeared) entitled "Social Revolution and the East," which appeared in *Zhizn Natsional'nostei* in 1919 (see appendix A).

Sultan Galiev's central idea, and the one from which Rubinstein extracted his metaphor, was that "the fire of the revolution no longer burns in Western Europe." In retrospect, we know that Sultan Galiev was right, but in 1919 when all Bolshevik leaders, including Lenin, waited anxiously for the crisis which they were sure would come in Germany, he was considered a dangerous heretic. His heresy did not stop there, moreover. The European proletariat, he argued, was weak to the point of collapse: "In no way can we say confidently that there is enough strength in the Western proletariat to overthrow the Western bourgeoisie." Therefore, the socialist revolution in Western Europe, in his opinion, was doomed to failure.[22]

From the beginning, he declared, the communist movement had been aimed in the wrong direction. "It was necessary that . . . the Russian Revolution from its very first days should develop into a worldwide revolution," he contended, " . . . otherwise the socialist revolution in Russia will have lost all of its inner meaning."[23] Of course, Lenin and the leading Russian Bolsheviks envisaged precisely that—a world revolution—but, as Sultan Galiev explained, they were looking at an entirely different world:

> The disasters of the socialist revolution in the West compelled us to accept the simple truth that without the participation of the East, it is impossible for us to achieve the international socialist revolution.[24]

Genuine "proletarian" nations can be found only in the East, he continued. Hence, the East is the linchpin in the revolutionary process. "Deprived of the East," he concluded, " . . .Western imperialism will wither and die a natural death."[25]

The European socialist revolution could still be salvaged, most Muslim national communists agreed, but this would require a fundamental reassessment by Russian Bolsheviks of the dynamism of the Western proletariat and of the revolutionary potential of the peoples of the East. "Soviet power could not find a better ally than the toiling masses of the East," argued Narbutabekov, the delegate from Turkestan, at the Congress of the Peoples of the East in Baku in September 1920:

> But during the last three years, the West European proletariat, which is the most active element of the world revolution, has not yet decided to give us serious aid despite our repeated appeals. The complete fiasco of the general strike of July 21st [1920] is proof that the West European proletariat is unable to help the revolution [in Russia]. Consequently, we must organize without delay our work in the East in a rational manner, taking into account its religious, economic, and social conditions. There is no other solution for Soviet power.[26]

As it became increasingly clear that the Russian leadership of the Communist party was unwilling to shift the thrust of the revolution eastward—indeed, that the revolution was focused inward instead—the majority of Muslim national communists accepted the more dramatic postulate of the Tatar communist Enbaev, a comrade of Sultan Galiev: "We believe that the worldwide colonial revolution is unavoidable and that this revolution will be the beginning of the Socialist revolution in the West."[27] This axiom was to become the earmark of national communist revolutionary movements everywhere: the socialist revolution must begin at the source of its strength—in the colonial East.

To "easternize" the socialist revolution meant to change the basis of its support and leadership entirely. Instead of an alliance between the European proletariat—whom the national communists considered to be docile and servile to imperialists' interests—and the Asian peasantry, an alliance advocated by the Komintern, Sultan Galiev and his followers envisaged a purely Asian revolution consisting of an alliance between peasants and the revolutionary national bourgeoisie. The latter would lead the revolution, they declared, thereby proving that they were not above assigning a prominent, albeit crucial role to themselves. At the Baku Congress, Turar Ryskulov explained why:

We cannot count on a purely communist revolution in the East. It will have a national and petty bourgeois character, but with time it will become a social movement. The revolutionary workers organizations being too weak in the East, petty bourgeois democrats must assume the leadership.[28]

This was agreed to by nearly all Muslim national communists and formalized in the "Thesis Concerning the Tasks of the Proletarian Revolution in the East," which appeared in *Zhizn' Natsional'nostei* in July 1920:

The national liberation movement in the East is directed mainly by the merchant bourgeoisie and the progressive clergy. It is necessary that the communist proletariat supports the revolutionary national movement, whatever may be the forms of government of these countries and the immediate aims of these movements.[29]

Once again the national communists demonstrated their willingness to alter basic Leninism in order to adjust revolutionary doctrine to their own conditions. Where Lenin advocated a temporary alliance between the European proletariat and the Eastern national bourgeoisie, Sultan Galiev and his comrades not only changed the qualifications for membership in the former class—by labeling all oppressed peoples as "proletarian"—but insisted that this alliance be made permanent.

While the revolution in the East held out hope for a successful socialist revolution in the West, it is clear that the Sultangalievists had focused their attention elsewhere. Spreading the revolution—which logically should begin in the East by their calculations—back to the West was considered to be secondary to the widespread mobilization of proletarian nations. Commenting on the April 1920 conquest of Azerbaidzhan by the Red Army, Sultan Galiev fantasized publicly about the possibilities for penetrating these areas:

The sovietization of Azerbaidzhan is a highly important step in the evolution of communism in the Near East. Just as Red Turkestan is playing the role of the revolutionary lighthouse for Chinese Turkestan, Tibet, Afghanistan, India, Bukhara, and Khiva, Soviet Azerbaidzhan, with its old and experienced proletariat and its already consolidated Communist party—the Hümmet party, will become the Red lighthouse for Persia, Arabia, and Turkey. . . . The fact that the Azeri language is understood by the Turks of Istanbul, the Persians of Tabriz, the Kurds, the Turkic peoples of Transcaucasia, the Georgians, and the Armenians, will increase the international political role of Soviet Azerbaidzhan. From Azerbaidzhan we could hurt the British in Persia, hold out our hand to Arabia, and lead the revolutionary movement in Turkey until it becomes more or less an independent class struggle.[30]

For Sultan Galiev, the sovietization of Azerbaidzhan, or for that matter the sovietization of any of the non-Russian territories of the Soviet Union, did not connote at this early stage Great-Russian dominance of those areas, as we are inclined to interpret that process today. Instead, it meant the freeing of local cadre from Russian control so that they might transport the revolution in a more organic sense into their natural spheres of influence. Russian communists, to the contrary, were incapable of leading the revolution beyond purely Russian areas because they were "ignorant and afraid of Asia," an expression which recurred frequently in this period in the writings of the national communists. Any association between the Russian members of the Communist party and native communist organizations in the East, therefore, should be restricted, argued al-Harizi (probably a pseudonym) in *Zhizn' Natsional'nostei*. "Appearing in the East under the sole flag of the Russian Communist party, we condemn ourselves to failure because our enemies will denounce us as simple successors to former Russian imperialism." The revolution must be carried across Soviet borders into the East by "Muslim and Oriental communists."[31]

"The proximity of the victory of the world socialist revolution obliges us to pay special attention to the most backward peoples of the East," wrote Sultan Galiev in 1918. "We, communists, must help our younger brothers. We Muslim communists, with our better knowledge of the languages and the customs of the Eastern peoples, must play a capital role in this sacred task."[32] Not unlike the Russian Bolsheviks, who claimed for themselves the role of "elder brother" (*starshii brat*) among the ethnic groups of the Soviet Union, the Muslim national communists were prepared to advance their own revolutionary experience as proof of their right to leadership among their coethnics and coreligionists in the colonial world.

Each of the Muslim national communist leaders considered his own national group to be the proper channel for the transmission of revolutionary ideas to the East. Sultan Galiev's description of his own countrymen is typical:

Living in an immense territory from the Middle Volga and the Urals, to Siberia and Central Asia, Tatar workers were the best conductors of revolutionary energy in the territory which they inhabited and to even farther places, in the entire East.[33]

In the Caucasus, Nariman Narimanov, a former Hümmetist and chairman of the Communist party of Azerbaidzhan, saw his countrymen as a conduit through which revolutionary ideas could flow to the Middle East. Convinced that Azerbaidzhan would become the springboard for revolution into "all states and nationalities professing Islam," and that "in ten years they will achieve what they were unable to accomplish in a hundred years,"[34] Narimanov appealed to the Russian Bolsheviks to grant full independence to Azerbaidzhan, thereby unleashing her revolutionary force into this fertile milieu.[35] Even Najmuddin Efendiev-Samurskii, first secretary of the Daghestan *obkom*, argued that his country was the most logical starting point for the transmission of revolutionary ideas:

If the interests of the World Revolution are taken into consideration, it must be recognized that instruction in the Azeri language can be of greater service than [instruction in] Russian. Daghestan is an oriental country, which has preserved contacts with all the neighboring oriental countries. On the other hand, our country, having entered the orbit of the revolution, can and ought to serve as the bond of union between the Soviet Union and the East, and, more than any other region of the Union, it should become the channel of communist ideas toward the Near East, which speaks and understands Turkish. The Turkic language will enable Daghestan to enter into relations with all the peoples of the Near East.[36]

In light of the revolutionary events which have shaped the colonial, or Third World in the last half-century, the Sultangalievists' evaluation of the East as a more favorable focus for socialist revolution than industrial Europe would seem to have been a correct one, although at the time it surely would have required a significant leap of faith even by the most astute revolutionary. For the Muslim national communists, who could project into their assessment of other colonial societies that which they knew or assumed to be true in their own, the distance to be bridged between fantasy and possibility was considerably less. If revolution in the East was a carrot worth chasing, then the stick poised at their rear—the threat of renewed Russian domination—was an additional, and probably equal incentive toward this goal. It is conceivable that not all national communists shared Sultan Galiev's enthusiastic vision of the colonial world on the march, but that they chose to support his ideas energetically, if not wholeheartedly, in an attempt to create for themselves an arena for political action which the Russians could not or would not seek to control, whether for ideological considerations or for fear of alienating a substantial part of the world's population to the concept of soviet power. This tension between what was believed to be possible through independent action and what was certain if this action failed or was aborted prematurely is crucial to our understanding of why the Muslim national communists behaved as they did in the 1920s and why other national communists behave as they do today.

Whatever their reasons, Russian Bolshevik leaders rejected from the beginning any role for the East in the making of a socialist revolution. One might argue, in fact, that it was in the early 1920s in their dealings with the Muslim national communists—and not in 1927 in Shanghai, in the 1930s in their failure to lend full support to Mao Tse-tung's revolutionary army, or in the 1940s when other roads to socialism achieved followings of their own—that Soviet leaders first jeopardized whatever influence they might have had over national liberation movements in the Third World. Their opposition to the Eastern strategy was public and unrelenting. In general, they insisted that it was impossible to postpone the internal class struggle, rejecting outright Sultan Galiev's concept of "proletarian nations." Zinoviev's declaration at the Baku Gongress is typical: "We support the Turkish national movement, but at the same time we consider it our sacred duty to call on the oppressed peasants of Turkey to fight all rich and all oppressors."[37] National liberation movements are understandable but misguided, argued Bela-Kun at the same congress: "Liberation from the yoke of foreign oppressors alone will not give real liberty [to Eastern peoples]. It is necessary for them to liberate themselves from their own oppressors."[38] Even Pavlovich-Weltman, the only professional orientalist among the Old Bolsheviks, insisted that the national liberation struggle in Persia, India, and Turkey would only serve to bring native capitalists to power. "We must never forget this simple truth," he warned the delegates in Baku, "the peoples of the East can win their liberty only through an alliance with the [Western and Russian] proletariat. . . . The salvation of the East can come only through the victory of the Western proletariat."[39] Therefore, the Russians concluded, a socialist revolution starting in Asia was out of the question.

The Baku Congress proved to be a watershed in the plans of the national communists; it was from this point that they began to assume the role of "deviationists," both in their own eyes and in the eyes of the Russian Bolshevik leaders. Although not yet in open opposition to the Soviet regime, they made clear in their writings and correspondence that they understood that the Russian Communist party and the Komintern never would ally themselves to an asiocentric strategy but more likely would move gradually closer to the policies of the former czarist government.

After 1923, having lost his positions in the Russian Communist party for his deviationist tendencies, Sultan Galiev tried for a final time to create, at least in theory, a structure which could embrace the proponents of the Eastern strategy and set it in motion. This was his Colonial International. By this time Sultan Galiev had discarded completely any thoughts of cooperation with the Russians; the Colonial International was to be a formal announcement to them that the reversal of the relationship between the oppressors and the oppressed was to be institutionalized: the latter would now seek actively and systematically to establish hegemony over the former.[40] Russia, czarist or Soviet, he was careful to point out, would always belong to industrial Europe, the oppressors. The Colonial International was to be independent of the Komintern and all European communist parties, including the Russian Communist party, if not opposed to them.[41] "We think that the plan to replace one class of European society by the world dictatorship of its adversary—that is, by another class from this same society—will bring no significant change in the situation of the oppressed part of humanity. Even if there would be a change, it would be for the worse, not for the better."[42] The Komintern and the European communist parties, he concluded, are dominated by representatives of industrial societies and therefore no positive change was possible. Sultan Galiev envisaged a Soviet Union split between the Russians, who were to belong to the Western Komintern, and Central Asia, the Caucasus, the Middle Volga, and the Urals, which would side with the Colonial International. Eventually, the entire world would be divided along these lines, the industrial nations standing together with the colonial nations stretched in a circle around them.

The Struggle for Organizational Independence

These strategies for dividing the world into mutually exclusive ideological categories were from the beginning beset with practical difficulties arising from the conflict between the national communists, who sought to create organizations and train cadre to formulate and implement decisions made at the local level, and the Russian Bolsheviks, who constantly strove for greater centralization by investing Russian Communist party leaders alone with the power to decide at the center all important minority issues. The conflict over local autonomy took different forms in different ethnic areas of the new Soviet state; for the Muslim national communists, it was not a struggle between local factions, some of which believed that Moscow's dominance should be sanctioned. Those Muslims who felt this way never represented more than an insignificant minority. Instead, the vast majority of Muslims were united behind a leadership which placed autonomy from the Russians above all else. The struggle for organizational independence from the Russians was carried on in two important areas: the formation of independent or autonomous communist parties and the formation of national military units.

Independent or Autonomous Communist Parties

As we mentioned earlier, the acceptance of Marxist doctrine and of the communist organization in Muslim regions during the Civil War was a spontaneous phenomenon which was prompted and organized by native leaders. It was an autonomous movement which in the beginning had no organizational ties to the RCP (b). Therefore, the struggle with the Bolsheviks originated from this premise: that autonomy was not something to be granted to the native communists by Moscow, but on the contrary, that this was something which the Bolshevik "internationalists" *must* accept if they were to remain true to their Marxist revolutionary creed. Ideological purity aside, it soon became clear both to the Muslim national communist and to important Bolshevik leaders in Moscow that they were locked in a conflict of basic interests: while the former mobilized to consolidate their hold on whatever autonomy they had snatched during the revolution and in the early stages of the Civil War, the latter mobilized to recentralize authority, to take it back. The result was a classic institutional battle, with both sides employing essentially the same strategy. By the creation of a series of committees, bureaus, and party organizations in rapid succession, the national communists attempted to expand their sphere of autonomy by investing each new institution with more authority over and responsibility for native affairs than the one that preceded it. Stalin, who was rapidly consolidating his influence in all matters concerning minorities, answered these demands by creating special organizations of his own and by modifying the scope of decision making and the criteria for selecting cadre of the Muslim organizations. The result of Stalin's institution building was to erode substantially with each successive evolution the authority of native leaders to decide the nature of their relationship to the center, the structure and membership of their local organizations, and, ultimately, their ability to act as a united force against Russian opposition. Stalin adopted different tactics against the Tatars, in Azerbaidzhan, and in Turkestan.

The Tatars. The Muslim Socialist Committee of Kazan was the first important organization created by the national communists. It was formed in April 1917 by Sultan Galiev and Mulla-Nur Vahitov after the first revolution. The guiding themes were openly pan-Islamic, with only a superficial Marxist veneer. Despite these obvious ideological blemishes, the Muslim Socialist Committee of Kazan and its leaders were tolerated by Stalin, largely because at this juncture the Bolsheviks were in no position to oppose it.

In early 1918, Stalin moved to co-opt this committee, or at least to bring it more under Moscow's control, by creating in Moscow the Central Muslim Commissariat (Muskom), which subsumed under its control the Muslim committees in all cities of the Middle Volga and the Urals. This hierarchy was controlled through the Muskom by former nationalists who had joined the new regime. This served Stalin's purpose of centralizing native decision making, thus rendering it more susceptible to a frontal assault, but at the same time it provided influential national communists with a platform from which they could transmit their ideas to the borderlands.

In March 1918, Vahitov moved to insure this transmission by calling in Moscow the Conference of Muslim Toilers of Russia. At this conference the Socialist-Communist Muslim party was created for "all revolutionaries who accept the program of the RCP (b)," but it was not joined organically to the Russian Communist party. On the contrary, the Central Committee and the Executive College of the new party, under the leadership of Mulla-Nur Vahitov, Sultan Galiev, and Burhan Mansurov, advised their followers not to join the RCP (b) but to pledge their allegiance to a purely Muslim Communist party. At this early date they already were aware that the Russian Communist party "could become a chauvinistic, imperialistic Great Russian organization."[43]

Following the Czechoslovak uprising, Vahitov, Sultan Galiev, and their companions in June 1918 transformed the Socialist-Communist Muslim party into the Russian party of Muslim Communists (Bolsheviks) at the First Conference of Muslim Communists in Kazan. Its creators granted to this new party a separate but equal status as the RCP (b). The Central Committee was elected by the members of the party, and not nominated by the Central Committee of the Russian Communist party. Eleven members—all Muslims—sat on this Central Committee; party membership was restricted to Muslims alone, both Russian and foreign (mainly Turkish prisoners of war). As one Soviet historian later wrote, this was pushing dangerously close to another antipathetic situation:

> The Conference made a gross political mistake when it transformed the Muslim Communist Organization into an independent political party with an autonomous Central Committee. By making this mistake, the delegates followed the road of the Bund.[44]

The Muskoms under this arrangement were to become the regional organs of the Russian party of Muslim Communists.[45]

By fall 1918, Moscow's relative position vis-à-vis the Muslim borderlands in the East was considerably stronger; Kazan had been recaptured from the Czech legionnaires and Kolchak's armies had been driven back. Stalin chose the First Congress of Muslim Communists in November 1918 (to be distinguished from the aforementioned First Conference of Muslim Communists) to launch his counterattack against the rapidly proliferating Muslim claims of autonomy. Rejecting outright Sultan Galiev's proposal for a federal system with an autonomous Muslim Communist party, which the latter based on the premise that Muslims themselves were better placed to propagate communism in the East, Stalin forced the congress to regroup all Muslim communist organizations in a special section of the RCP (b). The appellation "Russian party of Muslim Communists" was dropped in favor of the more modest "Central Bureau of Muslim Organizations of the RCP (b)." Stalin himself assumed the chairmanship of this new organization. The Central Committee of the now-eclipsed Russian party of Muslim Communists was renamed the Central Muskom, with Sultan Galiev at its head; the regional Muskoms were subordinated to it. At this time Sultan Galiev was still a decision maker. Now, however, decisions which formerly had been submitted only to Muslim organizations for implementation passed directly through the Central Committee of the RCP (b). In his capacity as chief of nationalities affairs, Stalin placed himself at a critical junction in the decision-making road, and it was from here that he began to manipulate centrifugal movements back into line with Soviet policy. Thus, at a time when Sultan Galiev's prestige was growing rapidly among his national communist comrades (Vahitov had been shot by the Czech legionnaires some months earlier), his administrative and organizational freedoms already were being undercut by Stalin.[46]

In early 1919, Stalin took two more steps to reduce Muslim organizational autonomy. First, the Central Muskom was replaced by the "Tatar-Bashkir Commissariat" of Narkomnats, whose sphere of activity was further diminished. Second, the "Central Bureau of Muslim Organizations of the RCP (b)" was renamed the Central Bureau of Communist Organizations of the Peoples of the East. The former change clearly was intended to reduce the influence of Sultan Galiev and the other prominent Tatars by focusing them specifically on Tatar-Bashkir affairs and away from pan-Islamic and pan-Turkic notions, and away from any claims they might have advanced to represent all Soviet Muslims. The renaming of the Central Bureau completed this process by stripping the Muslim movement of the word *Muslim* itself, and, hence, of its legitimacy. Henceforth each ethnic group was instructed to deal individually with the center. A resolution of the Eighth Congress of the RCP (b) which took place in the spring of 1919 left no ambiguity:

> The Congress considers necessary the existence of a unified and centralized Communist party with a unified Central Committee which directs all activity of the parties in all territories of the RSFSR. All decisions of the RCP (b) and of its guiding organs are compulsory for all Party organs, regardless of their national composition.[47]

Stalin in this manner scored a total victory over the Tatar national communists on the issue of organizational independence.

Azerbaidzhan. The old Social Democratic Muslim party, the Hümmet, remained throughout the period of the independent Azerbaidzhan Republic (1919–20) an exclusively Muslim party; Russians, Armenians, and Georgians were systematically excluded. After the reconquest of Azerbaidzhan by the Red Army, the Hümmet was accepted as the building stone for the new Communist party of Azerbaidzhan, which was created in February 1920. Exclusivity was dropped in favor of a policy which permitted members of all nationalities. Signifiicantly, Nariman Narimanov, the former president of the Hümmet, was made the first secretary of the Central Committee of the Azerbaidzhan Communist party. In fact, the leadership of the party remained for many years (until their purge in the 1930s) in the hands of former Hümmetists.

Turkestan. The struggle for organizational independence took a more dramatic turn in Central Asia; eventually Lenin himself was to intervene. The conflict centered in Tashkent, which was in 1920 the headquarters of a number of Eastern communist party organizations including the Persian Adalet, the Turkish Communist Organization of Mustafa Subhi, as well as Chinese, Indian, Bukharian, and Khivian communist groups. Cut off from Moscow during the first years of the Civil War by the Orenburg cossacks and by Kolchak's armies, Central Asia remained until late 1919 under the control of the Tashkent soviet, an organization which was dominated by left Socialist Revolutionaries and manifestly hostile to non-Russian natives.

With the reestablishment of contacts between Tashkent and Moscow, the first, relatively weak native Muslim communist organizations began to agitate for recognition and independence from the RCP (b). Conflict with the center first became genuinely apparent in January 1920 with the convening of the Fifth Regional Conference of the Communist party (Bolshevik) of Turkestan in Tashkent. At this conference Turar Ryskulov, a Kazakh who in terms of his activist inclinations and innate intelligence can be considered Sultan Galiev's counterpart in Central Asia, presented an important report on the "national question," which had been ratified the day before by the delegates to the Third Conference of Muslim Communist Party Organizations of Central Asia which was being held in Tashkent at the same time. On the basis of Ryskulov's proposal, the Fifth Conference voted to change the name of the Autonomous Soviet Republic of Turkestan into the "Turkic Republic" and of the Communist party (Bolshevik) of Turkestan into the "Turkic Communist party." This reorientation to ethnic identity instead of the former territorial criterion for membership had an immediate consequence: only ethnics from the Turkic republics (Central Asia, Kazakhstan, Tatarstan, Bashkiria, and Azerbaidzhan) could belong to the new communist organizations; nonnatives—that is, Russians and other Europeans—by definition were excluded.

The official *History of Communist Organizations of Central Asia* notes correctly that this was a manifestation of "pan-Turkic nationalism." Ryskulov's proposal, its authors rightly argue, "would have severed the Communist party of Turkestan from the RCP (b), and Turkestan from the RSFSR."[48] Moreover, this move flew in the face of the decisions of the Eighth Congress of the RCP (b), which in November 1918 specifically forbade local communist party autonomy of this sort. Nonetheless, a majority of the delegates to the Fifth Conference approved Ryskulov's proposal.

The Central Committee of the RCP (b) in Moscow was not inclined to do so, however. To counter Ryskulov's move they ordered General Frunze, commander of the Turkestan front and a member of the Turkkommissiia, to intervene. Sufficiently intimidated by Frunze's violent criticism of Ryskulov, the Turkkommissiia on 24 February rejected the offensive proposal. This condemnation of organizational separatism was followed by an 8 March 1920 resolution of the Central Committee of the RCP (b) "On the Autonomy of Turkestan." According to this resolution, "On the territory of Turkestan there can be only one Communist party with one Central Committee. The Communist party of Turkestan is only a regional organization of the RCP (b), and Turkestan is an autonomous republic of the RSFSR."[49]

Ryskulov and his companions rejected this decision and dispatched a delegation of their own to Moscow in June 1920 to argue their case before Lenin. Their demands were fourfold: (1) suppression of the Turkkomissiia; (2) limitation of the authority of the Turkrevkom; (3) withdrawal of Russian elements of the Red Army from Turkestan; and (4) formation of a purely Muslim Turkestani army.[50] It did not take Lenin long to refuse each of these demands, thereby reasserting the primacy of the RCP (b) over all regional and non-

Russian communist organizations, but at the same time indicating that he considered Central Asian nationalism to be a major obstacle to state consolidation.[51] The following spring (1921) the Tenth Party Congress of the RCP (b) echoed his concern with these separatist tendencies in what probably was the first official attack on "pan-Turkic deviationists":

> Native communists . . . not entirely liberated from the ghosts of the past, tend to overestimate the importance of national particularism . . . . They tend to neglect the class interests of the Toilers and to confuse them with so-called national interests. They do not know how to distinguish the second from the first and ignore how to orient the work of the Party exclusively toward the toiling masses. This situation explains the emergence of the bourgeois-nationalism which, in the East, sometimes takes the form of pan-Islamism and pan-Turkism.[52]

National Military Units

Ryskulov's demands, in addition to their openly pan-Turkic bias, pointed to a more immediate threat to the consolidation of Soviet power in the borderlands, that of the existence of independent Muslim army units of considerable strength and conviction. Both national communists and Russian Bolsheviks recognized the importance of these military units. For Sultan Galiev, they represented both a vanguard force for spearheading his plans to organize the East and, in the struggle for Communist party organizational independence, a potential trump card to play against Stalin's move to strip native organizations of their rapidly diminishing autonomy. For the Russian Bolsheviks, the national military units represented a direct threat to their attempts to recapture the borderlands and, once these areas were secured, to establish central control.

Like Mao Tse-tung some years later, Sultan Galiev looked on the native Red Army units as important forums for the politicization of native cadre. In a sense, the army would replace the nonexistent trade unions and workers' organizations for this purpose, but through its various media to those in the ranks would flow not the abstract ideas of proletarian internationalism but practical realities of national communism and the objectives of the Eastern strategy. The size of this audience was impressive: in July 1918 there were approximately 50,000 Tatar-Bashkir fighters attached to the Sixth Red Army on the Eastern front; by early 1919, the number of Muslim soldiers in all areas numbered between 225,000 and 250,000, virtually all of them under the command of Muslim officers. Sultan Galiev envisaged a "Socialist Muslim Army" which would be opened to all Muslims who expressed sympathy with socialism and who sought "to preserve the honor and the glory of the victories of the proletariat" and "to extend the socialist revolution to all countries of the Muslim East." And once again, Sultan Galiev extolled the special resolve of his own countrymen, the Tatars: "The Tatar fighters of the Red Army were bringing into the faraway *kishlaks* of Central Asia, to the *yurts* of Siberia and to the *auls* of the Caucasian mountains, the red flag of the class struggle. They were the pioneers of the social revolution in the East."[53]

It is difficult to say with certainty when Sultan Galiev articulated more fully his concept of a Socialist Muslim Army, but probably it was after 1923 when he was out of favor and relegated to minor positions within the bureaucracy. We must rely on secondary sources for this information, which suggests that, after 1923, his ideas, while still in circulation, were confined mostly to underground or semiunderground transmission. It is certain, however, that at least Lenin and Stalin among the Russian Bolshevik leadership were aware of the potential danger which the national units posed to Russian control. As early as mid-1917, the Bolshevik All-Russian Military Conference took the following stand on the formation of these units in the Ukraine:

> The conference is convinced that the formation of national regiments, in general, is not in the interests of the working masses, although the conference does not deny the right of each nationality to form such regiments, and the conference expresses its complete assurance that the proletariat of the Ukraine together with the proletariat of all Russia, interested in the substitution of an all-peoples' militia for the regular army, will fight against the establishment of national regiments in the Ukraine which are completely separate from the peoples' army.[54]

When it was practical—that is, when the Bolshevik war effort no longer required the participation of national units to shift the balance in the Civil War in their direction—the formation of national units was discouraged. By May 1918, the Collegium of Narkomnats restricted this right to given nationalities, and only then with the caveat that everything possible should be done to prevent these units from falling "into the hands of nationalists and bourgeoisie."[55]

Muslim military units in mid-1918 fell under the control of the Central Muskom and the Muslim Military Collegium headed by Sultan Galiev. In this capacity, Sultan Galiev and his comrades in the Central Muskom were empowered to appoint and dismiss political officers working with Muslim units, a responsibility with obvious political possibilities. As we have seen, however, the national communists' organizational and administrative advantages by late 1918 had been subordinated almost *in toto* to the hierarchy of the RCP (b), with Stalin sitting comfortably at the apex. The Russian Bolshevik campaign against the national military organizations, in fact, paralleled closely their campaign against the independence of other native organizations, a fact which suggests that both campaigns were coordinated by Stalin. By the end of 1918, for example, at about the same time that all native communist political organizations were subordinated to the RCP (b), all Muslim regiments were placed under the exclusive command of the Red Army. By a decree of the Sovnarkom in June 1919, the Muslim Military Collegium was replaced by the Eastern Department for Political Administration of the Revvoensovet, whose jurisdiction extended only to the areas of training and supply of the Red Army. These injunctions severely limited the opportunities for spontaneous action or even unified dissent by the national communists, leaving their sphere of influence confined largely to the world of revolutionary ideas.[56] One Muslim institution which did survive for some months was the Institute for Muslim Officers in Kazan; in fact, it was created only in September 1919. While we know little about the teachers employed in this institute or the nature of the curriculum, it is reasonable to assume that this organization, too, was closely monitored by Moscow, if in fact it was not intended solely as a means to reeducate nationalist Muslims to the party line.

The Republic of Turan: A Revolutionary Springboard

With their organizational base cut away from under them and their independent military units diluted in the larger Red Army, the national communists after 1919 espoused increasingly radical solutions to their national problems, suggesting, perhaps that there is an inverse relationship between political reality and revolutionary imagination. It was in this period, 1919 to 1923, that Sultan Galiev elaborated his Eastern strategy and probably—although not publicly—the foundations of the Colonial International. The concept of the Republic of Turan by comparison was more realistic but less realizable, as it was proposed at a time when all signs pointed to a revitalized Russian domination of the former Russian Empire.

Our understanding of the Republic of Turan is limited to the attacks leveled against it by Soviet historians who were charged with unmasking the "national deviationists," in particular Sultan Galiev, after 1923. His arrest in that year and his subsequent demotion to perfunctory positions within the RCP (b) forced him and many of his fellow national communists into open opposition to the Soviet regime. The idea of a Soviet Socialist Republic of Turan, therefore, was debated *in camera* without the benefit of public media by which this idea could be circulated, a function which the journal *Zhizn' Natsional'nostei* had fulfilled so well in the past.

The concept was two-sided. Because no Muslim national communist would accept Stalin's four criteria for nationality—territory, language, psychological makeup, and economy[57]—they rejected on principle Soviet plans for creating small, modern nations in the different ethnic regions of the Muslim borderlands. In 1924, they opposed the division of Central Asia into five national republics: Kazakhstan, Kirghizia, Uzbekistan, Tadzhikistan, and Turkmenistan. Instead, they insisted on the unification of the Muslim-Turkic world in a unified Turkestan, with the addition of the Middle Volga territories of Tatarstan, Bashkiria, and the Turkic (but Christian) Chuvash Republic; the Muslim areas of the North Caucasus; Azerbaidzhan; and Daghestan. This was to be the Republic of Turan. The population of this configuration would be seventy-five percent Turkic and approximately eighty percent Muslim. It would be independent and sovereign vis-à-vis the RSFSR. Leadership of this republic would be entrusted to a monolithic and highly centralized party (the names "Eastern Workers and Peasants Socialist party" and "party of Oriental Socialists" were suggested). Importantly, this party would be open only to Muslims.

The other side of the Republic of Turan was its potential as a springboard for launching ideas and cadre into Asia. In this sense, it was conceived by Sultan Galiev and other national communists as a way to operationalize the Eastern strategy. "To attract the Muslim proletariat to communism," wrote another Tatar communist, Said Galiev (not to be confused with Sultan Galiev), in 1920,

> we must offer him a national flag, which will act on him as a magnet.... If we want to sponsor the revolution in the East, we must create in Soviet Russia a territory close to the Muslim East, which could become an experimental laboratory for the building of communism, where the best revolutionary forces can be concentrated.[58]

The clandestine ERK party suggested in their program that a Turkestan renaissance was possible if railway links were established to India, Iran, China, and to Asia in general, thereby liberating Soviet Muslims from the "Russian monopoly." The ERK leaders, unique among the Muslim national communists, also sought to increase their education through contacts with *European* countries, "whose culture," they noted unsubtly, "is higher than the culture of our conquerors."[59]

The Republic of Turan is, to our knowledge, the last comprehensive program for Muslim ethnic and administrative unity espoused by the national communists. As we have shown, it was a problematic proposal from the beginning because it lacked support from the Russian center, an autonomous administrative base, and the military capability to bring it about in light of the Russian opposition. From 1923 to 1928 the national Communists were to fall increasingly into disfavor with Stalin and the Russian Bolshevik leadership in Moscow. After their liquidation, the struggle for national autonomy was carried out only on the local level, focusing largely on administrative problems and virtually devoid of pan-Islamic and pan-Turkic overtones. Their ideas, however muted in the Soviet Union, lived on. And while the great Republic of Turan was not realized in their lifetimes, and perhaps never will be realized, their ideas found other springboards to the underdeveloped world, leaving them a legacy of which they justifiably could be proud.

გაუმარჯოს კავკასიელ
ხალხთა ძმობას!

Да здравствует братство
всех народов Кавказа!

Four

Saltykov-Shchedrin   Ташкент это там где
бьют по морде.

Lenin   It would be unforgivable
opportunism if, on the eve
of the emergence of the
East and at the beginning of
its awakening, we should
undermine our prestige
there with even the slightest
rudeness or injustice to our
own minorities.

The Struggle for
Power and
the Liquidation
of the National
Communists

Self-Determination and
Counterrevolution

Between 1928 and 1938, Stalin went on the offensive against his real and imagined adversaries in the Communist party and in Soviet society as a whole. Thousands were tried and liquidated; others simply disappeared. Scholarly and popular treatments of this period are plentiful, ranging from the memoirs of those who survived and articles and books by Western specialists—such as Robert Conquest's *The Great Terror*—to the admissions of the post-Stalin leadership itself, most notably those of N. S. Khrushchev. It is curious, therefore, that the special circumstances surrounding the liquidation of the national communists, and particularly Muslim national communists, in this same period have received comparatively little attention by Western scholars.[1]

The problem is not a lack of source material. Indeed, a large literature is available both in Russian and in other major languages of the peoples of the USSR. The trials of the national communists, for example, were publicized widely in newspapers and other media which can be found in the West.[2] Instead, the problem appears to be one of acute Eurocentricism: the propensity of Western scholars to equate the Soviet Union with Russia in terms of such elementary criteria as ethnic composition, religion, and cultural background;

and to see the revolution and its aftermath as an exclusively Russian affair. Ironically, the Russian Bolshevik leadership itself in no small sense encouraged this confusion. In the early stages of the Russian Revolution and Civil War the majority of them discounted the importance of the "national problem," largely because of their own Eurocentrism, while a few conscientiously rejected as ideologically impure any revolution other than the urban European revolution of which, they believed, the Russian Revolution was simply the opening round.

Accounts of the liquidation of the national communists often are included as part of Stalin's larger campaign to liquidate all of his enemies while en route to commanding a position of unchallenged authority within the Communist party apparatus. This interpretation, while incomplete, certainly is true in part: Stalin's influential position in those organs which were directly responsible for minority affairs undoubtedly allowed him a relative freedom vis-à-vis his competitors for power to manipulate cadre and crucial sections of the Soviet bureaucracy to his own advantage. From this vantage point, one might argue, Stalin was able to define the parameters of "national deviation" and thereby to establish himself as the one Bolshevik most qualified to eliminate it.

It is important to bear in mind, however, that the fight against the "national deviationists"—or "bourgeois nationalists," "Mensheviks," "wolves in sheep's clothing," or "agents" of British, German, Japanese, or Turkish imperialism, as the indictments against the national communists read—began very soon after the revolution, although no collective accusation was made against them until after Sultan Galiev's arrest in 1923. The repellant idea of "Sultangalievism" was debated and condemned as early as 1923, long before Stalin had consolidated his hold over the Party. Moreover, the ultimate party line on the extent to which non-Russian national communist cadre would be allowed to interpret and implement decisions of the center, in light of their own understanding of purely national demands and requirements, was laid down in 1923—at the Twelfth Party Congress—when Lenin was incapacitated but still living. Liquidation of national communism and national communists began at this time; while actions against them were at first limited and selective, nonetheless they were continuous. These purges culminated in 1937–38. There can be little doubt that the remaining national communists who were liquidated in the late 1930s were removed on specific orders from Stalin. But earlier, in the mid-1920s, this was not necessarily the case. It is more likely that at this time national communists were condemned more by a consensus of the Russian Bolshevik leadership. Most Russian Bolsheviks were well aware of the threat of national fragmentation to the Soviet state.

73   The Struggle for Power and
the Liquidation of
the National Communists

Furthermore, Sultan Galiev and his fellow national communists had directly challenged the Leninists' ideological hegemony by elaborating other (and unmistakably anti-Russian) revolutionary theories. For the Russian leadership, what had once been incomprehensible or unimaginable was now becoming perfectly clear: that there was indeed a "national problem" which threatened the success, if not the legitimacy of the revolution itself. Therefore, while contemporary Soviet accounts of the rehabilitation of national communists like Turar Ryskulov or Fayzullah Khojaev stress that they were "victims of the cult of personality," it is appropriate to suggest that these men, Sultan Galiev, and others, hardly were the victims of the cult of one man but of an entire revolutionary party which never seriously challenged that it would rule an empire—a Russian empire.

The impression that the Russian Bolshevik leadership never intended to relinquish control of the borderlands prevailed among the Russian populations living in virtually every non-Russian territory of the Soviet Union, an impression which Lenin did little to dispel in his theoretical writings. The rise of national factionalism, argued Rubinstein in 1930 at the height of the national struggle for Tatarstan, was due to the misunderstanding of Lenin's nationalities policy by local Russian cadre.[3] If these cadre misunderstood the thrust of Lenin's opposition to Great-Russian chauvinism, they did not misunderstand the dominant centralist spirit of his disquisitions on the minorities and the socialist state:

> The right of nations to self-determination implies exclusively the right to independence in the political sense, the right to free political separation from the oppressor nation. Specifically, this demand for political democracy implies complete freedom to agitate for secession and for a referendum on secession by the seceding nation. This demand, therefore, is not the equivalent of a demand for separation, fragmentation, and the formation of small states. It implies only a consistent expression of struggle against all national oppression. The closer a democratic state system is to complete freedom to secede, the less frequent and less ardent will be its desire for separation in practice, because big states afford indisputable advantages, both from the standpoint of economic progress and from that of the interests of the masses and, furthermore, these advantages increase with the growth of capitalism. Recognition of self-determination is not synonymous with recognition of federation as a principle.[4]

Federation, Lenin argued, was objectionable because it delimited human groups on the basis of ethnic identity and not on the basis of class affiliation. To counter the possibility that nations within a federal state might choose to separate from that structure, Lenin devised an irrefutable circular argument.

In the first place, he contended, the socialist state, by its very essence, made national conflict unlikely because the guiding principle of international working class solidarity—a liberating principle—was substituted for the enslaving and narrow-minded concept of nationality. All members of the state, regardless of national origin, would come to see themselves as members of the united working class rather than as members of a nation. But this principle of socialist organization cut another way as well. Not only was national conflict unlikely in a socialist state because of the harmonizing effect of socialist relations, it was illegal as well because national dissent by its very nature implied that the values of nationality superseded those of working-class solidarity. By this formula, one who advocated secession for his nation—for whatever reason—was by definition a nationalist and an enemy of the revolution. Therefore, a national community could not agitate for secession from a former oppressor nation—and it is clear that Lenin was thinking about the Great-Russians in this respect—nor could it separate from the political superstructure which housed them both. Such a move would disrupt working-class solidarity and thereby endanger the revolution: in short, it would be a counterrevolutionary act.

If we understand that Lenin practically if not formally equated secession with counterrevolution, and that the right to self-determination, in his eyes, did not include the right to secede from a socialist state in order to agitate for relief from actual oppression, then it becomes clear that his condemnations of Great-Russian chauvinism were not intended to discourage minority nations from seceding from the empire. Instead, Lenin sought to reduce Great-Russian chauvinism because he understood that this would reduce tensions between Russians and minorities and thereby make less troublesome the latter's assimilation into an immutable multinational configuration. "We do not advocate preserving small nations at all costs," he wrote in 1914; "*other conditions being equal,* we are decidedly for centralization and are opposed to the petty-bourgeois ideal of federal relationships."[5]

Because this idea is central to Lenin's writings from early prerevolutionary days, it is difficult to explain the subsequent subordination of non-Russian minorities to Russian rule as "a revolution betrayed." It also helps us to understand Moscow's opposition to the national communists, who blatantly advocated not only secession but the shifting of the center of the revolutionary movement from Russia to the East. Lenin very early, in fact, established the principles by which these "deviationists" could be opposed on purely ideological grounds. The vast majority of Russians, for whom the works of Lenin had not yet become obligatory bedtime reading and who were not inclined toward abstract theoretical explanations, realized instinctively that

75   The Struggle for Power and
the Liquidation of
the National Communists

their new leaders would not dissolve in a few short years an empire which
their Russian ancestors had made over the course of many centuries.

Only S. Dimanshtein, a Bolshevik with an unusually broad knowledge of
the East, recognized Muslim nationalism as a potentially useful tool to Soviet
power, although his assessment was tempered by his understanding of the
inherent unpredictability of national movements:

> In the East, nationalism is in full development. We must not try to stop
> this natural movement, but we must try to canalize it. In the East, the
> main danger comes from the fact that nationalism grows more rapidly
> than the class consciousness of the toiling masses. If the problem is ap-
> proached in the wrong way, a crisis could blow up, which could bring the
> victory of the bourgeois separatist trends.[6]

Dimanshtein was reluctant to elaborate the "wrong way," but when his
recommendation appeared in *Zhizn' Natsional' nostei* in 1922, most Bolshevik
leaders probably had reached the conclusion that it would be wrong and
possibly disastrous to tolerate national communist movements.

The Southern Border: Turkey, Iran, and the Republic of Ghilan

Soviet options gradually were being circumscribed by events outside the
Soviet Union and by their estimation of the potential danger to the Soviet state
from unstable regimes on its borders, which might be prodded into anti-Soviet
activities by the hostile governments of the capitalist world. Therefore, the
Bolsheviks concluded, these unstable countries must be dealt with in such a
way as to remove the possibility that they might infect large areas of the
Soviet borderlands.

Here again the goals of the Muslim national communists clashed with those
of the Moscow leadership. The national communists, as we have noted,
argued that the revolution should be directed outward, to the East, and particularly into three states which they considered to be the richest in revolutionary
potential: Turkey, Iran, and China. Moscow, on the other hand, was attempting to consolidate the revolution at home, especially inasmuch as it was now
evident to most of the Russian leadership that the European revolution on
which they had placed their hopes would not be forthcoming in the foresee-
able future. Not only had the revolution failed to spread to Europe, but hostile
states along the Soviet border were reconsolidating in the aftermath of the
war, thereby raising before the Bolshevik leaders the specter of "capitalist
encirclement." Soviet efforts to break this encirclement on its western border

eventually led them to Rapallo; the southern border presented a much different problem. There, the border first had to be stabilized before it could be breached, and this required that the native forces who wanted to extend the revolution into the Middle East and who enjoyed significant territorial, ethnic, linguistic, and religious advantages over the Russians in these areas be brought under control. Revolutionary activity along the Soviet Union's southern border, Soviet decision makers recognized, would draw the attention of capitalist powers and invite them to intervene. It was this understanding which prompted the Russian representation at the Baku Congress in September 1920 to reject the arguments of the national communists as impractical and counterproductive to the revolution in general, without elaborating their fear that the safety of Russia lay in the balance. And it was this understanding, coupled with the Russian Bolsheviks' displeasure at seeing another revolutionary center proposed in their own revolutionary empire, that galvanized them into action against the national communists.

The radical "leftist" approach to the possibility of extending the revolution to the East which was advocated by Sultan Galiev and the Muslim national communists consisted in supporting all *revolutionary* movements in the colonial world, regardless if these movements claimed to be communist, socialist, or radical nationalist. On this premise they opposed any rapprochement with the Teheran government, and were hesitant toward the Kemalist movement in Turkey. Instead, they favored a policy of active support for the various Turkish Communist parties. They also backed the Persian Communist party and advocated armed intervention on behalf of the Jengeli guerilla movement in Ghilan. These movements, it was believed, were the harbingers of national revolution in their respective territories.

Moscow rejected this offensive strategy for a more cautious and defensive one. Forsaking their apparent ideological allies, the Russian leadership beginning in 1920 lent its support to the neutralist nationalist-bourgeois regimes of Kemal Ataturk in Turkey, Reza Shah in Iran, Chiang Kai-shek in China, and King Amanullah in Afghanistan. They were strongly influenced, no doubt, by the knowledge that popular uprisings—of whatever ideology—are difficult to control. The Basmachi rebellion in Turkestan and the Daghestani revolt provided them daily with a graphic illustration of the passion and unpredictability of spontaneous uprisings. Moreover, Zeki Validov, the president of the Bashkir Revolutionary Committee (Bashrevkom) and one of the first radical nationalists to "fellow-travel" with the Russian Bolsheviks, in June 1920 condemned the Bolsheviks and fled to Central Asia where he joined the Basmachi. Soviet leaders thus were reminded that the national communists were nationalists first and communists second, and that if national communist

77   The Struggle for Power and
the Liquidation of
the National Communists

allegiance to the Russian-made revolution were openly challenged by Moscow, they would turn against it. Worse still, it was feared that the national communists might infect entire revolutionary movements in the East with their anti-Russianism, thereby jeopardizing any chance the Soviets might have at influencing these movements in the future. Moscow's preference for neutralistic moderate regimes over revolutionary movements in the East underscores the limited nature of the October Revolution from the beginning as well as the inherent Russian distrust of forces which they neither could control nor understand.

It is difficult to determine which Soviet leader or leaders were responsible for articulating this defensive policy, although it probably reflected the true feelings of the majority of the leadership of the Party. In any event, it was echoed in a somewhat less pragmatic form by the Second Congress of the Komintern, which was responsible for devising a master plan for the propagation of socialism in the colonial and semicolonial world. According to the 1920 line of the Komintern, social and political conditions in the East were ripe for a national bourgeois-democratic anti-imperialist revolution. This revolution, if supported by the Western and Russian proletariat, could and *must* transform itself into a socialist revolution, the construction of socialism in the West being a prerequisite for a successful revolution in the colonial world. Therefore, local communist parties and groups were invited to cooperate with radical revolutionary bourgeois-nationalist organizations. The Komintern platform insisted that the two revolutions—the national against imperialism and the socialist against feudal landlords and the bourgeoisie—occur simultaneously: a direct refutation of the national communist premise that the national revolution must occur first and that the socialist revolution—the class struggle—must be put off indefinitely.

The full significance of the interrelated decisions to support neutralistic regimes in the countries along the southern border of the Soviet Union and to refrain from employing national communists of similar ethnic background to spread the revolution into these areas becomes more evident when we consider the revolutionary potential of two important border states in the period 1919 to 1921: Turkey and Iran.

Turkey, in particular, in 1919 was as rich in revolutionary possibilities as the czarist's empire had been in 1917. Like Russia, Turkey possessed a relatively important industrial proletariat; the war had left in its wake political, economic, and social conditions not unlike those of European Russia in the last years of the conflict: military defeat had been overwhelming; central power had nearly ceased to exist; economic ruin was almost total; and the country was occupied by foreign powers. Not surprisingly, many revolutionary socialist and communist parties made their debut in Turkey at this time. In February 1919, the Turkish Socialist party in Istanbul joined the Second International. In September of the same year a Leninist-oriented Socialist party of Workers and Peasants of Turkey was formed also in Istanbul under the influence of the German Spartakus Bund. Non-Turks, mostly Greeks, Bulgarians, and Jews, banded together in the International Association of Workers. In Moscow, in July 1919, Mustafa Subhi organized Turkish prisoners of war into a communist organization and initiated a Turkish communist newspaper, *Yeni Dünya,* which first appeared in Simferopol. Subhi moved this group to Baku, then to Batum in 1920, just after the area was conquered by the Red Army. From there, he continued to direct communist activities in Turkey.

A Turkish Communist party was founded in Ankara in June 1920. Of its three main leaders, one, Sherif Manatov, was a Bashkir member of Stalin's Narkomnats. In September 1920, in Baku, at the same time as the Congress of the Peoples of the East was being held in that city, Subhi formed another Turkish Communist party. Subhi's intent was to weld all communist organizations in Turkey and in Russia into one centralized party.

The fall of 1920 was the zenith of the Turkish communist movement, but it was also the high point of the Soviet-Kemalist honeymoon. Kemal had been successful in pushing back the British-supported Greek troops from Anatolia and, hence, was considered by the Soviet leaders to be a valuable ally in their campaign to break out of the "capitalist encirclement." Simultaneous Soviet support of both the Turkish Communist party and of Kemal would seem to be a literal application of the theories which were elaborated at the Second Congress of the Komintern and at the Baku Congress: an alliance of communists and radical nationalists. Furthermore, the Turkish Communist party at this time appeared to be sufficiently powerful to coerce Kemal into a second, socialist revolution or, failing at this, to seize power. But this was not to be. In January 1921, Mustafa Subhi and the entire Central Committee of the Turkish Communist party left Batumi for Turkey. On their arrival at Trabzon, they were arrested by the police and killed. The young Turkish communist movement therefore was crippled before it had any genuine opportunity to show its strength, and in the spring of that same year, Kemal organized yet another Turkish Communist party which would be directed by his government in order to remove any possibility for Russian-sponsored communist expansion in Turkey. Kemal's artificial Turkish Communist party was recognized as such by the Komintern, which withheld its official endorsement.

It has been hinted—without proof—that Soviet complicity with Kemal sealed the fate of Subhi and his comrades. In any event, the Soviet govern-

79 The Struggle for Power and
the Liquidation of
the National Communists

ment did not protest. On the contrary, the Soviets showed themselves more than willing to accept the Kemal regime and on 16 March 1921, they signed a "treaty of friendship and fraternity" with him to prove it. Even in 1922, when communism was officially outlawed in Turkey, it is doubtful that the Soviet leadership was overly distraught. Instead, it was hoped that the ascent of a strong democratic nationalist movement in Turkey, however much it delayed the penetration of communist ideas, would undercut the influence of Western powers in the Middle East. And one of the prerequisites for the consolidation of the revolution at home, Soviet leaders realized, was the immunization of their own borders to Western influence. Demetrio Boersner explains the origins of this Soviet ideological schizophrenia, which even today typifies their relationships with the Third World:

> [Soviet power was] agitating against Kemalist repressions of the left and attempting to take the leadership of the working masses away from the nationalists, while at the same time giving critical support to Kemal in all instances in which he seemed to take a stand against the Great Powers.[7]

In Iran the "objective conditions" for a socialist revolution also appeared to be opportune. Iran was under foreign occupation (Russians in the north, British in the south), its economy was devastated, agriculture stagnant, and its artisans and petty bourgeois all but ruined. In addition, Iran had a strong tradition of urban antifeudal and anti-imperialist uprisings, such as the Tabriz revolt in 1911. In Ghilan, near the Russian border, there existed a powerful rural guerrilla movement, the "Jengeli." This movement first appeared about 1913 as an anti-imperialist force, opposing both Russians and British. It was radically pan-Islamic; its leader, Mirza Kuchik Khan, was a religious figure, although the secondary leadership was drawn mostly from radical bourgeois intellectuals from Tehran and Resht. The rank and file were mainly Ghilani mountaineers. Armed and financed partly by the Germans and the Turks, at the end of the war this movement represented a highly mobilized and efficient military force on Russia's southern border.

Socialist ideas first reached the Jengelis after the collapse of the Russian Army in Iran in 1917, and the movement was free to concentrate its anti-imperialist campaigns exclusively against the British. Shortly thereafter, the Jengelis established contact with Azeri Hümmet and the Persian Adalet in Baku. In April 1920, the Red Army completed its conquest of Azerbaidzhan; and on 18 May 1920 a Soviet flotilla which was chasing a retreating White force across the Caspian landed in the Ghilani port of Enzeli. Admiral Raskol'nikov, the commander of the flotilla, at this time proclaimed the alliance of Soviet forces with the Jengelis. The new marriage was consummated on 4

June 1920, when Kuchik Khan inaugurated the Soviet Socialist Republic of Ghilan—the first such Soviet "satellite" to exist beyond the borders of the Soviet Union.

In June, the Adalet moved from Baku to Resht, and on June 20 they assisted in the formation of the Iranian Communist party (Bolshevik). In the spring of 1921 Soviet authorities dispatched a division of Red Army troops to Ghilan to support the new movement, the first—and last—time that the Soviet Army has lent direct military assistance to a nationalist-communist coalition beyond the borders of the Soviet state. Significantly, this division was composed entirely of Russians, both officers and men, with no Muslims from the Caucasus taking part. As in Turkey, and even before the Second Congress of the Komintern, Moscow initially opted for a literal but "hard" application of the Leninist line: to support an alliance between a local communist party (the Iranian Communist party) and a radical nationalist movement (the Jengeli).

Perhaps even more than in Turkey, conditions in Iran at this time seemed to justify the Komintern line. The government of the last Kadjar was despised by virtually all segments of Persian society, and its authority had eroded dramatically. British occupation forces were leaving the country, thus creating a situation which made direct action against the central government possible. In Tehran, radical nationalist forces were preparing an uprising. Only the Persian cossack brigade stood between the Jengelis and the capital. Also in the spring of 1920, two other radical nationalist movements surfaced in northern Iran—the movement of Sheikh Mohammed Khiabani, who controlled Tabriz, and that of the Kurdish chieftain Khoda Verdi Khan in Khorassan. Both were democratic leaders with strong sympathies for the Soviet experience. In fact, both had received aid from the Soviets in the Caucasus and in the Transcaspian region. Taken together, the movements of Kuchik Khan, Sheikh Mohammed Khiabani, and Khoda Verdi Khan between spring 1920 and fall 1921 were in control of the entirety of northern Iran. And all were friendly to Soviet power.

Muslim national communist leaders in the Soviet Union favored these developments and recommended in *Zhizn' Natsional' nostei* that the Soviet Socialist Republic of Ghilan receive the complete support of the Soviet government. Sultan Galiev and other national communists viewed the Republic of Ghilan as a test case, first of the Eastern strategy, and second of the possibility of cooperation between radical national movements and the Soviets. It is not unlikely that they looked on this experiment as a model for their own political relationship with the Russian center.

The national communists' hopes were misplaced, however, for it is reasonably certain that by mid-1920 Soviet leaders already had decided to assist

81   The Struggle for Power and
the Liquidation of
the National Communists

in the liquidation of the Jengelis. On 25 October 1920, an Iranian envoy arrived in Moscow and on 25 February 1921, the Soviets and Iranians signed a treaty of friendship similar to the treaties which were signed with Afghanistan (28 February) and, eventually, with Turkey (16 March). The first Soviet ambassador to Iran, Theodore Rothstein, assumed office in Tehran in April. In May, the Soviets suspended all aid to the Jengelis, including the withdrawal of all Red Army troops from Ghilan on 30 May.

These moves spelled the end for Kuchik Khan, but not before he had drawn a little blood in the balance. According to official Soviet historiography, the Iranian communists, with whom Kuchik Khan ostensibly was allied, attempted to transform the national, pan-Islamic movement into a socialist revolution. In a little-known incident, Kuchik Khan confronted his communist allies over the question of leadership of the revolutionary movement. The communists were not to survive this confrontation, which was held over a lavish feast. At some time between courses, Kuchik Khan renounced the vagaries of scientific socialism for the certainties of the sword, slaughtering the entire Iranian communist leadership in their seats. In September 1921, Kuchik Khan's forces, abandoned by the Soviets, were driven from Ghilan by regular Iranian army troops. Later, Kuchik Khan's body was found in the mountains of Talysh, where he had frozen to death while fleeing to northern Azerbaidzhan. At the same time, the Soviets abandoned their other potential allies in northern Iran, Sheikh Mohammed Khiabani and Khoda Verdi Khan. Like the Jengelis, both of these movements were crushed by the Iranian Army. Henceforth, Moscow supported the neturalist Reza Khan (the future Reza Shah). As they had done with Kemal in Turkey, the Soviet leadership chose to support a more conservative regime in Iran because it offered greater promise of being able to stabilize the country and by so doing to ward off Western intervention. By 1923, the Komintern would praise Reza Khan, the new prime minister, for "his progressive and anti-imperialist orientation."[8]

Twelfth Party Congress
and the Purge of Sultan
Galiev

What Zeki Validov's decision to join the Basmachis had suggested was demonstrated beyond doubt by Kuchik Khan and the Jengelis: national communists, or even nationalists with socialist inclinations, could not be trusted to lead their followers beyond a purely national revolution. Soviet leaders, and particularly Stalin, realized that what had happened in Turkey and Iran could happen at home if Soviet Muslim national communists were allowed to propagate their theories on revolution in the East and to enlist the support of other Muslim forces along Soviet borders as springboards for the revolutionary penetration of Asia. Stalin's first warning to the Muslim national communists came in January 1921 at the Conference of Turkic Peoples Communists of the RSFSR, a time when the Soviet government was renouncing revolutionary movements in Turkey and Iran and throwing its support to national bourgeois regimes. At this conference, Stalin attacked "the theoretical weakness of Turkic communists and their 'nationalism,' which is an obstacle to the development of communism in the East."[9] A stronger warning still was delivered in April 1921 at the Tenth Party Congress of the RCP (b).[10]

Throughout 1922, Stalin and the Muslim national communists maintained an uneasy truce at the official level; the superficial fabric of close personal cooperation remained untorn. Below the surface, however, Stalin already was moving against the Muslims. On his orders, the Communist party of Bukhara, one of the main bastions of Muslim national communist support, was purged thoroughly: 14,000 members were expelled, leaving a total membership of only 1,560. At the same time, Russian control was tightened over Bukhara and Khorezm, the two "protected" peoples republics and mainstays of Muslim autonomy, starting with the removal of the *jadids* from the Bukharian government. Finally, in late 1922 and early 1923, steps were taken to prepare for the *razmezhevanie* of Central Asia, the process by which the peoples of this region were divided into component "nations," thereby ending once and for all the Muslim national communists' dreams of a united Muslim-Turkic state—Turkestan.

The Twelfth Party Congress of the RCP (b) in April 1923 was a watershed in the struggle against the national communists, but even at this late date accusations were directed not against the Muslim national communists but against the Georgians. It is possible that Stalin still felt sufficiently unprepared to attack the Muslim national communists directly; he chose instead to confront his fellow Georgians. This tactic seemingly bore the marks of in-family criticism, but it proved to be serious criticism which shortly after the congress became the standard line of accusation against all national communists, including the Muslims. The struggle pitted Stalin, who dominated the congress, and his close Georgian associates, Grigorii Ordzhonikidze and Mamia Orakhelashvili, against the prominent old Georgian Bolsheviks Budu Mdivani and Filip Makharadze.

In his report, Stalin listed the offenses for which the Georgian national communists were being censured:

1. "Violation of party discipline," and especially of having sent a letter directly to Lenin without passing it through formal channels.

83   The Struggle for Power and
the Liquidation of
the National Communists

2. "Disobeying decisions of the Central Committee of the RCP (b)."

3. "Demanding special economic concessions for Georgia," which present a danger to Party unity.

4. "Local chauvinism" and "imperialism," for oppressing smaller nationalities in Georgia (Ossetians, Abkhazians, and so on), and for violation of the principle of equality of nationalities.

5. "The desire to obtain privileged positions for Georgians," at the expense of other nationalities.[11] Ordzhonikidze's report was more vicious: he accused the Georgian communists of cooperation with the Mensheviks in 1918–20; of retaining class enemies (landlords) in the Georgian Communist party; of granting amnesty to political enemies (Mensheviks); and of "leftism" and "adventurism" in foreign policy.[12]

Behind these often confused and trivial accusations lay two central issues. First, the Georgian Central Committee—and by implication the central committees of all local communist parties—were being directed to subordinate themselves entirely to the Central Committee of the RCP (b). Second, the nature of a "national problem" in the Soviet Union was fundamentally reversed. Russian chauvinism was no longer to be considered as the major obstacle to state integration. Instead, "local chauvinism" and "local nationalism" were now designated as the more dangerous. Lukashin, one of Stalin's followers, explained the new equation: "One fourth of the problem is caused by Great-Russian chauvinism and three quarters by local chauvinism." This was a simplistic, but highly significant reformulation of the Soviet nationality problem, for it provided a rationale by which minority communist parties could be attacked and forced into line. The resolutions of the Eighth and Tenth Party congresses against factionalism, when combined with these new resolutions against national deviations, provided Stalin with all the tools he required to subordinate any national organizations to central control. He was to employ these new weapons almost immediately against Muslim national communists in general and against Sultan Galiev in particular.

Sultan Galiev attended the Twelfth Party Congress in April 1923. On 25 May, the Tatar newspaper *Eshche* of Kazan launched a campaign against him, and in that same month he was arrested for the first time. At the "Fourth Conference of the Central Committee of the RCP (b) with the Workers of the National Republics and Regions," which took place on 9–12 June 1923 in Moscow, and which Stalin chaired, Sultan Galiev was thoroughly vilified, accused of deviations and treason, and ejected from the Communist party. Zeki Validov's treacherous precedent was brought up time after time; Stalin went so far as to accuse Sultan Galiev, like Validov, of having "passed from the camp of the Communists to the camp of the Basmachis.''[13] Of course, Stalin had trusted Sultan Galiev and defended him "as long as it was possible," or so he claimed, but then this trust was justified because

There are so few intellectuals, so few thinking people, even so few literate people generally in the Eastern republics and regions that one can count them on one's fingers. How can one help setting store by them? It would be criminal not to take every measure to save from corruption people of the East whom we need and to preserve them for the Party.[14]

The indictment of Sultan Galiev in the "Resolution Concerning Sultangalievism of the Conference of the Central Committee of the RCP (b) with the Workers of National Republics and Regions" was comprehensive and unsparing. The specific charges against him are worth quoting in their entirety because they show the interrelationship in the minds of Soviet tacticians between Moscow's efforts to centralize political power, the revolutionary situation along the Soviet Union's southern border, the elevation of local nationalism to a position of reproach above Great-Russian chauvinism, and the questionable allegiance of the national communists:

1. Sultan Galiev was nominated by the Party to a responsible job as a member of the Collegium of Narkomnats, where he took advantage of his position and relations which he obtained through his position with local workers in order to create with some workers of the national republics (Party members and non-Party members), who were not yet very solid in their convictions, an illegal organization. Its aim was to oppose measures taken by the central organs of the Party. He used conspiratorial methods and classified information in order to subvert the Party's decisions in the field of nationalities policy.

2. Sultan Galiev tried to use this anti-Party organization in order to destroy the confidence of the formerly oppressed nationalities in the revolutionary proletariat and he sought to oppose the union of these two forces—which is one of the essential bases of the existence of Soviet power and of the liberation of the Eastern peoples from imperialism.

3. Sultan Galiev tried to extend his organization beyond the borders of the Soviet Union. He tried to establish contacts with some of his partisans in Turkey and in Persia and to unite them around a common platform opposed to the true nationalities policy of Soviet power.

4. The anti-Party and objectively counterrevolutionary goals of Sultan Galiev and the very logic of his anti-Party works led him to treason, to an alliance with openly counterrevolutionary forces fighting against the Soviet regime. Thus, he established contacts with the Basmachis of Tur-

85   The Struggle for Power and
the Liquidation of
the National Communists

kestan and of Bukhara, who are supported by international imperialism
through one of their leaders, Zeki Validov.

5. The conference considers that the criminal acts of Sultan Galiev
against the unity of the Party and against the Soviet Republic, which he
admitted in his confessions, exclude him from the Communist party.

6. The conference realizes that the nationalist deviation of certain local
workers in the republics and in the regions is a reaction against Great-
Russian chauvinism, which is manifested in many mistakes made by Russian comrades on the spot. The struggle against this chauvinism is one of
the main goals of the Party. It is possible to consider the activity of Sultan
Galiev, at least during its earlier stage, as a reprehensible expression of
the nationalist deviation. But the conference is also obliged to note that
the anti-Party and anti-Soviet activity of Sultan Galiev could have been
stopped in the beginning or at least neutralized within the framework of
the Party *if the local Party workers themselves had fought the national
deviation in the Eastern republics,* especially in Tatarstan and in
Bashkiria, where Sultangalievism had a certain success. [Our emphasis]

7. The conference considers, therefore, that one of the missions of our
Party is to form truly internationalist and communist cadres among local
Party workers in the national republics and regions, chosen mainly from
the proletarian and semiproletarian milieu. They must be sufficiently
flexible to attract to Soviet work elements of the local intelligentsia who
are sufficiently loyal and tested to resist Menshevik, bourgeois, and
nationalist influences and to be able to fight simultaneously the national
deviation and survivals of national inequality which make this deviation
stronger.

8. Communist organizations in the national republics and regions must
exercise tight control in order to preserve the organizational and ideological framework of the Party. If the Party is to consider the nation and even
nationalist trends among the large popular masses, it cannot tolerate one
of its organizations becoming contaminated by these same trends. *A
communist can ask for a modification of the nationalities policy only
within the Party organization and only according to the strict line of the
Party.* [Our emphasis][15]

It seems that Sultan Galiev was never formally tried on these charges. In fact,
he was released from custody in June 1923, "in recognition of services
rendered to the revolution." Nonetheless, his arrest and indictment foretold of
a broader and more conclusive campaign against all national communists in
the Soviet Union. Significantly, Stalin had added to his personal arsenal the
one collective noun which by its very utterance could accuse, condemn, and
ensure the liquidation of national communists—*Sultangalievism.* Sultan

Galiev's arrest and subsequent indictment was a turning point in the history of the Russian Communist party, for it established to the present day a general pattern of accusation against non-Russian groups who might be so bold as to articulate in word or in deed their national aspirations. Other national communists who attended this conference and who could perceive the gravity of this change attempted to shift the blame away from Sultan Galiev and onto the Russian Bolshevik party itself, but to no avail. Skrypnik, in fact, went so far as to suggest that national deviations were inspired not by Sultan Galiev or other like-minded individuals but by "the incapacity of the RCP (b) to apply correctly the national program."[16]

Curiously, the condemnations of the Georgian national communists and of Sultan Galiev were not followed by any large-scale purge of national communist leaders. Instead, an uneasy truce between Stalin and his former allies set in, a relatively quiet period which was to last for nearly five years in their otherwise stormy relationship. The reasons why Stalin relaxed his pressure after these enthusiastic beginnings are unclear, but the answer probably lies in the danger the national communists posed to Stalin's grand design to accumulate power at the empire's center. The national problem, one might argue, was only one of the points contested by Stalin and his competitors. The national communists were neither useful allies nor effective emissaries for the revolution abroad, but they could tip the scales against Stalin if they chose to throw their support to one of his opponents, like Trotsky, Bukharin, or Zinoviev. As long as Stalin's power remained unconsolidated, therefore, the national communists would be warned but remain unmolested.

The National Communists Fight Back

In the years 1923 to 1928, the Muslim national communists enjoyed a short breathing space which they used to shore up their position. The purge of Sultan Galiev caused them to recognize that national autonomy or independence was a long way off, but this understanding only stiffened their resolve to penetrate deeper into the colonial world with their ideas and programs. Moscow rapidly was assuming an old face—that of Great-Russian imperialism; but, then, so was national communism becoming more national, without yet jettisoning its Marxism completely. During these years, Muslim national communists worked to strengthen their position in three ways: the organization of clandestine, conspiratorial groups; open opposition to the Russian policy of cultural, biological, administrative, and linguistic russianization; and the establishment of contacts abroad.

Mir-Said Sultan Galiev

Fayzullah Khojaev

Turur Ryskulov

Nariman Narimanov

Najmuddin Efendiev-Samurskii

Galimjan Ibragimov

Mulla-Nur Vahitov

Ahmed Zeki Validov

Ahmed Baytursun

Ali Khan Bukeykhanov

Mohammed Ayaz Iskhaki

Mir-Yakub Dulatov

Fuad Tuktar

Enver Pasha

87   The Struggle for Power and
the Liquidation of
the National Communists

The charge leveled at Sultan Galiev by the Fourth Conference of the Central Committee of the RCP (b) with the Workers of National Republics and Regions that he had engaged in conspiratorial activity, including that he had assisted in the formation of at least one clandestine organization, was probably true. At an uncertain date, probably in the spring of 1920, Sultan Galiev, Zeki Validov, and a group of prominent Muslim national communists—including, probably, the Kazakhs Ahmed Baytursun, Ali Bukeykhanov, and Turar Ryskulov, the Crimean Tatar Veli Ibrahimov, and the Uzbek Nizameddin Khojaev and maybe Fayzullah Khojaev—met in Moscow and founded the secret group Ittihad ve Tarakki ("Union and Progress"). We know of this group only through official Soviet sources which, logically enough, are somewhat less than complimentary. According to an article by Ya. Kh. Peters, the head of the NKVD in Central Asia, which was entitled "A Page of Treason,"[17] Ittihad ve Taraqqi pursued a threefold goal: to infiltrate national communist Turks into the Communist party and Soviet government apparatus; to obtain control over the educational systems in the Muslim republics in order to inculcate pan-Islamic and pan-Turkic ideals; and to establish contacts with counterrevolutionary organizations abroad and in Soviet Russia, especially with the Basmachis. There is enough evidence to suggest that these charges contained a modicum of truth. It is also safe to assume that Sultan Galiev's arrest in 1923 did not put an end to this conspiratorial activity.

According to various Soviet sources, it was between 1923 and 1928 that Sultan Galiev, out of prison and living in Georgia and in Moscow, most actively worked to create a system of underground secret organizations, centered in Moscow and Kazan, but with offshoots extending as far as Alma Ata and Tashkent. It also appears that many Muslim national communist leaders, who eventually were purged by Stalin, were connected to this organization, although the extent of their complicity remains unclear. Even Soviet sources refrain from describing these contacts as a centralized movement. The Muslim national communists in question probably included the Kazakhs Ahmed Baytursun, Ali Bukeykhanov, Mir-Yakub Dulatov, Turar Ryskulov, and maybe Smagul Sadvokasov, Mendeshev, Khozhanov, Seyfullin, and Sultanbekov; the Uzbek Fayzullah Khojaev; the Crimean Tatars Veli Ibrahimov and Firdevs; and, of course, almost all Volga Tatar Communist leaders.

The membership of these organizations appears to have been mainly of prerevolutionary *jadid* origin, intellectuals who had joined the new establishment and who were disappointed not by communism but by its Russian face; former officers and soldiers of Muslim units who had fought in the Civil War on the Red side; and former militants from radical national groups and parties, such as Young Bukharians, Milli Firqa, or Alash Orda.

It is difficult to determine the degree of contact and consultation between underground national communist organizations, but we can assume that organizations other than that for which Sultan Galiev was directly responsible did exist. We learn from the transcript of the 1938 trial of Fayzullah Khojaev, Akmal Ikramov, Rykov, and Bukharin, for example, that one such organization, Milli Istiqlal ("National Independence"), was created in Central Asia sometime between 1923 and 1928. In 1938, Akmal Ikramov admitted to being the leader of Milli Istiqlal, although one should bear in mind the nature of the forum to which this confession was rendered (and especially the use of the word *fascist,* which suggests quite strongly that this confession was more than a simple personal recantation): "In 1928, I was in fact one of the leaders of the counterrevolutionary nationalist organization, which in essence was a national fascist organization. It was called Milli Istiqlal. . . . Our ultimate object was to wrest Uzbekistan from the Soviet Union. . . ."[18] By this late date, however, all of Stalin's enemies were being tied to each other in an ever-expanding web of accusation. At his trial in 1938 (the "trial of the Anti-Soviet Bloc of Rightists and Trotskyites"), Rykov made the absurd and obviously prompted revelation that his "bloc" was connected to a Central Asian "pan-Turkic organization through the offices of Khojaev and Rys-kulov."[19] All went to the wall, and the truth of the matter was lost for all time. Yet, despite the exaggeration, fabrication, and lying which characterized the charges on which many prominent Russian Bolsheviks and national communists were tried and shot, there can be little doubt that the latter did indeed conspire.

Through their clandestine groups the Muslim national communists, after 1923, attempted to raise the anti-Russian consciousness of the native masses. Their real opposition to russianization—or "sovietization," which was rapidly assuming the outlines of Russian culture—was aimed at nearly all areas of public life, including language, literature, cultural affairs, and the interpretation of history. Their opposition to the linguistic division of the Soviet Turkic world after 1923 was especially pronounced. Seeking at first to have Kazan Tatar declared as the *lingua franca* of all Turkic territories of the Soviet Union (in fact, for some years in the early 1920s Kazan Tatar had served this function unofficially),[20] the Muslim national communists in 1926 fell back to a three-region linguistic strategy. Under this plan Kazan Tatar would become the language of the European part of the Soviet Union, Azeri would be the language of the Caucasus, and Chagatay would serve all Central Asia. They also opposed the introduction of Latin and later of Cyrillic alphabets, arguing instead for the universal use of the Arabic alphabet. All battles were lost. After 1928, Soviet authorities introduced first the Latin alphabet and in 1939 the Cyrillic. Nowhere was the Arabic alphabet retained.

89   The Struggle for Power and
the Liquidation of
the National Communists

Moreover, the territories of Soviet Islam were divided into some thirty-six separate nations, and a literary language was established, sometimes invented, for each.

Nearly all non-Russian communist leaders took part in this struggle, including those native leaders who until 1923 had opposed the national communists because they believed that cooperation with the Russians was possible. A typical example of this latter group was Galimjan Ibragimov, a Tatar Communist writer and political leader, who until 1923 had opposed Sultan Galiev. Like most native leaders, Ibragimov understood by the end of the 1920s that Russian imperialism was the most dangerous threat to Soviet Muslims. Prior to this, he had been preoccupied with fighting against what he believed to be a greater danger to Tatar society, religious obscurantism and various "survivals of the past" (*perezhitki proshlogo*), such as sexual inequality and cultural underdevelopment. In 1927, breaking completely with his past behavior, Ibragimov published a small pamphlet entitled *Which Way Will Tatar Culture Go?* (Tatar Miedeniyetine nindi yol blän barajaq?) in which he expressed openly nationalistic, pan-Turkic, and violent anti-Russian ideas.[21] The pamphlet proved to be his undoing, and he soon was arrested and charged with the following crimes: exaggerating the importance of national independence to the Tatars and idealizing prerevolutionary Tatar culture, underestimating the role of the Russian proletariat and overestimating the role of the Tatar intelligentsia, attacking only the "leftists" and ignoring the crimes of the "rightists," and comparing Russian communists to czarist gendarmes. Ibragimov died in prison in 1938.

Finally, Muslim national communists looked abroad, to the East, for support for their revolutionary theories, but on this count, too, they failed. Simply, they were men ahead of their time; their bold ideas concerning the revenge of the colonial world on the industrial West were not echoed beyond the borders of the Soviet Union. Where the ideas of Sultan Galiev were known, their proponents lacked either the means or the following to exploit them, and so it would remain for several more decades. Had they received encouragement from abroad, the Muslim national communists might have moved into armed opposition against the Russians. They were too much Marxists, on the other hand, to establish contacts with authentic "bourgeois" anti-Soviet forces abroad.

The Turning Point: 1928

In 1928, Stalin emerged as the undisputed leader of the Communist party of the Soviet Union, cleverly having defeated his Bolshevik adversaries for the job which Lenin vacated by dying. The disastrous communist experience in Shanghai in April 1927 and the Soviet retreat from Asia in general was formalized at the Sixth Congress of the Komintern, where it was insisted that revolutionary strategy could exclude cooperation between local communist parties and the national bourgeoisie, relying instead on "class against class" formula; a new line on the construction of socialism in the colonial world required that socialism first be successfully established in Soviet Russia and no more in the West or Central Europe before it could be exported. The New Economic Policy was slowly phased out, and the beginning of "socialism in one country"—symbolized by five-year plans—was phased in. *Korenizatsiia*—the policy which from 1921 had assured non-Russians of a certain percentage of administrative posts in their national territories—was ended, ostensibly for practical reasons: rapid industrialization required an army of trained technicians and specialists which the Russian people could supply but which the natives could not.

And in 1928, Sultan Galiev was arrested for the last time and sent to the Solovki camps. His ultimate fate is unknown. According to some sources, he died or was executed in prison; according to others he was released in 1938 and lived for some time in Saratov. All would agree, however, that from 1928, the power of his personality was lost to the national communists' cause, a loss which severely diminished the national communists' capacity to resist. These factors, taken together, provide a graphic picture of a revolution turned inward: a revolutionary elite less interested in the unborn revolution in Europe and in the colonial world, more interested in the affairs of its own state and particularly those of its largest ethnic group, the Great-Russian nation.

In this milieu the national communists had no future. They could count neither on the Moscow leadership to support their programs and ideas nor on powerful allies from abroad to force the Russians to make concessions on their behalf. Moreover, the national communists threatened Stalin's bureaucratic takeovers at the local level and therefore his claim on the overall Party apparatus. Worse still, they threatened in theory, if not in fact, Russian hegemony in a state which most Russians viewed as their own. These were unacceptable conditions for both Stalin and for the Russian people; and while we have no Solzhenitsyn-like chronicles to depict the purge of the national communists, we can be reasonably sure that even those Russians who were sent to the wall in the bloodletting of the mid-1930s approved of this action.

The liquidation of national communists, both Muslim and non-Muslim, began almost simultaneously in all parts of the Soviet Union. Even before Sultan Galiev's final arrest, Shumsky, the peoples' commissar for education in the Ukraine, was accused of "putting hope in the restoration of a bourgeois

91   The Struggle for Power and
the Liquidation of
the National Communists

government in the Ukraine with the help of armed forces of foreign imperialism.'' In the Middle Volga region, the arrest of Sultan Galiev was followed by a major purge of the Communist party of Tatarstan. In December 1928, the majority of the Tatar members of the Tatar Obkom were arrested, tried for "Sultangalievism" and "treason," and executed. In this group were Keshaf Muhtarov, chairman of the Central Executive Committee of the Tatar Republic; Kasym Mansurov, head of the propaganda section of this same committee; Rauf Sabirov, first secretary of the Tatar Obkom; Firdevs, a former leading member of the Milli Firqa; and many others. During the following January, a second sweep of this same organization netted among other "Sultangalievists" Mikdad Burundukov, peoples' commissar of education; Veli Iskhakov, vice-president of the Tatar *Gosplan;* and Mahmud Budeili, first secretary of the Tatar Komsomol.

At the same time, the Communist party of the Tatar Republic of Crimea was purged. Veli Ibrahimov, the first secretary of the Crimean Obkom, was arrested, tried, and executed for "counterrevolutionary activity," thereby making him at this time the highest-ranking Muslim national communist to be executed on Stalin's orders.

Moscow first claimed partial victory over Sultangalievism in November 1929 via a resolution of the Tatar Obkom (victory over Sultangalievism has been claimed many times since, but, as in the resolution quoted below, the party faithful are encouraged always to be on guard):

> The ideological and organizational destruction of Sultangalievism does
> not yet mean that our offensive against nationalism must come to an end.
> The Tatar Obkom invites all members of the Communist party to hunt
> down Sultangalievists, to reinforce the struggle against all kinds of
> nationalist manifestations among the backward masses, and to unmask the
> still numerous bearers of Sultangalievism in our Party and Soviet apparatus.[22]

This invitation was followed by a massive purge of various cultural, scientific, artistic, and literary institutions in the Volga-Ural region, including the Scientific Society of Tatarology of Kazan (fall 1929); the Oriental Institute of Kazan (spring 1930); the Tatar Literary Association "Dzhidigan" (fall 1930); the Communist party of Bashkiria (1931); the Union of Proletarian Writers of Tatarstan and the Tatar state publisher—Tatgosizdat (spring 1932).

In 1932–33 the purge of national communists moved to the Caucasus and was resuscitated in the Ukraine.[23] Nariman Narimanov, one of the central figures in Azerbaidzhani national communism, died in his bed—one of the few national communists anywhere in the Soviet Union to escape the executioner. Posthumously, however, he was thoroughly vilified as a "deviationist," "traitor," "agent-provocateur," "deserter," "bourgeois nationalist," and "anticommunist."[24] Between 1934 and 1937, nearly the entire Central Committee of the Communist party of Azerbaidzhan was purged and liquidated. It should not surprise us, perhaps, to know that the first to be purged and liquidated were former members of the Hümmet who had joined the Communist party, including Sultan Mejid Efendiev, chairman of the Central Executive Committee of the Communist party of Azerbaidzhan; Dadash Bunyat Zade, chairman of Sovnarkom; and Hamid Sultanov, the peoples' commissar of the interior.

After 1934, the Communist parties of Kazakhstan, Uzbekistan, Kirghizia, Tadzhikistan, and the Crimea were purged systematically. Eliminated were both those men who had joined the Communist party from various nationalist organizations, like the Alash Orda (Bukeykhanov, Baytursun, Dulatov) or the Young Bukharians, and those who began their political activity as Bolsheviks (Ryskulov, Mendeshev, Sadvokasov). Writers, historians, artists, and other cultural figures were purged and liquidated. Muslim clerics, regardless of their political sympathies, after 1935 were accused of acting as spies for Japan or Germany. By 1942 the number of working mosques had been reduced from 26,000 (in 1912) to 1,312. Even the leaders of the Union of the Militant Godless were charged with being Hitler's agents in the Soviet Union, demonstrating beyond any doubt the fervor of Stalin's campaign, if not its evenhanded application.

On the eve of World War II, national communism in the Soviet Union was dead. No underground national communist organizations survived the purges; the entire prerevolutionary intelligentsia in Muslim territories, and to a slightly lesser degree in the Ukraine, was liquidated. Protective barriers were established between whatever remained of the Muslim national communists and the two things which Sultan Galiev's ideas required more than anything else to succeed: the change of alphabets, which already has been noted, successfully isolated the new generation from its past; and a dense and deadly military barrier was erected along Soviet borders, thereby precluding, or nearly so, any chance that the ideas of the national communists could get out of the Soviet Muslim world and into the revolutionary East. More important still, this barrier made it increasingly unlikely that the ideas of the Muslim national communists soon would find their way *back* to their source from the East, where they had been carried by a few bold individuals in better times.

A Note on Rehabilitations

Following the death of Stalin in 1953 and Khrushchev's revelations of Stalin's crimes in 1956, a number of national communists were "rehabilitated," that

93 The Struggle for Power and
the Liquidation of
the National Communists

is, their names were once more made mentionable without accompanying pejorative adjectives. These rehabilitations may have been the result of fear in higher echelons of the Party that, with Stalin gone, centrifugal forces might appear in the borderlands. Therefore, rehabilitations might serve as a functional safety valve for the natives' pent-up resentment toward Moscow. On the other hand, the rehabilitations may have come automatically as part of "de-Stalinization." Although there is no clear pattern, it would seem to be significant that almost nowhere were important national communists rehabilitated unless they had been tried and condemned in the process of one of Stalin's judicial extravaganzas, Turar Ryskulov and Fayzullah Khojaev, for example. Moreover, the newspaper articles which generally hailed rehabilitation in most cases stressed that the victim had been a "victim of the cult of personality." Therefore, one might argue, if "Stalinization" had caused this mistake, then "de-Stalinization" by definition must correct it. On the other hand, many national communists who were liquidated in the mainstream or on the periphery of one of these extravaganzas have not been rehabilitated.

Perhaps more interesting than those who have been rehabilitated are those who have not. In Kazakhstan, for example, the minor figures Zhamdosov, Tozybakiev, and Asylbekov were rehabilitated, but important members of the Alash Orda, like Bukeykhanov, Baytursun, and Dulatov, remain in disgrace, as do those first leaders of the Communist party of Kazakhstan—Sadvokasov, Mendeshev, and others—who were purged in the 1930s but who were not former nationalists. Ryskulov, as we mentioned, was rehabilitated, but he had been tried in February 1938 in Moscow, and therefore his liquidation could be directly attributed to Stalin's madness. In Uzbekistan, a similar pattern appears to hold. Fayzullah Khojaev, who also was convicted with Bukharin and Zinoviev, and Akmal Ikramov have been rehabilitated, but important ideologues like Abdurrauf Fitrat, Münevver Kary, Cholpan, and members of the Chagatay Society have not.

One important figure who not only has been rehabilitated but extolled in several recent scholarly and popular treatments is the Azerbaidzhani national communist Nariman Narimanov. Officially, Narimanov did not fall to "the cult of personality," but neither was he rehabilitated in the same automatic sense as were Khojaev and Ryskulov. Instead, Narimanov's rehabilitation appears to have been prompted by local support for his role as a prominent Azerbaidzhani cultural figure, and this support was launched immediately after or even a bit before Khrushchev's speech. Several dissertations on Narimanov and his work have been written by students at Baku State University, and within the last few years a complete collected edition of his works has been published.

It is doubtful that any amount of local pressure could force the rehabilitation of Sultan Galiev. The man himself is seldom mentioned; only "Sultan-galievism" is discussed in official media, and when it is, it is always condemned. Nor have the names of the important Georgian national communists Filip Makharadze and Budu Mdivani been cleared. Ironically, no small number of fellow Georgians who at first were henchmen for Stalin but who later were executed by their master have been rehabilitated: Mamia Orakhelashvili, Shalva Eliava, Nestor Lakoba, Soso Buashidze, Gregorii Ordzhonikidze, Alesha Svanidze, to mention a few.

If there is a formula by which we may determine who can be rehabilitated and who cannot, it is difficult to recognize. Indeed, there would seem to be both different methods to rehabilitation—local pressure or central decree—and different types of rehabilitation itself (that is, cultural, historical, national). What is reasonably evident is that those national communists whose ideas and actions were the most infectious have not and probably will not be reestablished in favor, for this would illuminate a legacy which Soviet state builders would like to purge from Soviet memory.

1 МАЯ.
РАБОЧИМ НЕЧЕГО ТЕРЯТЬ, КРОМЕ СВОИХ ЦЕПЕЙ,
А ПРИОБРЕТУТ ОНИ ЦЕЛЫЙ МИР.
К. Маркс и Ф. Энгельс.

Five

Muammar Khadafi   By God, if Russia is truly
socialist, then we are not
socialist. We must search
for another principle to
realize justice, but we
won't call it socialism in
order to be independent.

The Legacy of
Muslim National
Communism

A legacy can be many things, from the statue which dominates a city square to the traces of a heroic legend which hide in the corners of a child's mind. It can be a living presence, like an army or a governmental system, or a body of ideas or disconnected notions about the past which float through the collective memory of a society. Legacies often are ambiguous or incorrectly attributed to soil from which they did not spring. They are the objects of much exaggeration and, just as often, the subjects of heated debates. In short, it is difficult to specify the precise nature of any legacy; and quantification of its various facets is virtually impossible.

The legacy of Muslim national communism of the 1920s in the Soviet Union and abroad raises all of these problems. Moreover, what is difficult to discern in free societies becomes even more obscured in states like the Soviet Union, where certain ideas cannot be expressed openly, where the interpretation of events must conform to rigidly established criteria, where institutions are regulated in accordance with doctrinal requirements, and where the human repositories of history can be eliminated quickly and easily, having no intrinsic value in the eyes of the State. In spite of these limitations—but perhaps because of them, for the glorification of the forbidden often exceeds that of the well-known—we can identify among the Muslim populations of the Soviet Union certain attitudes and feelings which probably can be attributed to the influence of the national communists and their ideas. We shall consider this problem first, and then turn our attention to national communism's legacy beyond Soviet borders.

Muslim National Communism's Legacy in the USSR

Stalin and his supporters completely destroyed all tangible manifestations of Muslim national communism and liquidated all important Muslim national communists in the late 1920s and 1930s. No institutional or human legacy exists; all organizations through which national communist ideas were spread and the men who spread them were eliminated. The existence of an ideological legacy—a body of ideas from which inspiration and guidance are drawn or around which courses of action are plotted—is problematic. The original writings of the national communists are not accessible to a younger Muslim generation, first because it is illegal to read them and, second, because the changes in alphabet have left this generation unable to read the many works of Muslim national communists which were written in local languages and in Arabic script. A few "reliable" individuals are granted access to the Russian periodicals and journals of this period in which it is possible to find essays by Sultan Galiev and others (*Zhizn' Natsional' nostei, Pravda Vostoka, Bakinsii Rabochi,* and so on), but it is doubtful that they are permitted to read many of the most important works and certain that they are not permitted to write about them even if they gain access. It can be argued, however, that the selective reedition of the works of national communists, like those of Narimanov, Khodzhaev, or Ryskulov, allows those who are truly interested in rediscovering the essence of the message of the national communists to read between the lines. It is likely that it is no more difficult today for a young Tatar to discover Sultan Galiev than for a Russian dissenter to discover Berdiaev.

The personal imprint of important Muslim national communist leaders on Soviet Muslim society is not a deep one.

> Sultan Galiev [writes Maxime Rodinson] does not seem to have left in the Muslim territories of the USSR a real spiritual legacy. One doesn't know what would happen if it were possible to create oppositional political parties. But what we may imagine concerning the aspirations of the peoples of these areas shows them to be far from Sultan Galiev. Their demands seem to be of a more reformist type . . . .[1]

This failure of Sultan Galiev and other national communists to leave a strong personal legacy is a significant one, given the "past-centered awareness" which is common to most Muslims (in contrast to Christian awareness which projects a "Golden Age" in the future). If it were possible today to rediscover even a very idealized Sultangalievism, which is what one might expect, the impact of national communism would be considerably more verifiable, yet this does not seem to be the case. That it is difficult to discover any reference to Sultan Galiev or to his fellow national communists in the unofficial expressions of Soviet Muslims suggests that the Soviet campaign to blunt the edge of the national communists' message by eliminating its messengers has been successful, or, on the other hand—but this is less certain—that the message from the beginning lacked mass appeal and subsequently was forgotten. The recurrent official Soviet attacks against Sultangalievism, however, indicate beyond any doubt that someone has not forgotten who he was and what he stood for.

National communism's legacy does not turn on the heroic personalities which the movement added to the current of Muslim history, however, but on the changed psychological atmosphere which the national communist movement helped to create. This psychological legacy feeds on the national communists' belief that communism is a legitimate, "natural," and logical stage in the long and painful, but glorious unfolding of Muslim history which began in 1552 and, they hoped, eventually would lead to the reestablishment of Muslim power and cultural renaissance. Communism, to be sure, is part of the "Russian period" of Muslim history, but national communists rejected the notion that an exclusive relationship must exist between the Russian nation and communist ideology. Muslim national communism, therefore, became communism without Russians—different in its aims, its doctrine, and its application. Muslim national communists insisted that communism could be made to serve a long historical tradition, that it could be naturalized and adapted to the Muslim sociopolitical environment.

This *état d'esprit* remains strong among Soviet Muslims today, as the following popular Uzbek poem illustrates:

My cradle was the territory of Great Asia,
The cradle that rocked Ulughbek and Avicenna,
The light in whose eyes has spanned a thousand years.
This is the world that led the caravan of history,
This Samarkand, this Bukhara—these two universes.
This is the cradle of Communism in the bosom of the East![2]

What is now widely accepted by Soviet Muslims is that it is unnecessary to search for a special "national way" to communism, as one cradle can house, nurture, and, to a significant degree, blend the two ideologies. To the contemporary Soviet Muslim elite, nationalism and communism do not stand in doctrinal opposition to each other or even in a determined sequence. Instead, they are considered to exist simultaneously within the same historical tradition but on different planes. Instinctively, these elites have inverted Stalin's famous formula to fit their own understanding of communism: Soviet Muslim society is "national in essence and socialist in form" and not the other way around. The militance which characterized the search of the Muslim national communists of the 1920s and 1930s for a "national way" to communism is gone, and the lesson which, ironically, the Russians themselves taught Soviet Muslims has come to stay: that, just as Ivan the Terrible can coexist amicably with Stalin, Andrei Rublev with Emelian Iaroslavski, and Alexandre Nevski with Demian Bednyi, so Timur can live side by side with Lenin, and the Turkic national epics, *Alpamysh* or *Manas,* can share a shelf with the writings of Marx and Engels.[3]

The belief that genuine communism is realizable only in the East because of the unique historical, political, social, and economic conditions which are peculiar to the non-European, nonindustrial world, remains strong in most Soviet Muslim regions. This, too, is part of the national communists' legacy, and in recent years the insistence of Soviet Muslims on the distinctive properties of their own brand of communism has intensified. James Critchlow, one of the most astute observers of Soviet Muslim affairs, notes that Soviet Muslim elites have undertaken to forge "a distinct personality" and a separate ideological base. "Soviet Moslem communism," he notes, "shows signs of being no longer a tame adjunct of Soviet strategy; in it are the seeds of a new ideological challenge and incipient threat to the 'democratic centralism' on which all Soviet administration is based."[4] This insistence has not become militant for reasons which we already have noted, but also because other forces have made militance unnecessary. The extraordinarily rapid Soviet Muslim population growth has diminished the importance of "revolutionary springboards," which from the beginning were intended to augment the size of the Russian Muslim population in a head-to-head showdown with Russia and the West. Muslim political and administrative unity, which was to be brought about under a "Republic of Turan," similarly has become secondary to Muslim cultural, intellectual, and psychological unity which is progressing, perhaps paradoxically, as the Muslim regions are sovietized and illiteracy is eradicated.

In addition, Soviet Muslim elites must be painfully aware that their claim to lead the revolutionary forces in the colonial world has been attenuated severely by one irrefutable fact: most of Asia, including such backward areas as Southern Yemen or Bhutan, is free and independent, and other Muslim peoples, like Bangladesh, currently are displaying an impressive amount of revolutionary zeal. In this regard, Soviet Muslims no longer are masters, but pupils. Maxime Rodinson warns of interpreting Soviet Muslim quiescence too literally. "They do not seem to be tempted by the role of propagators of the revolution in the East," he notes. "But perhaps the lid of official conformism hides other boiling realities."[5] Nonetheless, Rodinson is correct to argue that Soviet Muslim demands tend to be of a reformist and not a revolutionary type. The immediate objectives of Soviet Muslim elites are to secure greater local autonomy within the existing Soviet federation and to develop more influence in Moscow over central decision making regarding their regions.

In pursuit of these objectives, Soviet Muslims rapidly are accumulating important resources and advantages. One of their most significant resources is the fast-expanding size of Soviet Muslim populations. The low fertility rates and high infant mortality rates which were prevalent in Muslim regions fifty years ago have been reversed. Figures from the 1970 Soviet census indicate that Soviet Muslims now have fertility rates upward of 1,800 per thousand, while Great-Russians reproduce at only 863 per thousand. Muslim population growth appears most dramatic when shown in terms of absolute increases between the censual years of 1959 and 1970:

Ethnic Group[6]	% of Total Increase 1959–70	1959 (Millions)	1970 (Millions)
Great-Russians	13	114	129
Ukrainians	9	37	40
Belorussians	14	8	9
Uzbeks	53	6	9
Tatars	19	5	6
Kazakhs	46	3.6	5.3
Azerbaidzhanis	49	3	4.3
Tadzhiks	53	1.4	2.2
Turkmens	52	1	1.5
Kirghiz	50	.9	1.5

A recent extrapolation of this trend projects a high-end total of some ninety million Soviet Muslims by the year 2000 (see appendix F). Thus it would appear that the new Muslim communists can count on an immensely larger potential following—barring any unforeseen events—for their brand of Eastern communism than the Muslim national communists could count on in the 1920s.

This demographic shift will color virtually every facet of Muslim-Russian relations. The percentage of the Russian population in all of the Muslim republics is declining as a result of the native population explosion, but also from the emigration of Russians from these areas. This change accompanied—and perhaps was at least in part precipitated by—the emergence of a new Muslim elite. This new elite has increased its representation in the official apparatus, in educational institutions, in technical and scientific occupations, and in political representation at both the local and state levels. The result is a significant *de facto korenizatsiia,* the formula first tried in the 1920s to assure the assignment of a certain percentage of trained natives to important posts within their own republics. Critchlow notes the paradoxical aspect of these educational and occupational inroads:

> The new elites presumably owe their status to Sovietization which has given them modern professional training and an economic and social structure in which to use it. At the same time, they suffer from a paradox of Soviet society: the system encourages minority education but restricts the occupational mobility of the Moslem graduates toward the center. They are victims of discrimination with respect to admission to the All-Union political-administrative apparatus which is the real seat of power and position. Members of the Soviet Moslem elite have a vested interest in the system, but to the extent that it blocks their advancement at the republican level they must push to improve the position of their Republic.[7]

This "enforced parochialism" ultimately strengthens the special self-identity of Muslims to their sociopolitical environment. It also strengthens the new Muslim elites' commitment to fashion an ideology which better explains their vision of a more independent relationship vis-à-vis the Russian center and of a more elaborate role for their societies in the affairs of the non-Western world.

In many respects the new elites differ from the Muslim national communist elites of fifty years earlier. Where the latter came from different social backgrounds, from both secular and nonsecular schools, and from a number of different political traditions, the new Soviet Muslim elite is more uniform in its experience and its attitudes. Nearly all have been russianized equally, employing Russian as a second or professional language, and most are educated in local Russian schools. They are younger than their Russian counterparts. Most, in fact, were born in the late 1930s and 1940s. As intellectuals, the new elites are less sophisticated than their predecessors, less iconoclastic, paradoxically more traditional, and less revolutionary. The majority probably are the sons of peasants (the working class still was almost nonexistent in the 1930s and 1940s in Muslim areas with the exception of Baku), and this background exerts a deep and lasting influence over them. The impetus which they lend to *mirasism*—the resuscitation of the ancient past—is considerable, despite the official Soviet campaign against this movement.

Before the demographic shift was recognized and before the processes of sovietization threw many Russians and Muslims together for the first time, it was widely assumed by Soviet policy makers that national differences in the Soviet Union gradually would diminish through the biological assimilation of smaller peoples by larger ones and that this would result in a withering of the significance of national boundaries. As late as 1961, this idea was formalized in the Party program. The mechanism would be two-staged: in the first, *sblizhenie,* the peoples of the Soviet Union would draw closer together; and in the second, *sliianie,* they would merge—both biologically and spiritually— into one people. No one in the Soviet leadership or in the ethnic populations at large doubted that this formula signified the Soviet leadership's desire to russianize all non-Russians, that the Russian language, cultural standards, and behavioral norms would become the only acceptable bases for all the peoples of the Soviet Union.

The 1970 Soviet census and other recent sociological data, however, de-stroyed whatever illusions Soviet leaders may have harbored for the success of these assimilationist policies among Soviet Muslims. In short, to judge by language criteria or the rate of intermarriage between Muslims and non-Muslims, Soviet Muslims demonstrated almost no inclination to assimilate to the Russians, in spite of the latter's intensive and ongoing campaigns to promote this result. Nor was it found that national boundaries became less significant with increased contact between Russians and Muslims; the census, in fact, indicated that in 1970 less than one percent of Central Asians lived outside of their nominal ethnic territories. These territories remain compact and largely immune to Russian pressures.

Not only are Soviet Muslims not assimilating to Russian culture either within or outside of their native republics, but it would appear, at least in the case of one of the most dynamic Central Asian Muslim groups, the Uzbeks, that other smaller Muslim peoples are slowly assimilating to them. The out-lines of this process are still unclear. There can be little doubt, however, that many Uzbeks see themselves as the natural leaders of Soviet Muslims, much as Sultan Galiev and the Volga Tatars saw themselves in the 1920s. It is not unlikely that the Uzbeks have begun to view themselves vis-à-vis other Soviet Muslims in the same way the Russians portrayed themselves in terms of all other minorities in the USSR—as the "elder brother" (*starshyi brat*). This posturing has some justification. The Uzbeks are the largest of the Soviet Muslim populations and one of the fastest growing. They have a strong economy (the world's first or second largest cotton exporter) which has translated into political representation at the center. Moreover, the cultural splendor of Uzbekistan has been restored and upgraded in terms of both its ancient symbolism—such as the restoration of the cities of Samarkand, Bukhara, and Khiva—and as a center—mainly through Tashkent—for the conduct of formal economic, diplomatic, and cultural relations with Muslim countries of the Middle East and Afghanistan.

The "opening" of Soviet Muslim territories, and particularly through the door of Tashkent, is certain to have more than a superficial impact on the new Soviet Muslim intelligentsia. The first effect of these broadened contacts—and perhaps the most ominous for future Russian leaders in Moscow—is the expanded awareness by Muslim elites of a new universe of social and political alternatives and the realization that a sociopolitical universe which includes only Russians and Soviet Muslims is too confining. Foreign Muslims now are numerous in the main cities of Central Asia and especially in Central Asian universities. On the other hand, more Soviet Muslims than ever before are representing the Soviet government abroad in various capacities, and particularly as emissaries to other Muslim countries.[8] The intensity and regularity of contacts between Soviet Muslims and Muslim outsiders is difficult to ascertain, as are the long-term effects of these relationships. One possibility among many requires our attention. Foreign Muslims who come to the USSR and who host Soviet Muslim delegations abroad often belong to new Asian and African states which have only recently been freed from European tutelage. The leaders of these new states not infrequently take their inspiration for economic and political development from some form of socialism. An "Egyptian way," a "Libyan way," or a "South Yemeni way" to socialism, to mention only a few, resemble on a very basic level the national communism of the Muslim national communists, at least inasmuch as these various national "ways" generally subordinate everything, including the concept of class struggle, to the consolidation of the national liberation movement. The ideas of Sultan Galiev, furthermore, are known to some of the leaders of these national liberation struggles. One must wonder when it will be that Soviet Muslims, under the stimuli of events taking place in the Muslim world beyond their borders, will begin to examine again the ideas of their own national communists, ideas whose existence is already suspected but which, ironically, may return to the Soviet Union from the outside.

Soviet Muslims and particularly Central Asian Muslims led by the Uzbeks, in recent years have displayed an assertiveness in their relations with the Russian center, certainly due in part to their formidable population growth and fast developing economic power, but also to the changing perception many

Muslim elites have of themselves and their societies. One probable result of
the opening of Central Asia to outside influences is the stress laid by local
Moslem writers on the "federal" nature of the Soviet Union, on the
gosudarstvennost' (the quality of being a state), and on the status of each
Muslim republic as a separate socialist state on a larger spectrum of socialist
states.[9] Yet one senses that the elites of Soviet republics like Uzbekistan see
themselves not so much in terms of those political, social, or cultural characteristics which they share with Eastern European socialist states like
Czechoslovakia or Rumania, but instead more as a Third World nation, albeit
one whose immediate future will hold development before national struggle
and not the other way around.

Paradoxically, official Soviet efforts to build a federation which is
"socialist in content, national in form," because of some important successes, ultimately may have the effect of making national integration more
difficult and native demands more prevalent. New Soviet Muslim ethnic units
which possess distinct administrative, economic, and political characteristics
and which conform to identifiable ethnoterritorial boundaries have come into
being. Whether these "nations" have become nations in fact, with a true
sense of national consciousness based on an identifiable distinct culture, remains to be proved. It is certain that one culture, "Irano-Turkish Islamic"
culture, remains common to almost all Soviet Muslims, and that with the
spread of mass education this common patrimony has become more widely
understood and supported than it was fifty or sixty years ago.

Regardless if something resembling a modern national consciousness is
emerging in the Muslim republics of the Soviet Union, the fact that Soviet
social planners have attempted to build "nations" by creating literary languages, by supporting cultural heroes, by educating a new native intelligentsia, and by delimiting specific national territories has provided Soviet Muslims with a "national" metaphor for future demands and dissent. Moreover,
by providing individual Soviet Muslim ethnic groups with the cosmetics to
paint themselves as separate and distinct from each other, while at the same
time demanding that they integrate into a Russian-dominated system, Soviet
social engineers have aided the process of differentiation between Muslims
and Russians more than between Muslim ethnic groups, whose differences
remain relatively marginal.

The Soviet leadership, of course, may choose to squash any "national"
demands from Muslim republics in their infancy, but any move of this sort
now must be tempered with the knowledge that serious damage almost certainly will be done to Soviet influence in the Third World, as the Muslim
"nations" of the Soviet Union, and particularly Uzbekistan, have been

exploited heavily in the Third World as models of "national development" under Soviet power. It is conceivable that the price that the Soviet leadership will have to pay for this exploitation is to permit their model "nations" to behave more as real nations—with well-defined and articulated political, economic, cultural, and social concerns. What impact this permissiveness might have on processes of Soviet state integration is unclear. At the very least it offers to the enterprising Muslim elite a fertile and fluid arena for political maneuver and intrigue.

Soviet strategy consistently has sought the destruction of pan-Turkic and pan-Islamic allegiances and movements in the Muslim regions of the USSR through the fragmentation of the Dar ul-Islam and the reconstitution of these peoples into separate and distinct nations. This strategy has included a massive expenditure on the reeducation of the affected peoples to think of themselves both ethnically and culturally in terms of smaller national units and spiritually in terms of their overriding allegiance to the Soviet state. By encouraging the unequal development of one Muslim "nation," such as the Uzbeks, Soviet strategists in theory could make these distinctions permanent.

In practice, however, it is doubtful that a policy of conscientious unequal development of Soviet Muslim nations would go far toward instilling the inhabitants with distinctly national self-identities, or that, even if these efforts were partially successful, it would be of real political consequence in the internal affairs of Soviet Muslims. In the first place, the imperial background of Central Asia remains very strong. In fact, under Soviet nation building this legacy has been proclaimed anew in the course of the restoration of ancient national monuments, the creation of a literary heritage, and the identification of national heroes—all of which go far beyond purely "national" criteria and back into a more universal tradition. It should prove difficult to carve new nations from a thousand-year-old empire.

In the second place, the Central Asian Muslim world has always been hierarchical, with one dynasty claiming for itself the right to lead all Muslim faithful. Therefore, the elevation of the Uzbeks to a more privileged position among Soviet Muslims could be viewed by other Muslim elites as a favorable sign and not as an evil omen; as every Muslim knows, his past was made glorious by the exploits of strong dynasties.

Finally, the ascendency of one Muslim ethnic group to a position of power and leadership does not signify that an alien culture will be forced on those Soviet Muslims who are less dynamic. On the contrary, the cultural roots which the Uzbeks today are adopting in accordance with the Stalinist formula to be "national in form" are not from the "Uzbek" past, but from the common past of all Central Asian, Kazakh, and Middle Volga Muslims. The imposition of "Uzbek culture" on other Muslim "cultures," therefore, would be equivalent to forcing the thing on itself, and the offspring of this rape, we may assume, would be a thoroughbred of no mean proportions.

All of the factors mentioned above—that is, the quickening and large population growth of Soviet Muslims; the creation of a new Muslim elite; the failure of russianization in Soviet Muslim regions; the rise of the Uzbeks as a Muslim "elder brother"; the opening of Soviet Muslim territories to non-Soviet influences; and the paradoxical effects of Soviet nation building—all contribute to make the sociopolitical milieu of Soviet Muslims a changing and unpredictable one. These conditions by themselves, however, do not translate automatically into an intensification of centrifugal forces and a diminution of integrative forces. In fact, all speculation on the future of Soviet Muslims should be tempered by a knowledge that strong integrative pressures have succeeded in binding many Soviet Muslims, including Muslim elites, to the Soviet system. Soviet social engineering, however, has not succeeded in transforming the Soviet Muslim into the *Homo Sovieticus* envisioned by the more naive propagandists.

Each of these factors, moreover, strengthens the Soviet Muslim's sense of his own distinctiveness from other peoples of the Soviet Union, and particularly from the Russians. The ongoing strength of Islam, even in the face of sustained Soviet official campaigns to erase "survivals of the past," continues to be a source of spiritual, cultural, and historical unity. The tenacity of Muslims to cling to these roots can be seen in the lively and expanding network of underground, "unofficial" Islam which has sprung up to replace that "official" observance which is forbidden by the Communist party.[10]

It is impossible to say, of course, whether the conditions noted above plus the cement of Islam are sufficient to inspire a pan-Turkic or pan-Islamic movement of the kind which the national communists sought for in the 1920s. The sovietization of the Muslim peoples, on the other hand, has eliminated one of the major impediments to political unification faced by the national communists in the 1920s and 1930s. Where the Muslim elites of that earlier period expressed their opposition to the Soviet system and to the Russians from religious belief or through political viewpoints, institutions, and movements which ranged from the most conservative antimodernism to the most revolutionary socialism, Soviet Muslim elites today nearly all are communists. And while most of Sultan Galiev's important ideas probably have been forgotten or forcibly expunged from the public memory, it is significant that notions of pan-Turkic and pan-Islamic action have not been, as recent Soviet campaigns against "Sultangalievism" and "pan-Turkism" demonstrate.[11]

It is difficult to determine the precise targets of official Soviet attacks on "Sultangalievism," and it may be that they are intended to counter the arguments of Western scholars, who have taken an interest in the Soviet "nationality question," as much as they are aimed at real deviations in Soviet society. Yet these criticisms and condemnations ironically serve to remind the Soviet Muslim public of the existence of the national communists, as well as to keep alive at least the barest outline of national communist ideas. Other critiques of national communism in the 1920s and 1930s undoubtedly now are being carried into the Soviet Union from the outside. This trend is likely to increase, barring any unforeseen crackdowns on diplomats, scholars, businessmen, and tourists from the West, the Middle East, and Japan, who are the logical conduits for these materials.

The legacy in the Soviet Union of the Muslim national communists of the 1920s and 1930s, then, is a legacy "in the air" which is intuited as much or more than it is understood in all its particulars. For the ordinary Muslim, this legacy is a way of looking at his society and knowing instinctively that communism is an integral part of the larger sweep of Muslim history. For the Muslim modernizing elite, it is the specific knowledge that Muslim communist development is not the same as Russian communist development, and that a communism without Russians is possible if not desirable. For Muslim intellectuals who have an intimate knowledge of who the national communists were and what they stood for, for unbridled youth who have looked through the newly opened window on the East and have begun to champ at the bit that restrains them, and for the romantics and dreamers of forbidden dreams, this legacy is one of courageous example and self-sacrifice for a noble cause, as well as a nagging incentive to renew that cause, to regain leadership in the Muslim world, and to claim the future.

National Communism beyond the Borders of the Soviet Union

Some forty-five years after the liquidation of the national communists in the Soviet Union, their ideas about the synthesis of nationalism and communism, about the complementary nature of Marxism and Islam, about Asia's role as the progenitor of revolution, and about the division of the world into oppressed and oppressors in one variant or another had penetrated into virtually every corner of the Third World. It is impossible to say with certainty that in each instance these ideas were carried beyond Soviet borders by persons who possessed an intimate knowledge of national communist programs or who were on intimate personal terms with the Muslim communist leaders themselves. In fact, it is likely that responses similar to those of the Muslim national communists developed simultaneously in different parts of the colonial world into which socialism had been injected as a cure for imperialism and colonialism. Whether these ideas were transferred or whether they were native-born is much harder to determine than in the transfer of technology, where the origins of mechanical apparatus and special techniques and applications are nearly always immediately identifiable to the trained eye. Ideas—and particularly political ideas—on the other hand, seldom escape being significantly transformed when transmitted from one society to another, from one culture to another. Often they are molded by the carrier, and by the time they reach their intended destination much of their original plumage is gone and in its place are new markings which belong to the culture into which the ideas are being transmitted. So it was with the transfer of Marxist ideas to the Soviet Muslim nationalists; so it would become with the transfer of Muslim national communism into the non-Soviet world.

We can identify some of the transmission belts for national communist ideas to the non-Soviet world; others must remain within the realm of speculation, as we lack the material to prove these links conclusively. To trace them all would require a separate study going far beyond the one proposed here. Instead, we intend to suggest briefly the potency of Muslim national communist ideas by showing how they were adopted and modified by a few important political figures and movements in the colonial world.

From 1920 to 1923, Moscow was a revolutionary bazaar, the meeting place for all Asian, African, and Latin American revolutionaries of all racial and political colors. Moscow during these years lacked many of the social and material amenities of life, as it still does; radicals of all trends flocked to it anyway, for while they could find more pleasing weather and more exotic foods in Istanbul or Djakarta, Moscow had what no place else in the world could offer at that time—it had a bona fide revolution. The political atmosphere in the Soviet capital was unique—perhaps more so than at any previous time, and certainly more so than in the decades which followed. The Bolsheviks who encouraged foreign revolutionaries to come to Moscow and who received them were not yet overly punctilious about the purity of the many doctrinal positions which were championed by the newcomers. Almost anyone was acceptable at this time, and all were free to discuss the most daring and heterodoxical ideas, as long as these ideas proved beyond question the strength of the articulator's anti-imperialist sentiments.

This atmosphere encouraged contact among the non-Russian revolutionaries, and therefore it should come as no surprise that many of the ideas of the Muslim national communists undoubtedly were learned and carried from the Soviet Union by relative unknowns. A number of especially important meetings took place during this period, including three Komintern congresses (the Second in 1920, the Third in 1921, and the Fourth in 1922), the Congress of the Peoples of the East in Baku (September 1920), and the Twelfth Congress of the RCP (b) (April 1923). Each of these meetings was attended by Muslim national communists and foreign revolutionaries, where the ideas of the former were discussed openly.

The most important center for the transmission of these ideas was the Communist University of the Toilers of the East (Kommunisticheskii Universitet Trudiashchikhsia Vostoka, or KUTVa). Opened in September 1921, KUTVa remained an extremely active and influential forum until 1924, when its staff was purged for the first time (the staff was purged again in 1927 and in 1930 as heterodoxical socialist ideas became less acceptable to the Soviet regime). KUTVa from the beginning became the intellectual headquarters for revolutionary high cadre from the colonial world. It was there that they encountered the ideas of the Muslim national communists in a more intense and systematic fashion. Among the permanent teachers who were responsible for the ideological indoctrination of these revolutionary recruits from abroad were almost all of the important Muslim national communist leaders, including Sultan Galiev, Turar Ryskulov, Nariman Narimanov, Najmuddin Efendiev-Samurskii, Galimjan Ibragimov, Ahmed Baytursun, Fayzullah Khojaev, and Mir-Yakub Dulatov. Foreign communsits who were invited to lecture and to administer at KUTVa included the Indian Manabendra-Nath Roy, the Dutchman H. J. F. M. Sneevliet, and the Iranian Sultan Zade, all of whom eventually were to espouse political ideas resembling those of Sultan Galiev's. The first two, in fact, were outspoken in their defense of the primordial role of colonial peoples in the world revolution before the Second Congress of the Komintern. Like Sultan Galiev, they insisted that the success of the revolution in Europe was tied directly to and depended upon the success of the revolution in the East. KUTVa's students were no less impressive. They included men who would change the shape of communism in the world by giving it an Eastern face: the Japanese Sen Katayama, the Indonesian Tan Malaka, the Chinese Liu Shao-Shi, the Turks Nazim Hikmete, Vala Nureddin and Şevket Süreyya Aydemir, and the Vietnamese Ho Chi Minh.

The ideological purity of the instruction at KUTVa certainly was suspect early on, if not for the mixed politics of the faculty and students then for the materials recommended for student reading. Among doctrinal works recommended to students, for example, were the writings of Otto Bauer and Karl Renner, hardly the stuff that Bolsheviks are made of. In this cosmopolitan environment national communist ideas could be elaborated and debated at length. From KUTVa, the conveyance of these ideas abroad by their non-Soviet practitioners was natural and unimpeded.

One clear example of national communist ideas traveling abroad with a KUTVa student is that of the Indonesian Tan Malaka, once leader of the Indonesian Communist party. Like Sultan Galiev, Tan Malaka understood the necessity of allying Islam, nationalism, and Marxism. He charged at the Third Congress of the Komintern that "the hostility toward Islam and pan-Islamism expressed at the Second Komintern Congress had damaged the position of Communists in Indonesia."[12] From 1922 to 1927 the official Komintern agent for the entirety of Southeast Asia and Australia, Tan Malaka broke with Stalin at the Sixth Congress in 1928. The new party which he formed, the Partai Republik Indonesia (PARI), to rival the official Partai Komunis Indonesia (PKI) was founded on Sultan Galiev's principles of a blending of orthodox Marxism and pan-Asian nationalism. "The PKI emerged as a supranational Soviet instrumentality and PARI as a revisionist movement espousing what was later to be characterized as 'national communism,'" notes one historian. "The orthodox communists took the global view that they served Indonesia by serving Moscow's goal of reshaping the world in the Soviet image. Tan Malaka took the nationalist view that he served Indonesia by supporting Tokyo's goal of 'Asia for the Asians.'"[13] The case of Tan Malaka is one of obvious borrowing from the Soviet national communists. Had Sultan Galiev or his compatriots been able to implement their ideas in the Soviet Union, it is likely that their own course would have resembled that of Tan Malaka.

At about the same time that Tan Malaka broke with Stalin over important doctrinal issues and began to organize around national communist ideas in Indonesia, the Indian communist Manabendra-Nath Roy also left the Soviet camp. Roy's important connections with the communist movement in Asia—and especially in India and China—make him, along with Tan Malaka and possibly Ho Chi Minh, probably the main channel through which Soviet Muslim national communist ideas were spread to the Third World. Yet another possible channel was the network of Iranian Marxist refugees who sought sanctuary in the Soviet Union in the 1920s, like Sultan Zade, as well as those leaders of the Azerbaidzhan democratic regime who fled to the Soviet Union after 1946. The latter group was subjected to the standard treatment which Stalin reserved for those of his foreign fellow communists who had failed: they were arrested, incarcerated, and deported to Siberia. In the 1960s, some who survived managed to return to Iran. Our incomplete information about the survivors suggests that most remained true to their Communist ideal, although their faith in the Russians was spent. It is possible that their influence on the communist movement in Iran today is responsible for the emergence within the Tudeh party of a strong religious-nationalist wing which in a curious way attempts to reconcile radical Islam and Marxism.

A third channel is less ambiguous. In 1954 the leader of the Algerian Liberation Movement, Ahmed Ben Bella, was kidnapped by the French and imprisoned. During his imprisonment, he had an opportunity to read an earlier work by one of the present authors on Sultan Galiev,[14] which he received from sources known to the authors. When he became president of the Algerian Republic, Ben Bella was fond of quoting Sultan Galiev's ideas and in particular that of the "Colonial International." In a 1964 interview, Ben Bella removed any doubt surrounding his own inspiration when he declared that he was very impressed by the ideas of a "Russian" Marxist, Sultan Galiev.[15] It is probable that Ben Bella's advocacy of Sultan Galiev's ideas infected other African leaders, including his successor Houari Boumedienne and Libya's Muammar Khadafi.

Liu Shao-Chi carried national communist ideas to China from KUTVa where he had been a student. It is also probable that many unknown Chinese and non-Han Chinese, who may have lived along the Central Asian borders, augmented this formal transfer with their more intimate knowledge of Soviet Asian society.

Chinese revolutionaries, led by Mao Tse-tung, also stressed the imperative need to root the revolution in national culture while rejecting Western influences. In his *On New Democracy,* Mao Tse-tung displayed his own intellectual debt to the national communists when he wrote,

> New-democratic culture is national. . . . It belongs to our own nation, and bears our national characteristics. . . . So-called "wholesale Westernisation" is a mistaken viewpoint. China has suffered a great deal in the past from the formalist absorption of foreign things. Likewise, in applying Marxism to China, Chinese Communists must fully and properly unite the universal truth of Marxism with the specific practice of the Chinese revolution; that is to say, the truth of Marxism must be integrated with the characteristics of the nation and given a definite national form before it can be useful; it must not be applied subjectively as a mere formula. Formula-Marxists are only fooling with Marxism and the Chinese revolution, and there is no place for them in the ranks of the Chinese revolution. China's culture should have its own form, namely, a national form.[16]

One of the most unique cases of the spread of national communist influence is that of José Carlos Mariátegui. Born in 1894 in the town of Moquequa in Southern Peru, Mariátegui became one of the most original early Latin

American Marxists; and his ideas are directly related to those of Sultan Galiev and the Muslim national communists, whose work Mariátegui may have known.

Mariátegui spent 1919 to 1923 in Europe, mainly in Italy, where he became deeply interested in the evolution of socialism and especially its development in the Muslim East. He followed closely the trials of the revolutionary movement in Turkey and in China. Moreover, he was well acquainted with the discussions which took place at the Congress of the Peoples of the East in Baku in September 1920 and probably with the debates which transpired in other early Soviet revolutionary forums. Back in Peru in 1923, he began to elaborate a revolutionary doctrine for Peru, a "Peruvian way to communism," which had clear antecedents in Muslim national communism.

Mariátegui searched for the foundations of Peruvian communism in the structure of the ancient Inca Empire—"a perfect socialist and collectivist structure"—which was, he insisted, "the most advanced organization of primitive communism in the entire world history."[17] Much as Sultan Galiev had sought a national way to Marxism in the traditional past of the Mongol empire, so Mariátegui hoped "to rediscover in history and in Peruvian reality the deep roots of a 'natural' socialist development."[18] Like Mao, Mariátegui rejected mechanical applications of Western Marxism to Peruvian conditions. "Our socialism would be neither Peruvian nor even socialist," he declared, "if it is not unified with national demands."[19] And like Ahmed Baytursun's claims on behalf of his fellow Kirghiz, Mariátegui maintained that "when the Indian will make his own socialist idea, he will serve it with a discipline, a tenacity, and a strength seldom attained by any proletarian of another origin."[20]

Sultan Galiev and other Muslim national communists had argued that communism could be built in a nonindustrial society; that, in fact, it was only in the nonindustrial world that genuine communism could be constructed. The colonial world, with few exceptions, had no proletariat and, therefore, the foundation on which communism must be established was the revolutionary peasantry led by bourgeois intellectuals. In this way the rural masses of the Third World ceased to be the objects of the world revolution and became its subjects instead, the revolution's main driving force. Thus, national communism inverted the orthodox Marxist-Leninist theorems that the revolution was to be born in the industrial areas of the cities from which it would spread from city to city and eventually bring down the imperialist capitalist regime in power. Instead, the opposition of the countryside to the city is a dominant theme in national communism. Under Mao Tse-tung, this idea was developed to the fullest, based largely on the Chinese communists' own revolutionary experience. "Since China's key cities have been occupied by the powerful imperialists," he argued, " . . . it is imperative for the revolutionary ranks to turn the backward villages into advanced consolidated areas . . . from which to fight their vicious enemies who are using the cities."[21] It was this same revolutionary experience which led Lin Piao to coin another axiom of Chinese-style revolution which the Muslim national communists had suggested in their writings and debates some years before: "To rely on the peasants, build rural base areas and use the countryside to encircle and finally capture the cities—such was the way to victory in the Chinese revolution."[22]

Only a short theoretical leap was required to pass from the encirclement of the cities by the countryside to the encirclement of the entire industrial world by the underdeveloped world. Lin Piao made this leap in 1965:

> In a sense, the contemporary world revolution also presents a picture of the encirclement of the cities by the rural areas. In the final analysis, the whole course of world revolution hinges on the revolutionary struggle of Asian, African, and Latin American peoples who make up the overwhelming majority of the world's population. . . . Taking the entire globe, if North America and Western Europe can be called "the cities of the World," then Asia, Africa, and Latin America constitute "the rural areas of the world."[23]

The Soviet Union, Lin Piao took pains to point out, was one of the "cities of the world," and, therefore, "the imperialists, the reactionaries and the Khruschev revisionists . . . will be swept like dust from the stage of history by the mighty broom of the revolutionary people."[24] The Chinese, who see themselves as the *primus inter pares* among "rural areas of the world," drew the appropriate conclusions from this major theoretical revision of orthodox Marxism and reassessed their own revolutionary role accordingly. Their doctrinal split with the Soviet Union and the enhanced Chinese military capacity encouraged this new line.

Chinese leader P'eng Chen was one of the first to spell out what has become a given of Chinese revolutionary strategy in the aftermath of an era of Sino-Soviet cooperation. Breaking decisively with orthodox Marxism and unequivocally adopting national communist tenets of the 1920s, P'eng Chen announced in 1965 that "the primary responsibility for bringing about the world revolution had shifted away from the working-class movements of the industrialized countries in the West to the national liberation movements in the backward areas of the Third World."[25]

Sultan Galiev, of course, had forecast the reversal of the relative positions of the industrial world and the colonial world. Oppressed "proletarian nations" would establish hegemony over those industrially advanced areas of the world that possessed only proletarian classes. For the Algerian leader Ahmed Ben Bella, this was the cardinal principle in the blueprint for the advancement of underdeveloped peoples. "It is of crucial importance," he declared at the Cairo Conference of Nonaligned Countries in 1964, "that coexistence should govern relations among the great powers, but it is more than that. It also involves peaceful coexistence between the small countries and the great powers. It therefore implies a change in the present relations between great and small states and enforcing the role of the latter in international affairs."[26]

Ben Bella's successor, Houari Boumedienne, added a new twist to this argument that has become increasingly popular among small nations in Africa, Latin America, and Southeast Asia. "In the past the world was divided into two blocs, the Communist and the Capitalist," Boumedienne noted; "today it is, in our opinion, composed of two parties, the rich and the poor, or the inhabitants of the North and the South."[27] This new dichotomy, North versus South, alters significantly the East-West polarity accepted by the Muslim national communists and most of the non-Soviet national communists prior to the Second World War. In the 1920s, of course, many of the small African nations that today command an unprecedented amount of media attention had not yet been heard from. The North-South dichotomy, however, is a significant development in national communist theory for two reasons. First, it removes Islam as the single most important unifying element in any Third World coalition, a condition which the Muslim national communists might have been willing to accept but which they were unable to perceive in the early 1920s. The North-South dichotomy relies more heavily on another element of national communist doctrine, that of the oppressed versus the oppressor, or the rural and underdeveloped against the urban and industrial.

Second, like the coalition envisaged by Sultan Galiev, advocates of the North-South dichotomy continue to stress the natural solidarity of "proletarian nations" and to reject what they consider to be the artificial and forced solidarity of Soviet-dominated communist parties. Colonel Muammar Khadafi, president of Libya, reaffirms and explains in his "Greenbook" the correctness of the North-South dichotomy. And he excludes from the southern camp not only Moscow—which Sultan Galiev also excluded from his "Colonial International"—but Peking as well.[28] Thus, for most national liberation movements which declare themselves to be oriented toward the communist world, Peking—despite its genuine claims to underdevelopment—ironically falls into a category hereto inhabited only by the Soviet Union: its material and spiritual encouragement are sought and accepted by the leaders of national liberation struggles, but in almost no instance will Peking be given command of the national movement itself, and the Chinese image will always be measured against other "Northern" great powers and not against other "proletarian nations" which share with China some common features of underdevelopment.

Almost without exception, the main tenets of Muslim national communism as they were articulated by Sultan Galiev and his companions in the 1920s have been adopted in a like or slightly modified shape by virtually every present-day national liberation movement which claims Marxism as its dominant ideological element. These ideas which slowly penetrated the Third World were not orthodox Marxist ideas or even some kind of a parallel Marxism; they were nationalist ideas in Marxist clothing, what Maxime Rodinson calls *Nationalisme Marxisant.*[29] Paradoxically, the rampant ideological heterodoxy which bore Marx's name was spawned in no small part by the organization which was entrusted with the task of purifying Marxist-Leninist doctrine among revolutionary representatives from the colonial world—the Third Communist International. In the early years of the revolution the Komintern was the scene of sincere debates on revolutionary strategy for the colonial world, including the ideas of Sultan Galiev and the Muslim national communists (and therefore, it too became a school for the education of colonial elites in the ideas of national communism).

But from 1928 to 1941, while the purge of the Soviet national communists was in full swing, the Komintern's policy in the East oscillated between two extremes. The first was a strategy of "class against class," which usually meant that local communists were invited to sacrifice everything to the dubious possibility of an immediate social revolution. Implicit to this strategy was the breakup of native nationalist and anti-imperialist forces in favor of proletarian ones at a time when the former—bourgeois and/or aristocratic national leaders—still enjoyed the confidence of the native masses. The outcome of this strategy could only be the liquidation of native colonial communist parties, whose memberships were derived largely from active nationalists and whose immediate aim was not social revolution but national liberation.

At the other end of the spectrum was the strategy of the "common front." Among other things, this strategy signified the reinforcement of ties between members of the local Communist parties and various antifascist—but nonrevolutionary—groups in Western countries. This strategy also demanded a high ante from native nationalists, whether they were members of the local communist party or not. In order to keep the "front" united, they were required to reduce or repress their national claims on their colonial masters and to lower the volume of their dissent generally.

Neither of these two strategies offered Komintern members from colonial lands much chance of succeeding in fulfilling their national goals; little by little they began to desert the Komintern and to return to their homelands or other more fertile revolutionary pastures. The official Komintern line remained very outspoken about the fight against imperialism, as in this passage from the 1928 program—never abandoned officially: "The fighting and brotherly alliance with the Toiling Masses of the Colonies remains one of the main goals of the world industrial proletariat, which exercises hegemony and which has the leadership of the struggle against imperialism."[30]

Steadily, however, the Russian Revolution was being turned inward, as we have already seen in the case of Turkey and Iran, and the real meaning of Stalin's benediction to the New Economic Plan, that "the World Revolution can only be sustained by Soviet grain," became clear. Grain it would have to be, for Soviet political and spiritual support gradually was being withdrawn in favor of a more *étatist,* less revolutionary strategy. Komintern affairs became secondary in the eyes of Soviet leaders to the building of socialism in one country, and non-Soviet revolutionary forces in the colonial world which were represented in the Komintern were reduced to a standby revolutionary reserve. "In the capitalist countries," lamented Indian communist M. N. Roy, "there were communist parties which could be helped with confidence that they were dedicated to the cause of social revolution. But in the colonial countries, similar instruments for revolution were absent. How then could the Communist International develop the national liberation movement there as part of the world proletarian revolution?"[31] The answer was that it could not and would not, as the Komintern rapidly became one more adjunct of the Stalinist system in the Soviet Union. Colonial communist parties, notes Rodinson, "remained basically subordinated to the world strategy of the International, which was centered on the world of the white man, and they were closely dependent on the European communist parties."[32]

If a colonial communist party were to break into this inner circle of communist parties and out of the ranks of the "revolutionary reserve," it had to compensate for the absence of an industrial proletariat, which constituted at that time, according to the Komintern line, the only legitimate foundation for a social revolution. Three alternatives were available. The first, which was advocated by the Bolshevik-dominated Komintern, consisted of substituting the assistance of fraternal socialist countries—a thinly disguised euphemism for Soviet interference—for the nonexistent native proletariat. By this formula, a communist party would be established with Soviet help and with Soviet cadres if necessary; and this communist party, then, would automatically become the representative of the (nonexistent) working class. After the eventual victory—and force was never ruled out—a real industrial proletariat would be created to provide these representatives with a constituency.

A second alternative—which was to prove to be moderately successful for many national liberation struggles after World War II—was to ally the peasantry and the native bourgeoisie in a fight against the imperialists and, eventually, against the imperialists' native allies. Victory in this struggle theoretically would open the door to the formation of a genuine working class and, consequently, to the birth of a regular proletarian communist party.

Finally, there existed the possibility of a purely peasant revolution—which meant only peasant leadership and excluded any alliance with the native bourgeoisie—with the aim of immediate social revolution. This seems to have been the least popular option. To date, the most notable example of a purely peasant revolution is the Cambodian Khmer Rouge movement.

For nearly all of the colonial revolutionaries associated with the Komintern the first alternative was unacceptable because this would lead to a strong and unwanted Russian influence in their national lives. For despite the fact of the Russian revolution—or perhaps because of it—most colonial communists remained skeptical of Russian and European communism. Many members of the Komintern, which had its headquarters in Moscow, had heard the Muslim national communists warn that Russian communism was not by definition different from Russian czarism, that it could be simply the bearer of neocolonialism. It is also likely that those who were not frustrated by the early transformation of the Komintern into a Great-Russian forum became sufficiently enlightened to quit the new Workers State when, in the early 1930s, the national communists were liquidated by the Bolsheviks, thereby rendering the warnings more credible.

It is in the rejection of this alternative by colonial radical elites that we can detect the strong influence of the Muslim national communists. Between 1928 and the end of the Second World War, these elites gradually came to eschew the Russian direction of the Komintern and its goals, which had been fixed in accordance with Soviet self-interest. More consciously aware that they could be abandoned quickly by the Russians if the general strategy of world revolution was altered to secure purely Russian ends, colonial radicals slowly but steadily moved toward a position not unlike the Jewish Bund before 1917 and almost identical to that of Sultan Galiev in the 1920s. Thus, they were gradually coming to reject the Komintern on strategic grounds.

Ideologically, the Komintern's Western-oriented line was no less palatable. Muslim national communism had touched a raw nerve in psychology of colonial revolutionaries which the Russians continually aggravated by their clumsy handling of Komintern strategy and doctrine. Orthodox Marxism alone could not effect this change, although it, too, spoke of oppression and misery. But orthodox Marxism did not speak of nonindustrial society—except as a kind of "idiocy" to be avoided—and therefore orthodox Marxists and even Russian Marxist-Leninists could not comprehend or simply refused to admit the inherent revolutionary dynamism of the East. Jealousy affected many Russians, probably most. Smug and self-satisfied that they had accomplished with the West's own tools what the West had been unable to do—to make a revolution—Russian leaders were niggardly in sharing the spotlight with anyone, especially with nonwhites and peasants from the wastelands of the globe whom they considered to be lacking in culture, if not in civilization.

National communism, on the other hand, spoke poignantly and succinctly of colonial reality, while at the same time it pointed a way out of Western domination. It exploited the anger of native nationalists and urged them to act, but to act as individual nations in concert under the banner of the oppressed East against the oppressing West. National communism and *Nationalisme Marxisant,* which are part of the same phenomenon, were not simply adaptations of Marxism to fit local conditions. More than this, they were specific and vociferous rejections of everything Marxism stood for: class struggle, internationalism, the destruction of traditional society, atheism, the city, the working class, industrialization, and, most of all, the dominance of the Western world. As the Komintern under Russian prodding and intrigue came to adopt these latter values, its demise—and that of Russian leadership in the Third World—was logical and unavoidable. Its failure was the ideological failure of orthodox Marxism to come to grips with non-Western conditions and the strategic failure of a revolutionary party which chose to patronize its eager adherents with promises while systematically abandoning its own revolutionary aims.

Rodinson's *Nationalisme Marxisant,* a phenomenon common to the entire colonial world where pure nationalism is covered by a thin veneer of Marxism or pseudo-Marxism, comes close to what Muslim national communism was in the 1920s and probably would look like today, had it been allowed to flourish. Rodinson's explanation of this phenomenon suggests that Sultan Galiev's reasons for embracing Marxism—or what he believed to be Marxism—are now more widely acceptable among Third World elites than ever before. Nationalism continues to provide the essence and Marxism a model for secular and modernist development, an efficient means of social organization, and a common front against the imperialist enemy. Just as in 1917–18 in Russia new communist Muslim groups were born from the nationalist elite and not from the indigenous socialist parties, so the *Nationalisme Marxisant* movements now are born in the nationalist camps of their respective societies and not within the communist party organizations already in place. This parallel should remind us of the relationship between Marxism and nationalism in the nonindustrial world which Sultan Galiev and the Muslim communists understood and elaborated in detail. It should also make us aware of the strength and utility of wearing Marxism cosmetically, a theme to which we shall return in the final chapter.

ВСЕМИРНОЕ
ВООРУЖЕНИЕ НАРОДОВ

 Изд. ст. Полит. Управл. Одесск. Окрвоенком.

Six

From the bazaar of Central Asia   Вот придут Китайцы,
они вам пропишут.

Conclusion and Prospects

Muslin national communism was an attempt to combine and synthesize three ideologies: the Islamic religion, which may modify its temporal "form" but never its element of eternal truth; nationalism, a temporal ideology which always is changing form, programs, and essence but never its ultimate goal; and Marxism, whose social goals generally were regarded by the Muslim national communists as superfluous, but not its power to mobilize elites and masses. National communist leaders adopted Marxism out of sincere conviction that it could solve their national problem. For them Marxism was a flexible doctrine. They rejected its major tenets except the most essential, that the time of the underdogs was at hand. From this realization they derived the concept of "proletarian nations" which would avenge the exploitation by the imperialist world. It made little difference to the Muslim national communists that the Marxism which they took as their own bore little resemblance to what Karl Marx had written. They stripped socialism of its original appointments and wrapped it in native cloth. In this attire, the socialism of the Muslim communists spoke of oppressed nations, national liberation, a Muslim way to communism, and Eastern strategy, but seldom of the proletariat, capitalism, or class struggle. Eventually these native socialists clashed with the more powerful Russians, who spoke of all the things which the Muslim national communists ignored and who were in search of a national communism of their own. In the end the Russians won: Muslim communist organizations were rolled up and their leaders liquidated.

It is impossible to know what Muslim leaders like Sultan Galiev thought privately about their selective use of Marxism. Some may have recognized the contradictions which were inherent to the adoption of Marxism as the basis of their national struggle. Most, however, seized on the one central theme in Marxist thought, that it was time to stop thinking about the world *in abstracto* and change it. For the Muslim communist of the 1920s, the world to be changed was the Dar ul-Islam. The first step of this change would be the expulsion of Russians from Muslim lands, followed by the linking of Russia's Islam more closely to the Muslim world abroad. Communism promised to achieve at least the first of these goals by turning the oppressed against the oppressors, Muslims against Russians. Sultan Galiev and his comrades in this sense were genuine communists and not simply cryptonationalists who had managed to infiltrate the Communist party. Their differences with the dominant Russians were of a national, not a political character. Like the Russians of Stalin's time and after, Muslim national communists fought for a socialism with a national face, for a "socialism with a *tübeteika*," not for a "socialism with a human face." No Muslim Solzhenitsyn or Dubcek rose to challenge Sultan Galiev's interpretation of Marxism. The Muslim national communists sought to build Marxism—as they understood it—without Russians, with a minimal Russian presence, or with the Russians in a subordinate position, but not a socialism without Lenin or Stalin, on the condition that these revolutionary leaders could be naturalized. Lenin and Stalin were foreign imports; Vuludimir Linin Iliyas oğlu and Yusuf Estalin Basariyūn Zāde grew closer to home.

The destruction of Muslim national communism over fifty years ago presumably did not dampen the enthusiasm of other Muslims, both within the Soviet Union and outside, to attempt a synthesis of its component ideologies. The lesson which most Muslim leaders seem to have drawn from the Soviet Muslim experience is that Russian socialism and Muslim socialism are of a different piece and that in the 1920s the former simply proved to be stronger than the latter. Some Soviet Muslims felt and continue to feel that socialism and Islam in their essentials can coexist and that a culture can be built which is socialist in essence and Muslim in form—or the opposite.

The early attempts by the Muslim national communists to "Marxify" Islam in recent years have been followed throughout the Islamic world by the inverse process of "Islamizing" Marxism. In his *Marxism et Monde Musulman*, Maxime Rodinson gives many examples of this trend. More recently, other even more curious efforts in this direction have appeared in Iran. One

"Islamic Marxist," Ali Shari'yati, for example, argues that the Shi's expectancy of the return of the twelfth, hidden Imam corresponds to revolutionary awareness among radicals. The legendary one-eyed opponent of the twelfth Imam, Dajjal, becomes Marcuse's one-dimensional man. Ali Shari'yati refers to the impending global revolution against despotism and imperialism as "the second battle of Badr."[1]

The "Islamization" of Marxism suggests that many Muslim leaders have reversed the order of the two in their own minds in terms of the power of each to mobilize revolutionary energies. Islam is acquiring new meaning as a mobilization system in their eyes; radical Muslim ideologies, like the Ikhwan al-Muslimin ("Muslim Brothers") or Muammar Khadafi's neo-Jamaleddin al-Afghanist pan-Islamism are challenging—often victoriously—the spread of communism in the Third World. "We adopt Marxist economic analysis because we believe that it is the only one valid for the economic development of our country," explains former Algerian President Ahmed Ben Bella, "but we do not espouse the Marxist ideology because we Algerians are Moslems and Arabs."[2] Ahmed Ben Bella's priorities are the priorities of many Muslim leaders who pretend to be socialists. Islam, *Qawm* (people), *Millet* (nation), and *Vatan* (fatherland) come first, and only after these a utilitarian measure of Marxism. "Some evil-minded persons say that we are propagandists for Communisms," the Algerian president reminds us, "but we tell them that we come with an Arab and Islamic mission and that our motto is Arabism and Islam. . . ."[3] This "Islamization" has not progressed to the same extent in Soviet Muslim territories as it has beyond Soviet borders, largely because the Soviet Muslim must employ a severely limited official Soviet lexicon which constrains him from articulating openly many of the ideas of his Muslim brethren abroad.

Several forces may speed up this process in the Soviet Union in the next few decades. In the first place, Muslim national communist ideas have taken root in nearby China; the Chinese actively propagandize them along the Sino-Soviet border in Central Asia and Kazakhstan. Not surprisingly, the keynote of Chinese propaganda is the "colonial oppression" of Central Asian peoples at the hands of the Russians, the same theme which Sultan Galiev and his comrades did so much to elaborate. The following Chinese example is typical:

Sharpening contradictions among the various nationalities have become another serious problem confronting the Soviet revisionists. Brezhnev and company are stepping up the implementation of the Great-Russian chauvinistic policy under the deceitful slogan of "a new historical entity of people." From Transcaucasia to the Central Asian region, from the

Baltic coast to the shores of the Black Sea, there have been large-scale struggles waged over the past five years by the people in various union republics against Great-Russian chauvinistic oppression and assimilation of nationalities. This has been proved by the big purges carried out one after another by the Brezhnev renegade clique in these republics.[4]

Chinese attacks often contain references to Russian racism, Soviet "social-colonialism," and oppression by the "new czars," as well as slogans such as "Asia for the Asians."[5] Thus the Chinese serve the function of keeping alive in the minds of many Central Asians the fact of their subordination to a colonial power on one hand, and the dream of a pan-Asian solidarity on the other.

The Chinese until recently have been unlikely candidates to lead or inspire Central Asian Muslims, as they are by traditional Muslim standards the infidels par excellence—"Bot-parasts," true idol worshippers. The hostility of Central Asian Muslims toward the Chinese is evident in the folklore and in the *dastans* of the peoples of Turkestan. The revolt of the Dungans and the Uighurs in Sinkiang in the second half of the nineteenth century strengthened this hostility, and there can be little doubt that it survived the October Revolution in Russia. The Sino-Soviet split, on the other hand, cast China into a purely Asian role. This fact seems to have created a new basis for understanding between the Chinese and the Muslims of Central Asia; so much so, in fact, that a prominent Russian dissident recently felt it necessary to explain the often-heard warning, this chapter's epigram, from Muslims to Russians in the streets of Central Asian cities: "Wait until the Chinese come. They will show you!"[6] How deep this sentiment runs is difficult to judge at this writing, but it should become clearer in the near future.

In the second place, the opening of Central Asia, regardless of how tentative, to outside Muslim influences offers Soviet Muslims an alternative both to Russian socialism and to Chinese socialism. The natural and logical source of Muslim inspiration lies in the Muslim Middle East rather than in China. Turned in this direction, Soviet Muslims, who already are socialists—at least in form—might be tempted to assume the leadership in any efforts to synthesize Islam and socialism abroad.

But the future of Soviet Islam depends mainly on the Russians at the center. More and more of them are beginning to realize that the benefits accruing from their Muslim colonies may not be worth the real and psychological costs. *Samizdat* carries many statements by disgruntled Great-Russians—who believe that most non-Russians—and especially Central Asians—should be jettisoned from the Union of Soviet Socialist Republics before it is too late. Others believe that Russian control of these areas should increase, and the silly pretense of equality should be discarded. Even Alexander Solzhenitsyn, despite his deeply Christian ethic, falls rather callously in the latter group when he addresses the relationship of Crimean Tatars to what he sees as a Russian state: "The Tatar yoke over Russia has forever lessened our possible responsibility [*vina*] toward the remnants of the Horde."[7] For Solzhenitsyn as for many others, *Tatar* refers more generally to Muslim Turks, irrespective of national distinctions. This current resurgence of Great Russian ethnonationalism in the long run may do more to dictate the future of Soviet Muslims than anything which the Muslims themselves could do.

The Great-Russians are not without several options. Theoretically, genocide could be one, either through actual physical liquidation or through forced assimilation. Yet, while this may be a feasible—but so far relatively unsuccessful—way of dealing with smaller Muslim groups like the Crimean Tatars and the Meskhetian Turks, it is hardly so for some forty million Muslims who are broken up into larger and more compact groups. Forced deportation to Siberia or the offering of attractive incentives to migrate there is another option. Once again the numbers become prohibitive, and all available evidence suggests that Central Asian Muslims are not inclined to migrate. A third option would be to get rid of Central Asia, Kazakhstan, and perhaps Azerbaidzhan altogether. Some Great-Russian dissenters advocate this alternative. It is hard to believe, however, that these voices are heard in high councils. Few Soviet leaders are likely to forget that they came to power because of their commitment to hold the Union together. Finally, the Great-Russians can do nothing at all, other than to attempt to maintain the status quo. Whether the integrative forces which the Soviet leadership has initiated can defuse the centrifugal ones which are becoming more apparent and which are likely to intensify under the conditions we discussed earlier is a question which will hold our attention for the next few decades.

As for the Muslims, some, like their predecessors in 1917, certainly wish to remain part of a Soviet state, either monolithic or decentralized, but with some important qualifications. Demographic trends, they believe, gradually will cause the Soviet Union to lose its Russian character and to acquire a more pronounced Turkic and Muslim profile. In this event—provided that the Soviet leadership opts for the status quo, which is likely—Great-Russians, will be obliged to share increasingly more power with the Muslims, leading to a Russian-Muslim partnership (an idea which was advanced first in 1883 by Ismail bey Gaspraly in his *Russko-Musul' manskoe Soglashenie*) with the possible division of power between Russians and Muslims. Finally, some

Soviet Muslim intellectuals may already be agitating not only for an increased autonomy within the Soviet system but for outright independence, although this trend, if it exists, is difficult to identify.

Soviet Muslims are now midway through their sixth decade under Soviet rule, and this by itself should warn us that change, if it comes at all, could be far in the future. Central Asia and the Muslim Caucasus still look like colonies in a Russian empire. But like all colonies, they both feed and are fed by their master. The real ties which bind Muslim regions to Russia are demonstrably strong; a degree of symbiosis is present in their relationship. Still it would be wise to heed the warning of Albert Memmi when he writes,

> A day necessarily comes when the colonized lifts its head and topples the always unstable equilibrium of colonization. For the colonized just as for the colonizer there is no way out other than a complete end to colonization. The refusal of the colonized cannot be anything but absolute, that is, not only a revolt but a revolution.[8]

Sultan Galiev and his fellow Muslim national communists moved into this unstable equilibrium but could not topple it, leaving behind them only a body of potent political ideas and a legacy of action through courageous example. For today's Soviet Muslim, this heritage is potential energy, a testimony to the inherent dynamism of his society. Muslim national communism is a revolutionary strategy for the colonial world and it will find adherents wherever colonialism exists, whether in the Soviet Union or abroad. As a strategy, Muslim national communism closes the gap between the realm of abstract thinking and the necessity to act. Herein lies its appeal to those who seek to change their lot and have the courage to do so.

3-й конгресс мусульманских коммунистических организаций, объявивший национал-тюркистский пантюркистский уклон в среде «националов»

تۈركىستان مۇسۇلمان كوممۇنىستلار تەشكىلاتىنىڭ ئۈچىنچى قۇرۇلتايى ۋە قۇرۇلتاى ئۇلۇڭ مىللەتچىلىك رەۋەندەرلىك تۈرەندى.

Appendix A

Sultan Galiev

The Social Revolution and the East

From *Zhizn' Natsional' nostei*, 38(46), 1919. For French version of A. Bennigsen and C. Quelquejay, see *Les Mouvements Nationaux chez les Musulmans de Russie* (Paris, 1960), pp. 207–12.

The socialist revolution in Russia is only the beginning, one of the stages of the international socialist revolution. Sooner or later, it must take the form of a revolutionary struggle, of a desperate and decisive fight between two irreconcilable enemies, between two opposing forces, the international proletariat and international imperialism. The Civil War now raging within the boundaries of the former Russian Empire must expand and become deeper, both in its internal and in its external manifestations. Gradually, with the development of the revolution, new peoples and new countries will be drawn willingly or unwillingly into this war, which appears to be the last worldwide butchery of humanity. This is inevitable and unavoidable. The old world has become much too decrepit. It is groaning and collapsing. All the earth thirsts for and demands renewal, an entirely new harmony. The decisive moment has come, not only for individuals but also for entire peoples and governments, each of whom must honor his fate and irrevocably decide on which side of the barricade to place himself. Whether you want to or not, you must take part in this war, and consciously or unconsciously become either "White" or "Red."

Indeed, the October Revolution had still not occurred, when in Russia labor and capital, the proletariat and the bourgeoisie, two hostile forces, had already begun to differentiate themselves, to define themselves and to prepare themselves for the decisive struggle.

The October Revolution was only a moment in the collision between these forces in Russia when the Russian bourgeoisie, crushed in its homeland, was compelled to concentrate the remainder of its forces on the outskirts of Russia and in the countries of the Entente, where, for a more or less short term, it was guaranteed a comparatively "free" existence.

But from that moment the antirevolutionary struggle, which had been developing continuously, acquired an international character. In the campaign against the victorious workers and peasants of Russia not only the Russian, but also other units of the international bourgeoisie have been taking part, at first separately, then united. The League of Nations has become the general staff of their forces, where all the counterrevolutionary forces of the world come together as in a focal point. It is being transformed into a "Black International," uniting all the forces which in one way or another might serve as a barrier to the development of the revolution.

Such are the premises of the international socialist revolution at the present. And only in proceeding from them can we foresee the forms which its development may take in the future.

One of the practical problems which we must face at the present time, and which we must quickly resolve, is the "Eastern question." This problem is one of the inevitable and unavoidable phases in the natural development of the world socialist revolution. Even if we did not want to recognize it, and instead ignored it, it would stand before us in all its intricacy and internal and external complexity. We would be wrong if we limited ourselves to a superficial solution of the question. It needs thorough and completely attentive study, in its socioeconomic and international aspects.

We must examine all the possible concrete forms which the international class struggle might take in the East and define, once and for all, our relationship to it, with all the ensuing consequences.

We assume that the general course of international socialist policy taken by us is correct and that there is no need of correctives. Nevertheless, one must be aware that the problem of the East is in need of serious correction. However grievous this may be, one must admit that up to now all of the measures which we have taken as regards the establishment of correct mutual relations between Soviet Russia and the East were random and mere palliatives. In this sphere, the firm execution of a systematic and decisive policy confidently undertaken was completely inperceptible.

At worst, it was a simple reflection and acknowledgment of our weakness as, for instance, when Russian troops were recalled from Persia. At best, it was a mere expression of sympathy, and a platonic promise of support for the revolutionary aspirations of the East [as, for example, after the uprising in Afghanistan against the English].

In this respect, our actions began to take a more or less defined character only from the moment of the disasters of the socialist revolution in the West, when the very development of events (the defeat of the Spartakists in Germany, the failure of the general strike protesting against intervention in Russian affairs, and the fall of the Hungarian Soviet Republic) compelled us to accept the simple truth that, without the participation of the East, it is impossible for us to achieve the international socialist revolution. But even at the present moment these measures do not yet have that defined and established character which the laws of the correct development of the socialist revolution demand of them. The task of the present article is to give a more or less complete analysis of this question.

From *Zhizn' Natsional'nostei*,
39(47), 1919.

The Soviet system, as an expression of communism, is the antithesis of the bourgeois-capitalist state. These two systems cannot peacefully coexist side by side. They can tolerate one another only temporarily, until one side having obtained a preponderance of forces, however slight, will inevitably attack the weaker one.

By virtue of the basic law of the development of the socialist revolution, it was necessary that the Russian Revolution, from its very first days would develop into a worldwide revolution; otherwise the Soviets in Russia would have become only a small oasis in the raging sea of imperialism, risking obliteration each minute by the waterspout of the worldwide imperialist bacchanalia.

The leaders of the October Revolution understood this situation perfectly well and tried to channel it in the direction of the international current. And it could not have been otherwise, or the socialist revolution in Russia would have lost all its inner meaning.

But in a tactical sense this process of development of the revolution was directed incorrectly. It appeared correct in some of its outward manifestations (the Spartakist moment in Germany, the Hungarian Revolution, and so on) but in its totality it had a one-sided character. This one-sidedness consisted in the fact that almost all the attention of the leaders was turned toward the West. The task of transforming the October Revolution into an international socialist one was understood as the transmission of the mechanical energy of the

Russian Revolution to the West, that is, to that part of the world where the contradiction of the class interests of the proletariat and the bourgeoisie appeared most sharply and openly and where, for this reason, there seemed to exist a relatively solid basis for the success of the class revolution.

But the East, with its population of one and a half billion, enslaved by the West European bourgeoisie, was forgotten. The basic processes in the development of the international class struggle continued, bypassing the East, and the Eastern question and the problem of "revolutionizing" the East existed only in the minds of a scattered few, who were no more than a drop of water in the raging sea of the revolution.

Because of the ignorance of the East and because of the fear which it inspired, the idea of the participation of the East in the international revolution was systematically rejected.

It is true that the West European states, including their ally America, appear to be the countries where all the material and "moral" forces of international imperialism are concentrated, and it would seem that their territories are destined to become the chief battlefield in the war against imperialism. But in no way can we confidently say that there is enough strength in the Western proletariat to overthrow the Western bourgeoisie. This bourgeoisie is international and worldwide, and its overthrow demands a concentration of all the revolutionary will and all the revolutionary energy of the entire international proletariat, including the proletariat of the East.

In attacking international imperialism only with the West European proletariat, we leave it full freedom of action and maneuver in the East. As long as international imperialism, represented by the Entente, dominates the East, where it is the absolute master of all natural wealth, then so long is it guaranteed of a successful outcome in all its clashes in the economic field with the working masses of the home countries, for it can always "shut their mouths" by satisfying their economic demands.

Our hopeless expectations of revolutionary aid from the West in the course of the last two years of the revolution in Russia eloquently confirm this thesis.

But even if the West European worker succeeds in obtaining a victory over his bourgeoisie, we would still inevitably collide with the East, because as a last resort, the West European bourgeoisie, following the example of its friend in distress, the Russian bourgeoisie, would concentrate all its forces in its "outlying districts," and first of all in the East. It would not hesitate, in the course of suppressing the socialist revolution in Western Europe, to utilize the ancient national and class hatred of the East toward the West, which is always alive in the breast of the East toward Western Europe as the bearer of the imperialist yoke, and it would launch a campaign of blacks against Europe.

We not only admit this as a possibility, but we are convinced of it; the two-year experience of the struggle of the proletariat in Russia against its bourgeoisie has taught us a great deal in this respect.

From *Zhizn' Natsional'nostei*,
42(50), 1919.

Examining the East from the socioeconomic point of view, we see that almost all of it is the object of exploitation by West European capital. It is the chief source of material for European industry, and in this respect it constitutes highly inflammable revolutionary material.

If it were possible to compute the degree of exploitation of the East by Western capital, and in this connection, its indirect participation in the emergence of the power of the European and American bourgeoisie which have exploited and continue to exploit it, then we would see that a lion's share of all the material and spiritual wealth of the "whites" has been stolen from the East, and built at the expense of the blood and sweat of hundreds of millions of laboring masses of "natives" of all colors and races.

It was necessary for tens of millions of aborigines of America and Africa to perish and for the rich culture of the Incas to be completely obliterated from the face of the earth in order that contemporary "freedom-loving" America, with her "cosmopolitan culture" of "progress and technology" might be formed. The proud skyscrapers of Chicago, New York, and other cities are built on the bones of the "redskins" and the Negroes tortured by inhuman plantation owners and on the smoking ruins of the destroyed cities of the Incas.

Christopher Columbus! How his name speaks to the hearts of the European imperialists. It was he who "opened" the road to the European plunderers in America, England, France, Spain, Italy, and Germany; all of them participated equally in the plundering, the destruction, and the devastation of "native" America, erecting at her expense their capitalistic cities and their bourgeois culture. The invasions of Europe by Tamerlane, Gengis Khan, and the other Mongol princes, in all the cruelty of their devastating strength, pale before what the Europeans have done in this America discovered by them.

The thesis expressed in the beginning of this article is strikingly confirmed by the entire subsequent development of Western European imperialism when, having plundered "native" America, and having sated itself with her, it turned its attention to the East, with India as its main goal, which, almost from the first days of the appearance of the European imperialism, has not ceased to arouse in it a feeling of greed.

The entire history of the Crusades and all the long series of later bourgeois imperialistic wars in the East represent a carefully calculated policy of economic enslavement of the East by West European feudalists and their descendants, and this policy has finally been crowned with an almost total success.

If we would examine the relations between the West European countries and the East during the last phase, that is, in the beginning of the imperialistic World War, we would see that at this time the East was squeezed and convulsively writhing in the clutches of international capital.

All Asia and all Africa were divided by Europe into "spheres of influence," with only formal and fictional acceptance of the "independence" of some of the more outstanding states such as China, Persia, and Turkey.

The great imperialist war was the last stage of this policy, the stage where international imperialism, sensing its imminent demise, declared war on itself.

Today the victory of the Entente over Germany has provided a temporary solution to the Eastern question—Entente rule being imposed on the East.

But already today, although the situation is not yet completely clear, the contradictory interests in the East of the basic components of the "Holy Alliance" are beginning to be visible, and sooner or later a serious confrontation is bound to occur between the powerful imperialist states, all competing for first place in the piratic "League of Nations."

We must never forget that, if on the one hand the East as a whole is completely enslaved by the West, on the other hand its own national bourgeoisie applies a no less heavy "internal" pressure on the laboring masses of the East.

We ought not for a minute forget the fact that the development of the international socialist revolution in the East must in no case limit itself only to the overthrow of the power of Western imperialism, but must go further. After this first stage, a second stage must be reached. This second stage is the complex question of overthrowing the Oriental clerical-feudal bourgeoisie which pretends to be liberal, but which is in reality brutally despotic and which is capable, for the sake of its own selfish interests, to instantly change its stance toward its former foreign adversaries.

We must always remember one thing: the East on the whole is the chief source of nourishment of international capitalism. In the event of a worldwide socialist civil war, this is a factor extremely favorable to us and extremely unfavorable to the international imperialists. Deprived of the East, and cut off from India, Afghanistan, Persia, and its other Asian and African colonies, Western European imperialism will wither and die a natural death.

But at the same time the East is the cradle of despotism, and we are not in the least safe from the possibility that, after the overthrow of West European imperialism, an Eastern imperialism will emerge, which is for the time being still under the heavy pressure of its European colleague. There is no guarantee against the possibility that the feudal lords of China, India, Persia, or Turkey, having liberated themselves with our help, will not unite with imperialist Japan and even with some other European imperialism, and will not organize a campaign against their "liberators" in order to save themselves by this means from the contagion of "bolshevism."

Appendix B

Sultan Galiev

The Tatars and the October Revolution

From *Zhizn' Natsional'nostei*, 24(122), 1921.

Before undertaking a study of the role of the Tatars in the socialist revolution in Russia one should call to mind, if only briefly, the level of their social and political development before the October Revolution.

The history of the revolutionary movement among the Tatars can be divided into two periods: (1) the nationalist period, from 1905 to the February Revolution, and (2) the democratic, petit bourgeois period between the February Revolution and March 1918, when the "democratic" petit bourgeois intelligentsia was crushed by the combined forces of the Tatar and Russian proletariats. These two phases were directly dependent on political and social conditions which existed in Russia as a whole.

The waves of the Revolution of 1905 left their mark on the social, political, and cultural life of the Tatars; it shook the already weakening patriarchal structure of their society, leaving them open to ideas of the socialist revolution.

Thus we witness the awakening of a nation oppressed by czarism, condemned to cultural and economic degeneration and even to extinction. New forces, freed from oppression, were set in motion and new paths of development were impatiently sought after.

In the large Tatar centers of Orenburg, Kazan, and Astrakhan, newspapers and magazines were published in the national language. Tatar literature and

Tatar theatre were born and a new secular school system replaced the archaic traditional religious schools: the *medressehs* and the *mekteps*.

Young writers made their appearance in literature and in literary criticism. The question of the emancipation of women was taken up by the press and in literature, and, after a tenacious struggle, Tatar women gained access to schools, society, and the theater. True, all this happened within the restricted limits authorized by the czarist regime, but even under these conditions, emancipation played a very significant revolutionary role.

During this period all social and political activity took place under the banner of national renaissance of the Tatars. A fierce struggle was taking place on the subject. The revolutionary faction of Tatar society comprised of young people and students, especially those who had received a European (Russian) education, saw the salvation of the Tatar nation to lie in the acceptance of Western European culture and in the radical destruction of all that was old and outdated, of all that hindered their initiation into that culture.

In the beginning, the camp of their opposition included only hardened fanatics, defenders of the ancient forms of Tatar social life. But progressively, as this movement spread and gained in strength, those who only recently had been "innovators" and "revolutionaries" came over to swell the ranks. Already at the time of the February Revolution three tendencies in Tatar social life could be distinguished: (1) the *qadymists*, avowed reactionaries who edited the magazine *Din ve Magisat* at Orenburg and who were allied with organizations such as Soyuz russkogo naroda ("Union of the Russian People") and Sirat al-Mustaqim ("Association for the Salvation of Muslims"), directed by the last prerevolutionary mufti of the Russian interior and of Siberia, the monarchist Bayazidov. This group waged battle against the revolutionary movement through their intermediary, the czarist police. (2) The moderate intelligentsia and the liberal bourgeoisie, centered on the one hand around the newspapers *Quyash* and *Yulduz* of Kazan and the *Tormush* of Ufa (the moderate group) and, on the other hand, around the newspaper *Vaqt* of Orenburg (less moderate). (3) The revolutionary intelligentsia centered around the newspapers *Il* and *Süz* of Ayaz Iskhaki and of *Ang,* published at Kazan by Galimjan Ibragimov, and so on.

It is evident that, given the conditions of the times, Tatar political thought could not go beyond certain limits; alone, it was incapable of resolving the problems raised by history. These problems could only be resolved by the revolution—that which history itself would confirm in time to come.

Until the February Revolution, the social and political objective of the Tatars was national renaissance. At the time of the February Revolution this objective was replaced by that of national independence. The latter was at times construed as national cultural autonomy, and at other times as territorial autonomy in the form of an independent state, the population of which would have a Tatar and Bashkir (Idel-Ural) majority. This claim was put forth clearly and concisely at the "constituent congresses" and Tatar conferences beginning with the First Pan-Russian Congress of Muslims (May 1917 at Moscow) up to the Second Pan-Russian Congress of Muslims at Kazan.

The petit bourgeois Tatar democracy feverishly prepared itself for this "independence." All the "pan-Russian" organizations were in its hands: the Executive Committee of the Pan-Russian Muslim Central Council (Ikomus) was presided over by the famous Menshevik Caucasian Ahmed Bey Tsalikov; the Pan-Russian Muslim Army Council (Harbi Shura) was at its service, not to mention the Milli Idare (National Board of Tatars of the Volga and of Siberia); and the Millet Mejlisi (National Assembly) convened at the time of the October Revolution.

Preparations for independence proceeded on the military as well as on the political level. The SR Tatars, Ayaz Iskhaki and Tuktarov, allied with the KD, such as Sadri Maksudov, "worked" the Tatar intelligentsia, the women, and the *mullahs*, while the Mensheviks allied to the nationalists "organized" the Tatar soldiers. Everywhere, on the front and in the rear, national Muslim (Tatar) units were formed: companies, regiments, squadrons, and so on. These units were concentrated at Kazan, Ufa, Orenburg, and partly at Astrakhan.

During and after the October Revolution all these bodies rose against us. Certain ones tried to equivocate, but as their maneuvers came to naught, sooner or later they had to show their hostility to the proletarian revolution.

From before the October Revolution, the "Ikomus" and the "Harbi Shura" had drawn closer to Kerenskii. At the time of the offensive of the wild division of Kornilov on Petrograd, the Ikomus played a dominant role in slowing its progress. At the time of the coup d'état of October at Kazan the leaders of the Harbi Shura allied themselves with the provisional government: they entered its "Revolutionary Committee" and sought to pit Muslim units against the insurgents. The National Assembly directed by Sadri Maksudov also adopted a hostile position. When the leftist faction of the assembly directed by the SR leftist Tatars and Bashkirs insisted on the recognition of Sovnarkom and wanted to send a congratulatory telegram the assembly refused.

At this point a new stage in the social and political life of the Tatars began. Already at the First Pan-Russian Muslim Congress at Moscow (May 1917) a leftist faction had appeared, directed by socialist leftist Muslims, which was to play an important role in the Tatar revolutionary movement.

At the Second Pan-Russian Muslim Congress, reassembled at the end of July at Kazan, the socialist Tatars of the Left already seemed an organized force. On the day the congress was inaugurated the leader of the Tatar socialists of Kazan (SD Bolsheviks), comrade Mulla-Nur Vahitov, gave an important speech against the KD and the social-opportunist Tatars, while the leftist SD, directed by Galimjan Ibragimov, showed themselves very active in the Left wing of the congress.

When the coup d'état of October broke out, the socialist Tatars of the Left already represented a perfectly stable revolutionary faction. Most of the members of the Muslim (Tatar) Socialist Committee belonged to the First Revolutionary Staff of Kazan formed during those days in October (Mulla-Nur Vahitov, M. Sultan Galiev, K. Yakubov, and Ya. Chanyshev) and later played an important role.

On their side, the SR of the Left, grouped around the newspaper *Algan*, worked actively at Ufa.

After the liquidation of the Constituent Assembly, the Mensheviks and the SR Tatars adopted a violently hostile position vis-à-vis the power of the Soviets (by inciting the Muslims of Russia to armed struggle against Soviet power). The socialist Tatars of the Left saw as their mission the liquidation of pseudorevolutionary Muslim organizations, a task which necessitated a fairly long and arduous struggle.

At Petrograd, close to the Commissariat of the People and Nationalities, the Central Committee on Muslim (Tatar) Affairs of the Russian Interior and of Siberia was formed with comrade Mulla-Nur Vahitov, the president of the Muslim (Tatar) Socialist Committee, at its head. The Ikomus was liquidated.

But the most bitter struggle took place at Kazan against the Harbi Shura and at Ufa against the "National Parliament." The fight against the Harbi Shura was directed by the Muslim Socialist Committee of Kazan, which formed Red Guard units composed of Tatar workers and led energetic agitation among the Tatar units of the Harbi Shura, the workers, and the Tatar peasants. The decisive battle between the Harbi Shura and the Muslim Socialist Committee took place at the Second Pan-Russian Muslim (Tatar) Military Congress at Kazan in February and March of 1918.

There, the Socialist Committee constituted a faction of the Left which included leftist Bolsheviks and SR who played a historic role in the class struggle among the Tatars and the Bashkirs (since the Bashkirs took part in the congress).

In spite of their solid organization, the advocates of "democratic nationalism" were morally defeated at the Congress. (In its resolution concerning the Constituent Assembly, the Congress congratulated itself on its liquidation.) Feeling defeat to be close at hand, the leaders of the right-wing faction of the congress employed a strategem: profiting from the tactless attitude of certain of our comrades who rebuffed part of the leftist faction, they decided to risk everything, and proclaimed the so-called Idel-Ural State (which included Tatarstan, Bashkiria, the "government" of Ufa, a part of Kirgizia, the Mariis and Chuvash regions). But this desperate ploy did not succeed, for the Sovnarkom of the Republic of Kazan (the "government" of Kazan) decided to arrest the directors of the presidium of the Military Congress, thereby provoking a conflict between the two factions which was finally resolved to our benefit. The congress was dissolved, the military units of the Shura were disarmed, and its partisans were made to renounce the proclamation of national territorial independence of the Tatars.

The burden of the struggle against the National Assembly of the Tatars passed to the SR of the Tatar-Bashkir left at Ufa. No purpose would be served by recalling the importance of this struggle.

If, in the Harbi Shura we had to deal with the military force of the national block of the KD Tatars and social opportunists, the National Assembly represented their political strength and it was necessary to dissipate this strength at any cost, for they claimed to have seized power in the Transvolga and southern Ural regions and even tried to extend their influence to Central Asia. The people of Ufa succeeded brilliantly in this task and the National Assembly was dissolved.

With the liquidation of these bodies came a new phase in Tatar political life: the era of class differentiation. There were two aspects to this: the differentiation of classes in the countryside and the mobilization of the laboring masses in the Red Army.

The first task was assumed by the Muslim commissariats (Tatars and Bashkir), the second by the Central Military College (Tatar) close to the Narkomvoen. These two tasks were closely allied.

In the beginning the local Muslim commissariats played the role of revolutionary staff in the Tatar movement. Not only were they auxiliary political instruments of the local soviets, but they also served, in broader terms, as organs of power in both a political and an administrative sense. They accomplished an immense amount of work on the spot, especially in the areas of agitation, propaganda, and cultural activities. From another angle, work accomplished by the Military College was highly significant. It was aimed in two directions: first, the mobilization of the Tatars in the Red Army and their political education; second, the formation of Red military leaders and of political activists chosen from among the workers and poor peasants.

During its existence, the Central Muslim College was able to form several

Tataro-Bashkir battalions and regiments and two brigades of Tatar riflemen (which could be assimilated into divisions), and this in spite of the almost total absence of a working class. It opened to Muslims (Tatars) political courses and military courses for infantry and cavalry, as well as commanding posts. But its essential work took place on the front, in the political sections of the army. It was there that special sections were founded to satisfy the needs of the Tatars in the Red Army. In the wake of this, the number of Red Tatar combatants increased by leaps and bounds: at the time when the Civil War was at its peak on the Eastern and Turkestan fronts, the proportion of Tatar combatants in the Red Army exceeded fifty percent of the total number of combatants, and in certain units (for example, the Fifth Army) even reached seventy to seventy-five percent. Each Tatar unit had its own story. Suffice it here to recall the first brigade of Tatar riflemen that crossed all of Kirgizia and Turkestan and took part in the revolution at Bukhara, or again the Tatar battalion of reserves of Kazan which provided, in one year alone, seventy marching companies for the single front of Turkestan.

The Tatar combatants of the Red Army became the pioneers of social revolution in the East by carrying the red flag of class struggle to the distant *kishlaks* (villages) of Central Asia, to the *yurts* of Siberia, and to the *auls* of the Caucasus.

The courses for military leaders also played an enormous role in the development of the revolution among the Turks of Russia. In one year and a half, they trained thousands of Red Tatar military leaders for the fronts of Turkestan and the Caucasus.

A great deal was also accomplished in the fields of publishing and education by the Military College, which distributed among the Tatar combatants hundreds of thousands of copies of the newspaper *Qzyl Armiya* and political brochures published by the Central Muslim Military College.

Finally, the Military College put forth a concentrated effort to train specialists. It enrolled several hundred Tatar combatants in different specialized courses for wireless operators, military engineers, officers of the Staff Academy, and so on.

In speaking of Tatar units in the Red Army one should also mention their merits before the revolution. This was how the first Muslim (Tatar) regiment of Kazan, formed by the Muslim Commissariat of Kazan from the old Red Guards of the Socialist Committee, came to play a historic role in the battles against the White guards around Kazan even before the appearance of the Czechoslovaks.

For its part, the Muslim socialist regiment, aided by the Tataro-Bashkir battalion sent from Moscow by the Central Muslim Committee, helped crush the uprising at Kazan which the "Committee for the Salvation of the Homeland" had provoked, and aided in the liquidation of the staff of the SR leftists who were preparing to attack us.

The situation was similar at Astrakhan. The coup d'état of October had succeeded there thanks to the participation of Tatar units whose steadfastness and whose sacrifices had saved Astrakhan from counterrevolutionary attacks during the darkest days of Soviet Russia. The Muslim Military Commissariat of Astrakhan which had command of the Tatar units had always been on the side of the revolution.

The coal basin of Krivoi-Rog-Donetz supplied tens of thousands of Tatar Red Guards. At the time of the German imperialist offensive against the Ukraine, the units formed of Tatar workers sacrificed themselves in the defense of the soviet power. One single unit of mine workers, organized by comrade Bulushov, contained as many as 6,000 Tatar Red Guards. At the beginning of 1918 this unit covered the retreat of our forces before Kharkov and took part in the bloody battle before Likhaia-Tsaritsyn.

In conclusion it would be appropriate to say a few words about the importance of the Tatar Republic in the development of the social revolution in the East, for the Tatar factor was enormously important. All the cultural forces forged and shaped during this period in Tatarstan would become, in the future, the seeds of cultural development in our still underdeveloped eastern territories.

From this time on, the Urals, Siberia, Central Asia, Khiva, Bukhara, and even far-off Afghanistan sought cultural workers, teachers, journalists, and so on in Tatarstan. In this latter period, there was such a critical shortage of Tatar workers that Tatarstan itself was bled dry.

In drawing up the balance sheet of the fourth anniversary of the October Revolution and of the participation of the Tatars, it should be noted that the working masses and the poorer classes of Tatars did not take part in the revolution, but did help to spread it in the East. We must continue their efforts and infuse new vigor and strength into the revolutionary struggle. The Tatar Republic should be the base of this work. To take up anew the work in Tatarstan, to sustain the comrades already working in this direction, this is the task of the day which the revolution requires of us.

Appendix C

Sultan Galiev

The Methods of Antireligious Propaganda among the Muslims

From *Zhizn' Natsional'nostei*, 29(127) and 30(128), 1921.

The problem of methods of antireligious propaganda among the Muslims is very delicate and complex because of the place Islam occupies in Muslim life and because of the general social and political situation of Muslim peoples.

Naturally, for us communists, there is no doubt as to the necessity of antireligious propaganda, not only among the Muslims of Russia, but also beyond her frontiers. To us, all religions are the same. On this level the problem is clear and no analysis is necessary.

The difficulty appears only where methods of achieving the desired results as quickly and with as little suffering as possible are concerned.

Now, one can't hope to defeat an adversary without knowing him. To fight a force, whatever its nature, without knowledge of it, is to risk at least failure if not outright defeat. Therefore, before discussing methods used in the antireligious battle among Muslims, one should define Islam, if only in the broadest terms, and then see if the methods of propaganda established by revolutionary practice against other religions are valid here.

In analyzing this last point it becomes evident that for multiple reasons special methods should be employed in the antireligious campaign among the Muslims. For these same reasons, different methods should be adopted when dealing with different Muslim peoples.

The essential factor which determines the position of Islam is its youthfulness. Of all the "great religions" of the world, Islam is the youngest and therefore the most solid and the strongest as far as influence is concerned. All serious European Islamicists have recognized this fact. Islam has best preserved social and political elements, whereas the other religions emphasize above all ethnic and religious elements. Muslim law—the Shariy'at—is a code of law and of judicial norms that regulates all aspects of the earthly life of the believer. In it we find directions on how to pray, how to conduct oneself at work, in society, in the family, and in everyday life, down to the smallest detail. Moreover, many of its prescriptions have a clear-cut, positive character.

Suffice it to recall the obligatory nature of its instructions (the *hadith* of Mohammed: *Utlibu l-'ilma min al-mahdi ila-l-lahdi* [Aspire to knowledge from cradle to grave]); the duty to engage in trade and to work (*kasab*); the duty of parents to educate their children until they come of age; the institution of civil marriage; the absence of private property in lands, waters, and forests; the condemnation of superstitions; the prohibition of sorcery, games of chance, luxury, extravagance, jewelry in gold and silk clothing, the use of alcoholic beverages, usury, and cannibalism (the last point was important in North Africa); the establishment of a detailed and progressive system of taxes on produce and on goods (*Zakat, ushr*, and so on).

Even family law and the law of succession in Islam contained positive principles, for they regularized, at the time they were elaborated and even later, the anarchical situation of the pagan Arabs. Thus, for example, Islamicists consider the *hadith* of Mohammed on polygamy to be an expression of his desire to limit it.

Insofar as it is a religion comprising social and political motifs, Islam penetrates the spirit of the believer more deeply than other religions; it is therefore a more difficult and delicate task to combat its influence. The best proof of this lies in the personal position of Muslim clergymen, which is much more solid than that of representatives of other religions.

Take, for example, the situation of the Muslim clergy among us in Russia. Whereas among Russians we find one parish for every 10,000 to 12,000 inhabitants, among Muslims there is one mosque for every 700 to 1,000 souls and each mosque is served by at least three members of the clergy: the *mullah*, his assistant, and the *muezzin*.

The strength of the Muslim clergy can also be explained by reason of its social and political position among the Muslim population. The *mullah* is at the same time priest (in charge of religious rites), teacher (each *mullah* has a religious school connected to his mosque: *mektep* or *medresseh*), administrator (in charge of regulating estates, registering civil acts of state), judge

(competent in affairs of marriage, divorce, and succession), and at times even
a doctor of medicine.

Furthermore, the Muslim clergy are elected and this places them in a more
favorable and solid position than, for example, the Russian clergy. The Russian priest, appointed by the superior authorities, certainly has a lesser authority over his flock than does the Tatar *mullah* or the Uzbek *ulema* in his
mahalle. The latter consider themselves just the same to be "servants of the
people" and lend an attentive ear to their wishes. They are more democratic
and closer to the people, and exercise a greater influence on them than does
the village priest over the Russian *muzhik*.

The second factor which makes antireligious propaganda difficult among
the Muslims is the social and economic situation of all Muslim peoples during
the latter centuries. The decadence of Arab culture and of Turko-Tatar culture
(expulsion of the Arabs from Spain and the Turko-Tatars from southwest
Europe, conquest by Europeans of Muslim possessions in North Africa and
the Middle East, Russian domination of the Tatars, the Bashkirs, the
mountain peoples of the Caucasus and of the Turkic principalities of Central
Asia) has led to the political and economic submission of nearly all the 300
million Muslims of the world.

During the course of the last century the whole of the Muslim world was
exploited by West European imperialism and served as the material base of its
economy. This fact has profoundly marked the religion of the Muslims. The
expansion of western imperialism manifested itself first in the form of the
Crusades and later by economic conquest. But the majority of Muslims always felt this battle to be a political conflict, that is to say as a battle against
Islam as a whole. Moreover, the reverse would have been impossible, for in
the eyes of Muslims, the Muslim world forms an indivisible whole, without
distinction, nationality, or tribe.

Because of this, Islam was and still is, at least in the eyes of Muslims, an
oppressed religion forced to be on the defensive. In other words, the historical
evolution of Islam fosters a feeling of solidarity among the diverse groups of
the faithful and lends force to its proselytizing. These conditions make the
anti-Islamic campaign a difficult one.

In Russia the task is even more arduous, for in spreading antireligious
propaganda among the Muslims we risk comparison with the recent "adversaries of Islam"—the Russian missionaries who spent millions from public
funds in this "battle." It was not long ago that these inveterate reactionaries
swarmed over all the Muslim regions of Russia and spread throughout them
the nauseating odor of missionary corruption. Lately, moreover, these territories were covered with a dense network of "scholarly establishments,"

seminaries and religious academies destined to form "specialists" in the battle against "Mohammedism." Inept antireligious propaganda runs the risk of evoking this recent past in the Muslim mind and would only have very negative results.

Finally, when discussing the difficulties of anti-Muslim propaganda another important factor should be noted: the cultural backwardness of Muslims in general. We are not going to dwell on the subject, for no one denies that cultural backwardness and religious fanaticism go hand in hand, completing and mutually reinforcing each other.

Thus, the particular position of Islam, which can be explained on the one hand by its greater vitality due to its late appearance and on the other hand by the psychological state of the oppressed or only lately liberated Muslim peoples (the Muslims of Russia), necessitates an approach and new methods of antireligious propaganda.

What should these methods be?

First of all the problem must be faced prudently, in a spirit of practicality. Any bureaucracy and any aggressiveness should be avoided. The issue should not be one of an antireligious battle, but rather of antireligious propaganda. Once and for all we must wrest from our adversaries the weapons with which they can defeat us. We must proclaim loudly that we are fighting no religion as such, but wish only to propagate our atheistic convictions, as is our natural right. This kind of approach alone can ensure that we will not be confused with the retrograde Russian missionaries. We must make the Muslims understand that in spreading antireligious propaganda we are not continuing the work of the Pobedonostsev and of the Il'minski, but rather that of their own intellectuals, who recently, moreover, had been working in this same direction.

Then we must purge our ranks, once and for all, of the old missionaries, if indeed they have managed to infiltrate, and put Muslim communists in charge of organizing antireligious propaganda. On no account should bunglers or especially charlatans have any hand in this. It would only serve to discredit us in the eyes of the Muslim populace.

In the third place, antireligious propaganda requires a great deal of competence and should be undertaken in a practical manner. It is not enough to publish brochures or little articles with pretentious titles (no one will read them) or to organize conferences; we must carry on the campaign in daily life, by our example and activities; in other words, we must replace verbal agitation with acts of agitation. The person whom we wish to influence must never be aware that we are preparing to submit him to antireligious propaganda. Otherwise, alarmed and put off in advance, he will shy away from us. In this regard, the simple presence in a Muslim village or among Muslim workers of one true communist (atheist) who firmly disregards established Muslim rites would be more useful than many conferences or talks given by the most eloquent and convincing of orators. Muslims must become accustomed to having real atheists living in their midst. They must be put into close contact with someone who denies the existence of God and must be made to see this person as a positive, rather than a negative creature. They must understand that the atheist is not a devil in human guise as is customarily depicted, but rather a man like themselves—more positive, more cultured, more resolute, and more energetic. If you can manage all of this, then ideological victory is yours. Only the first step is crucial; the rest will be easy.

The actual method of conducting antireligious propaganda in Muslim provinces shows this exposé to be correct.

A mediocre agitator arrives in a village; he is a ferocious-looking Tatar, dark and threatening, with masses of long hair, a revolver and sword in his belt. He begins by insulting "Allah and his prophets," displays his "furious" atheism by stamping on the Koran or some other book considered sacred by the Muslims:

> You see, I trample the Koran and nothing happens. Therefore, this book is not sacred, therefore there is no Allah, etc.

The outbursts of these pseudoagitators produce the most disastrous impression on the population. "We wanted to seize and kill him on the spot," the peasants of one Tatar village told me, speaking of one such "orator," "but we changed our minds through fear that a punitive expedition would be sent against us for having killed a 'bulshavik.' "

On the other hand, they spoke in humorous tones, totally devoid of malice, and with sincere delight, of a talk given by a traveling Russian Bolshevik who told them funny stories about the village priests and the *mullahs*. "He was gay and simple and made us laugh; he explained to us how the Russian priests fool the people; and among ourselves we thought that our own *mullahs* are also crooks."

Such is the reality of life and we can't ignore it. I witnessed another case: in a Bashkir village, on the day of the Muslim feast of Aid-i-Qurban (a day on which all Muslim believers must go to the mosque), a youth followed the example of the only Bashkir communist of the village, the manager of the club, and refrained from going to the mosque.

However, propaganda by deeds must not exclude verbal propaganda. The latter must be used, but only where the ground has already been prepared. For example, why not organize public discussions on religion aimed at Muslim workers in the cities and then progressively spread out into the countryside. All this is possible, not only where verbal propaganda is concerned, but also for antireligious publications.

But it should never be forgotten that the principal difficulty as far as antireligious propaganda among the Muslims is concerned comes from their cultural backwardness and their political and moral degradation. The age-old oppression of Russian czarism left deep scars. Let us recall, as an example, that even after the formation of autonomous republics, the Muslims rarely participated in the administrative life of their republics. No antireligious propaganda will give the expected results as long as Muslims have not been liberated and made free and equal Soviet citizens, not only on paper, but also in fact. We must first of all improve public education in all its forms and at all levels, attract Muslims to the economic, administrative, and political agencies of the State wherever possible, and also spread and reinforce the work of the Party. All this is indispensable for success.

In conclusion we believe it would be useful to say a few words about the necessity of varying antireligious propaganda among the Muslims of Russia, according to their ethnic identity. This approach is necessary because of the great economic, social, and cultural differences among the different Muslim peoples of Russia. The general principles of antireligious propaganda previously discussed can only be applied to the problem as a whole. When it comes to dealing with the different ethnic groups, we must necessarily "individualize" and differentiate the propaganda, a task that would prove impossible without a knowledge of their particular customs and culture. The following analysis is a preliminary attempt in this regard.

Special Working Conditions among the Tatars

Certain factors particular to work among the Tatars are negative and tend to complicate antireligious propaganda; other factors, being positive, tend to facilitate it. Among the negative factors we should note:

1. The strength of the Muslim clergy. The Tatar clergy (Volga, Urals, the Russian interior, and Siberia) is better organized than say, for example, the clergy of Kirghizia or of Turkestan. This strength is explained by the fact that it was always in the forefront of the struggle against the Russian missionaries—and this gave it a great deal of experience—and also by the fact that during the past few years the clergy has undergone a profound internal transformation on the personal and organizational levels.

The "personal" or internal transformation of the Tatar clergy was caused
by the political pressure which the Young Turk intelligentsia brought to bear
on it after the 1908 Revolution in Turkey. Later on we shall describe its
characteristics and significance. The organizational reform took place after the
February Revolution, and after various congresses, meetings, and conferences. The Muslem clergy modified its internal constitution, making it more
staunch, more viable, more flexible, and more democratic, and placed at its
head a new spiritual directorate of the Russian interior and of Siberia.

2. The internal psychological reaction provoked by the "propaganda" of
the different Russian missionary associations and that of the "militants" of
the Union of the Russian People. This "propaganda" met with the natural
resistance of the Muslims and lent strength to their fanaticism. On this score
we can recall the massive emigration of Tatars to Turkey at the time of the
religious persecutions under Alexander III. The mark left by the activities of
these associations is still there and it will take decades to eradicate it.

The positive factors are as follows:

1. The proletarization of the Tatar masses. This was relatively more advanced than among the other Muslim peoples of Russia. The poverty of the
soil, poor harvests, constant famines, the weakness of local industries—both
primary and secondary, all facilitated this proletarization by forcing Tatar
workers to emigrate to the industrial regions of Russia.

Not long ago the number of Tatar workers in the coal basin of Krivoi-
Rog-Donetz alone reached the figure of 100,000 persons. Furthermore, tens
of thousands of Tatars work in the oil fields of Baku and Groznyi. Still others
are to be found in great numbers in the factories of the Urals and in the gold
mines of Siberia. Nearly half, if not more, of the dock workers on the River
Belaia, the Lower Kama, and the Middle Volga wereTatars. One could meet
them in faraway Murmansk and on the Amur where they worked in railway
construction. Poverty drove them from one end of Russia to the other, from
one mine to another, and the seeds of atheism were gradually sown in their
souls. They had no time to think of Allah when hunger urged them to work.
Uprooted from his homeland, leading a vagabond's life and taking his Russian
companions as examples, the Tatar worker broke the bonds which tied him to
his patriarchal life and thus destroyed the foundations of religious fanaticism.

2. A higher cultural level than that of other Muslim peoples of the Russian
borderlands. The last fifteen to twenty years which preceded the revolution
can be considered the era of national renaissance of the Volga Tatars. The
Russian Revolution of 1905 and the revolutions of the Persian democrats and
the young Turks contributed considerably to this awakening. From this time
on, Turkestan and Bukhara, until then considered the cultural centers of the

Tatars but in reality nothing but hotbeds of cultural obscurantism and religious fanaticism, began to cede place to Constantinople, Beirut, and Cairo. On their return to Russia the Tatar students with degrees from the universities of these cities propagated new ideas, ideas of culture and of progress. The Tatar people, five million souls in a deep slumber who were designated by the Tatar writer Ayaz Iskhaki as "the degenerate people," began to awaken. A bitter struggle started between the *qadymists* (traditionalists) and the *jadids* (innovators). Denominational Muslim schools—*mekteps* and *medressehs*— underwent reform and introduced secular studies. In 1906 the first theatrical production in the Tatar language was performed at Kazan and gave rise to a storm of protest on the part of the reactionary Muslim clergy and the fanatics in the population. After the 1905 Revolution, the first newspapers in the Tatar language appeared. Soon a great many Tatar newspapers and reviews appeared in all the large Tatar centers: Kazan, Astrakhan, Orenburg, and Ufa, and later even in Moscow.

In turn Tatar literature appeared and several large printing houses were founded at Kazan. The problem of women was now raised. The innovators pressed for a ban on the veil. The clergy and the *qadymists* opposed these changes. The innovators were cursed and in certain regions the new schools they had founded were closed; the schoolbooks written in the Tatar language on secular subjects were burned; teachers were lynched, and so on. But all this was of no use, for finally the innovators prevailed. In the end we witnessed the appearance of Tatar literature, Tatar theater, and a national Tatar school. Tatar women discarded the veil; the clergy was subjected to pitiless social criticism by the satirical papers of the time (*Chukish, Yashyn, Qormaq,* and so on) which considered this problem to be of great importance. The struggle between the *qadymists* and the *jadids* also spread to the clergy. All that was reactionary, decadent, and fanatical gravitated toward the *qadymists;* all that was new, wholesome, and revolutionary was drawn to the *jadids.* Among the latter appeared the reformers—such as, for example, Musa Bigiev, Abdullah Bubi, and Ziya Kemali. Musa Bigiev published treatises concerning certain specific points of casuist Islamic theology in which he attacked the archaic positions of the *ulema* (fetwatists). In the work *Rehmet-i Ilahiye*, he criticized opinion established for centuries that paradise is reserved for Muslims alone and, basing his argument on certain *suras* of the Koran, proved that paradise is not reserved only for Muslims but also for those *kafirs* (infidels) who merit it. For the Muslim fanatic accustomed to viewing the *kafirs* as "damned," this interpretation was truly revolutionary. Bigiev wrote another work in which he condoned the nonobservance of the Muslim law of fasting. This also provoked a storm of protests since until then the fanatical clergy, whose influence on the people was still too strong, had categorically rejected such a possibility.

Ziya Kemali and Abdullah Bubi were in the forefront of the struggle to reorganize the *medressehs*—upper and middle Muslim educational establishments. They founded Muslim upper schools where, alongside the study of the Shariy'at, "European" sciences were taught: mathematics, history, geography, natural sciences, social sciences. Before their involvement, the introduction of such subjects in parochial schools was considered to be real apostasy.

One *mullah*, a certain Ghafuri, in his brochure *İsabet*, even cast doubt on Muhammad's being a prophet. It is true that the author of this work was later taken back into the fold of Islam, but nevertheless his work left a deep impression on the Tatar conscience.

The reactionary section of the Tatar clergy endeavored to "preserve" Tatar society from these "young Muslims," at first by their rhetoric, and when this method proved ineffective, by ignoble denunciations to the czarist police accusing the innovators of "pan-Islamism," and so on. But all this was useless. Already, before the February Revolution, the fanatical reactionary clergy had ceased to be a political force and in its place appeared a new clergy, whose activity contributed to the weakening of the religious fanaticism of the Tatars.

3. The influence of the socialist revolution. The socialist revolution only served to deepen and enlarge the setting of the antireligious struggle among the Tatars. During the course of this struggle many former "revolutionaries" found themselves in the reactionary camp. The revolution also caused a schism in the ranks of the Tatar clergy. Two enemy camps were formed—on one side the "Red" *mullahs*, supporters of Soviet power, and on the other, the "White" *mullahs*, supporters of Kolchak and the Constituent Assembly, who, although in outward appearance recognized Soviet power, in reality worked underhandedly against us. It should be noted that everywhere the reactionary *mullahs* allied themselves with the counterrevolutionary Russian clergy, thus forming a "united front" against the "communist *mullahs.*" As an example one could cite the peasant uprisings in the spring of 1920 in the districts (*uezd*) of Menzelinsk, Belebei, and Bugul'ma, where the insurgents shot not only communists but also Tatar teachers and *jadid mullahs*.

We can conclude this account by saying that, among the Tatars, the time was ripe for antireligious propaganda and good results can be expected. In this instance the favorable factors outweigh the negative ones.

The Work in Bashkiria

The situation in Bashkiria is somewhat different. Here there is less of an attachment to religious fanaticism but at the same time traces of the superstitions of ancient animism are stronger. The weakness of fanaticism among the Bashkirs is explained by several reasons. The principal one is that the Bashkirs are still in the nomadic stage and they preserve the elements of tribal life. The example of the Kirghiz, the Turkomans, and the Arab Bedouin proves that the nomadic life never favored the development of religious fanaticism. All observers, westerners as well as easterners, have noted this. And this is easily understood. Nomadism puts man face to face with nature and, in the constant struggle for survival, leaves him little time to think of religion, much less to perform religious rites. We know that all religions are born in cities and only later spread to the countryside and desert.

A second factor restrained religious fanaticism among the Bashkirs: the fact that they did not receive Islam directly from the Arabs or the Persians, but from the Tatars, to whom they had already begun to assimilate culturally before their conversion to Islam. Among them, the Tatar *mullah* was the pioneer of Islam. It is easy to understand that, under these conditions, Islam was a foreign religion, artificially imposed. Finally, we should recall the class and racial antagonism between Tatars and Bashkirs due to purely economic factors: the more advanced Tatars oppressed the Bashkirs. Given this state of affairs, the Tatar *mullah* could have little influence on the Bashkir *auls*, and in the first serious conflict between the Bashkirs and Tatars (especially after the February Revolution, when the Bashkirs proclaimed themselves independent of the Tatars, and the Tatars opposed this), the Tatar *mullah* lost his position and his head. We know that, at certain times, the massacres of *mullahs* and of Tatar teachers in Bashkir villages took on a chronic character. Otherwise, the Bashkir attachment to superstitions can be explained by their cultural backwardness. Suffice it to recall that to this day they still have no literary language and always use Tatar. Literature, theater, and art all come to them via the Tatars.

The grounds for antireligious propaganda therefore do exist in Bashkiria. We must only make them more fertile.

The Work in Kirghizia (Kazakhstan)

The best results of antireligious propaganda should be looked for in Kirghizia. The nomadic Kirghiz are less inclined to religious prejudice and to fanaticism than the other peoples. Their conversion to Islam is reminiscent of that of the Bashkirs. Among the Kirghiz the clergy was exclusively Tatar (Kirghizia was subject to the Spiritual Assembly of Orenburg), and we must note as well that these were the weakest elements among the Tatar *mullahs*—the real dregs—who went there. Every summer the Tatar Muslim denominational schools sent an incalculable number of *shakirds* (seminarians) to Kirghizia with the intention of exploiting the naive Kirghiz in the name of religion. Those Tatars who, among their own could not even become *farrash* (mosque caretaker) there became *mullah-eka* (religious director). It is obvious that in this situation they could hardly create anything solid or durable. Also the morals and customs of the Kirghiz were untouched by outside influence. In Kirghizia Islam was not even able to alter the position of women. Whereas everywhere else they were reduced to the rank of slave, in Kirghizia women retained their liberty. The judicial limitations to which they were subject were customary in character and not religious.

Turkestan, Khiva, Bukhara

Working conditions in this region are completely different from those we encounter among the Tatars, the Bashkirs, or the Kirghiz. Until recently, Bukhara remained one of the main centers of religious fanaticism in Central Asia and its influence in Turkestan and at Khiva is still enormous. These territories have not yet crossed the evolutionary stage through which the Tatars have already gone. Literature, theater, and art, just recently developed among the Sarts [Uzbeks], are embryonic among the Bukharians and the Khivians. It was not until after the October Revolution that the Sarts saw the first secular school; among the Bukharians and the Khivians they have just been established, thanks, moreover to Tatar and Turkish intellectuals. The position of women has not yet been altered. The antagonism which we notice between the Sarts and the Bukharians on the one hand and the Tatars on the other is basically due to the fact that the fight against religious fanaticism and cultural backwardness in Turkestan was directed by the Tatars.

Only recently, in 1918, the Bukharian clergy, with the emir at its head, organized a grandiose pogrom against Tatars, massacring more than five thousand persons accused of being *jadids*. To fully appreciate the strength of Islam in Bukhara it is enough to recall that even after the Soviet regime was inaugurated the Shariy'at continued to be applied in many areas (for example, the system of duty in kind). It is true that in this regard the position of

Turkestan is somewhat different. Ever since the Russian conquest the position of Turkestan has been somewhat different; religion no longer takes the place of civil and administrative law. Nonetheless, religious fanaticism is still very strong there and the antireligious struggle more difficult and complicated than in Tatarstan and Kirghizia.

The antireligious campaign can only be waged there with the methods used by the *jadids* between 1905 and 1910 in the region of the Volga.

Azerbaidzhan, the Caucasus, the Crimea

As far as organizing antireligious propaganda is concerned, the position of Azerbaidzhan is more favorable than that of Turkestan. The proximity of Turkey, a more highly developed industry, the existence of a more or less conscious indigenous proletariat, and finally the more precocious cultural awakening (the first Tatar language newspapers appeared in Azerbaidzhan twenty-five to thirty years ago, whereas in Turkestan, the first newspaper in the Sart language was only published in 1915; we do not count the government newspaper published by the missionaries)—all this puts Azerbaidzhan several decades ahead of Turkestan and Bukhara. The evolution of Azerbaidzhan is comparable to that of the Tatars of the Volga, even though it is slower. It is certainly easier to spread antireligious propaganda there than in Turkestan or Bukhara.

In the Crimea we encounter the same favorable conditions. Here conditions are even more auspicious than in Azerbaidzhan, for religious fanaticism is even weaker. The Crimea occupies a position midway between Azerbaidzhan and Tatarstan.

The situation is more difficult in Daghestan and among the mountain peoples of the Caucasus. The traces of the recent İmamate (of Shamil and others), the maintenance of the *'adat* (customary law), the absence of any national literature (replaced by Arabic literature), and finally political and religious isolation—all this explains why the attachment to religious prejudice is stronger here than in the other Muslim regions of the Russian borderlands. Suffice it to recall that Shariy'at courts have recently been introduced in Daghestan and in many regions of the Republic of the Mountain Peoples. During the Civil War one could see villages and even whole tribes of mountain peoples taking part in the battle against the troops of Bicharahov and Denikin on the side of the Soviet forces, solely for religious motives: "Soviet power gives us greater religious liberty than the Whites," they said. In the ranks of the Red Army of the Caucasus are found Shariy'at squadrons and

units (the Shariy'at squadrons of the Kabardian *mullah* Katkakhanov numbered several tens of thousands of combatants).

The goundwork for antireligious propaganda is not yet prepared, or else is
as yet only very superficially so.

In closing and summing up our article, we must repeat that Islam is different from other religions in substance and because of its history, and that
other methods of propaganda are necessary to fight it. But it is also necessary
to adopt special methods for each Muslim nationality according to its own
particular geographic, historical, cultural, social, and economic characteristics; those which work well with the Tatars are worthless for the Kirghiz,
those suitable for the Muslims of Russia are not applicable in Afghanistan or Bukhara, and vice versa. Tactics appropriate to each one of them are
necessary, tailored to their psychology and ethos. One of the most pressing
tasks in our work of agitation and propaganda in the East should be a detailed,
in-depth study of this problem on the spot, and a serious analysis of it in the
Party press. Without the effort we will never be able to find solid footing and
neither will we be able to solve the problems facing us; we will never be able
to extricate ourselves from our present state of mental anarchy.

Appendix D

J. V. Stalin

Rights and "Lefts" in the National Republics and Regions

Speech at the Fourth Conference of the Central Committee of the RCP (b) with the Responsible Workers of the National Republics and Regions, 10 June 1923. "The Sultan-Galiyev Case." J. V. Stalin. *Works*, vol. 5, *1921–23*, (Moscow: Foreign Languages Publishing House, 1953), pp. 308–19.

I have taken the floor in order to make a few comments on the speeches of the comrades who have spoken here. As regards the principles involved in the Sultan Galiev case, I shall endeavor to deal with them in my report on the second item of the agenda.

First of all, with regard to the conference itself. Someone (I have forgotten exactly who it was) said here that this conference is an unusual event. That is not so. Such conferences are not a novelty for our Party. The present conference is the fourth of its kind to be held since the establishment of Soviet power. Up to the beginning of 1919 three such conferences were held. Conditions at that time permitted us to call such conferences. But later, after 1919, in 1920 and 1921, when we were entirely taken up with the Civil War, we had no time for conferences of this kind. And only now that we have finished with the Civil War, now that we have gone deeply into the work of economic construction, now that Party work itself has become more concrete, especially in the national regions and republics, has it again become possible for us to call a conference of this kind. I think the Central Committee will repeatedly resort to this method in order to establish full mutual understanding between those who are carrying out the policy in the localities and those who are making that policy. I think that such conferences should be called, not only from all the republics and regions, but also from individual regions and republics for the purpose of drawing up more concrete decisions. This alone can satisfy both the Central Committee and the responsible workers in the localities.

I heard certain comrades say that I warned Sultan Galiev when I had the opportunity of acquainting myself with his first secret letter, addressed, I think, to Adigamov, who for some reason is silent and has not uttered a word here, although he should have been the first to speak and the one to have said most. I have been reproached by these comrades with having defended Sultan Galiev excessively. It is true that I defended him as long as it was possible, and I considered, and still consider, that it was my duty to do so. But I defended him only up to a certain point. And when Sultan Galiev went beyond that point I turned away from him. His first secret letter shows that he was already breaking with the Party, for the tone of his letter is almost White Guard; he writes about members of the Central Committee as one can write only about enemies. I met him by chance in the Political Bureau, where he was defending the demands of the Tatar Republic in connection with the Peoples' Commissariat of Agriculture. I warned him then, in a note I sent him, in which I called his secret letter an anti-Party one, and in which I accused him of creating an organization of the Validov type; I told him that unless he desisted from illegal, anti-Party work he would come to a bad end, and any support from me would be out of the question. He replied, in great embarrassment, that I had been misled; that he had indeed written to Adigamov, not, however, what was alleged, but something else; that he had always been a Party man and was so still, and he gave his word of honor that he would continue to be a Party man in the future. Nevertheless, a week later he sent Adigamov a second secret letter, instructing him to establish contact with the Basmachi and with their leader Validov, and to "burn" the letter. The whole thing, therefore, was vile, it was sheer deception, and it compelled me to break off all connection with Sultan Galiev. From that moment Sultan Galiev became for me a man beyond the pale of the Party, of the Soviets, and I considered it impossible to speak to him, although he tried several times to come to me and "have a talk" with me. As far back as the beginning of 1919, the "Left" comrades reproached me with supporting Sultan Galiev, with trying to save him for the Party, with wanting to spare him, in the hope that he would cease to be a nationalist and become a Marxist. I did, indeed, consider it my duty to support him for a time. There are so few intellectuals, so few thinking people, even so few literate people generally in the Eastern republics and regions, that one can count them on one's fingers. How can one help cherishing them? It would be criminal not to take all measures to save from corruption people of the East whom we need and to preserve them for the

Party. But there is a limit to everything. And the limit in this case was reached when Sultan Galiev crossed over from the communist camp to the camp of the Basmachi. From that time on he ceased to exist for the Party. That is why he found the Turkish ambassador more congenial than the Central Committee of our Party.

I heard a similar reproach from Shamigulov, to the effect that, in spite of his insistence that we should finish with Validov at one stroke, I defended Validov and tried to preserve him for the Party. I did indeed defend Validov in the hope that he would reform. Worse people have reformed, as we know from the history of political parties. I decided that Shamigulov's solution of the problem was too simple. I did not follow his advice. It is true that a year later Shamigulov's forecast proved correct: Validov did not reform, he went over to the Basmachi. Nevertheless, the Party gained by the fact that we delayed Validov's desertion from the Party for a year. Had we settled with Validov in 1918, I am certain that comrades like Murtazin, Adigamov, Khalikov, and others would not have remained in our ranks. (*Voice:* "Khalikov would have remained.") Perhaps Khalikov would not have left us, but a whole group of comrades working in our ranks would have left with Validov. That is what we gained by our patience and foresight.

I listened to Ryskulov, and I must say that his speech was not altogether sincere, it was semidiplomatic (*Voice:* "Quite true!"), and in general his speech made a bad impression. I expected more clarity and sincerity from him. Whatever Ryskulov may say, it is obvious that he has at home two secret letters from Sultan Galiev, which he has not shown to anyone; it is obvious that he was associated with Sultan Galiev ideologically. The fact that Ryskulov dissociates himself from the criminal aspect of the Sultan Galiev case, asserting that he is not involved with Sultan Galiev in the course leading to Basmachism, is of no importance. That is not what we are concerned with at this conference. We are concerned with the intellectual, ideological ties with Sultangalievism. That such ties did exist between Ryskulov and Sultan Galiev is obvious, comrades; Ryskulov himself cannot deny it. Is it not high time for him here, from this rostrum, at long last to dissociate himself from Sultangalievism emphatically and unreservedly? In this respect Ryskulov's speech was semidiplomatic and unsatisfactory.

Enbayev also made a diplomatic and insincere speech. Is it not a fact that, after Sultan Galiev's arrest, Enbayev and a group of Tatar responsible workers, whom I consider splendid practical men in spite of their ideological instability, sent a demand to the Central Committee for his immediate release, fully vouching for him and hinting that the documents taken from Sultan Galiev were not genuine? Is that not a fact? But what did the investigation reveal? It revealed that all the documents were genuine. Their genuineness was admitted by Sultan Galiev himself, who, in fact, gave more information about his sins than is contained in the documents, who fully confessed his guilt, and, after confessing, repented. Is it not obvious that, after all this, Enbayev ought to have emphatically and unreservedly admitted his mistakes and to have dissociated himself from Sultan Galiev? But Enbayev did not do this. He found occasion to jeer at the "Lefts," but he would not emphatically, as a Communist should, dissociate himself from Sultangalievism, from the abyss into which Sultan Galiev had landed. Evidently he thought that diplomacy would save him.

Firdevs's speech was sheer diplomacy from beginning to end. Who the ideological leader was, whether Sultan Galiev led Firdevs, or whether Firdevs led Sultan Galiev, is a question I leave open, although I think that ideologically Firdevs led Sultan Galiev rather than the other way around. I see nothing particularly reprehensible in Sultan Galiev's exercises in theory. If Sultan Galiev had confined himself to the ideology of pan-Turkism and pan-Islamism it would not have been so bad and I would say that this ideology, in spite of the ban pronounced by the resolution on the national question passed by the Tenth Party Congress, could be regarded as tolerable, and that we could confine ourselves to criticizing it within the ranks of our Party. But when exercises in ideology end in establishing contacts with Basmach leaders, with Validov and others, it is utterly impossible to justify Basmach practices here on the ground that the ideology is innocent, as Firdevs tries to do. You can deceive nobody by such a justification of Sultan Galiev's activities. In that way it would be possible to find a justification for both imperialism and czarism, for they too have their ideologies, which sometimes look innocent enough. One cannot reason in that way. You are not facing a tribunal, but a conference of responsible workers, who demand of you straightforwardness and sincerity, not diplomacy.

Khojanov spoke well, in my opinion. And Ikramov did not speak badly either. But I must mention a passage in the speeches of these comrades which gives food for thought. Both said that there was no difference between present-day Turkestan and czarist Turkestan, that only the signboard had been changed, that Turkestan had remained what it was under the czar. Comrades, if that was not a slip of the tongue, if it was a considered and deliberate statement, then it must be said that in that case the Basmachi are right and we are wrong. If Turkestan is in fact a colony, as it was under czarism, then the Basmachi are right, and it is not we who should be trying Sultan Galiev, but Sultan Galiev who should be trying us for tolerating the existence of a colony in the framework of the Soviet regime. If that is true, I fail to understand why you yourselves have not gone over to Basmachism. Evidently, Khojanov and Ikramov uttered that passage in their speeches without thinking, for they cannot help knowing that present-day Soviet Turkestan is radically different from czarist Turkestan. I wanted to point to that obscure passage in the speeches of these comrades in order that they should try to think this over and rectify their mistake.

I take on myself some of the charges Ikramov made against the work of the Central Committee, to the effect that we have not always been attentive and have not always succeeded in raising in time the practical questions dictated by conditions in the Eastern republics and regions. Of course, the Central Committee is overburdened with work and is unable to keep pace with events everywhere. It would be ridiculous to think that the Central Committee can keep pace with everything. Of course, there are few schools in Turkestan. The local languages have not yet become current in the state institutions, the institutions have not been made national in character. Culture in general is at a low level. All that is true. But can anybody seriously think that the Central Committee, or the Party as a whole, can raise the cultural level of Turkestan in two or three years? We are all shouting and complaining that Russian culture the culture of the Russian people, which is more cultured than the other peoples in the Union of Republics, is at a low level. Ilyich has repeatedly stated that we have little culture, that it is impossible to raise Russian culture appreciably in two or three, or even ten years. And if it is impossible to raise Russian culture appreciably in two or three, or even ten years, how can we demand a rapid rise of culture in the non-Russian backward regions with a low level of literacy? Is it not obvious that nine-tenths of the "blame" falls on the conditions, on the backwardness, and that you cannot but take this into account?

About the Lefts and the Rights.

Do they exist in the communist organizations in the regions and republics? Of course they do. That cannot be denied.

Wherein lie the sins of the Rights? In the fact that the Rights are not and cannot be an antidote to, a reliable bulwark against, the nationalist tendencies which are developing and gaining strength in connection with the NEP. The fact that Sultangalievism did exist, that it created a certain circle of supporters in the Eastern republics, especially in Bashkiria and Tataria, leaves no doubt that the right-wing elements, who in these republics comprise the overwhelming majority, are not a sufficiently strong bulwark against nationalism.

It should be borne in mind that our communist organizations in the border regions, in the republics and regions, can develop and stand firmly on their feet, can become genuine internationalist, Marxist cadres, only if they overcome nationalism. Nationalism is the chief ideological obstacle to the training of Marxist cadres, of a Marxist vanguard, in the border regions and republics. The history of our Party shows that the Bolshevik party, its Russian section, grew and gained strength in the fight against menshevism; for menshevism is the ideology of the bourgeoisie, menshevism is a channel through which bourgeois ideology penetrates into our Party, and had the Party not overcome menshevism it could not have stood firmly on its feet. Ilyich wrote about this a number of times. Only to the degree that it overcame menshevism in its organizational and ideological forms did bolshevism grow and gain strength as a real leading party. The same must be said of nationalism in relation to our communist organizations in the border regions and republics. Nationalism is playing the same role in relation to these organizations as menshevism in the past played in relation to the Bolshevik party. Only under cover of nationalism can various kinds of bourgeois, including Menshevik, influences penetrate our organizations in the border regions. Our organizations in the republics can become Marxist only if they are able to resist the nationalist ideas which are forcing their way into our Party in the border regions, and are forcing their way because the bourgeoisie is reviving, the NEP is spreading, nationalism is growing, there are survivals of Great-Russian chauvinism, which also give an impetus to local nationalism, and there is the influence of foreign states, which support nationalism in every way. If our communist organizations in the national republics want to gain strength as genuinely Marxist organizations they must pass through the stage of fighting this enemy in the republics and regions. There is no other way. And in this fight the Rights are weak. Weak because they are infected with skepticism with regard to the Party and easily yield to the influence of nationalism. Herein lies the sin of the right wing of the communist organizations in the republics and regions.

But no less, if not more, sinful are the Lefts in the border regions. If the communist organizations in the border regions cannot grow strong and develop into genuinely Marxist cadres unless they overcome nationalism, these cadres themselves will be able to become mass organizations, to rally the majority of the working people around themselves, only if they learn to be flexible enough to draw into our state institutions all the national elements that are at all loyal, by making concessions to them, and if they learn to maneuver between a resolute fight against nationalism in the Party and an equally resolute fight to draw into Soviet work all the more or less loyal elements among the local people, the intelligentsia, and so on. The Lefts in the border regions are more or less free from the skeptical attitude toward the Party, from the tendency to yield to the influence of nationalism. But the sins of the Lefts lie in the fact that they are incapable of flexibility in relation to the bourgeois-democratic and the simply loyal elements of the population, they are unable and unwilling to maneuver in order to attract these elements, they distort the Party's line of winning over the majority of the toiling population of the country. But this flexibility and ability to maneuver between the fight against nationalism and the drawing of all the elements that are at all loyal into our state institutions must be created and developed at all costs. It can be created and developed only *if* we take into account the entire complexity and the specific nature of the situation encountered in our regions and republics; *if* we do not simply engage in transplanting the models that are being created in the central industrial districts, which cannot be transplanted mechanically to the border regions; *if* we do not brush aside the nationalist-minded elements of the population, the nationalist-minded petty bourgeois; and *if* we learn to draw these elements into the general work of state administration. The sin of the Lefts is that they are infected with sectarianism and fail to understand the paramount importance of the Party's complex tasks in the national republics and regions.

While the Rights create the danger that by their tendency to yield to nationalism they may hinder the growth of our communist cadres in the border regions, the Lefts create the danger for the Party that by their infatuation with an oversimplified and hasty "communism" they may isolate our Party from the peasantry and from broad strata of the local population.

Which of these dangers is the more formidable? If the comrades who are deviating toward the "Left" intend to continue practicing in the localities their policy of artificially splitting the population—and this policy has been practiced not only in Chechnya and in the Yakut region, and not only in Turkestan. . . . (*Ibrahimov:* "They are tactics of differentiation.") Ibrahimov has now thought of substituting the tactics of differentiation for the tactics of splitting, but that changes nothing. If, I say, they intend to continue practicing their policy of splitting the population from above; if they think that Russian models can be mechanically transplanted to a specifically national milieu regardless of the manner of life of the inhabitants and of the concrete conditions; if they think that in fighting nationalism everything that is national must be thrown overboard; in short, if the "Left" Communists in the border regions intend to remain incorrigible, I must say that of the two, the "Left" danger may prove to be the more formidable.

This is all I wanted to say about the Lefts and the Rights. I have run ahead somewhat, but that is because the whole conference has run ahead and has anticipated the discussion of the second item.

We must chastise the Rights in order to make them fight nationalism, to teach them to do so in order to forge real communist cadres from among local people. But we must also chastise the Lefts in order to teach them to be flexible and to maneuver skillfully, so as to win over the broad masses of the population. All this must be done because, as Khojanov rightly remarked, the truth lies "in between" the Rights and the Lefts.

Appendix E

The Program
of the
ERK Party

The organization of ERK (Party of Freedom) was conceived in the spring of 1919 when socialist groups of Tashkent and of Temjassovo (Bashkiria) decided simultaneously, though independently of each other, to organize autochthonous socialist parties to be incorporated as independent units into the Third International. In November 1919, representatives of Tashkent, Bukhara, Kirghizia, and Bashkiria met accidentally in Moscow and decided to unite their efforts to organize national-socialist parties and drafted a program of a unique party. The program consisted of twelve points. In the spring of 1920, it became clear that the Central Committee of the Russian Communist party would not admit the legal existence of an autochthonous socialist party, even if it were integrated in the Komintern. Thereupon, the representatives of the proposed party met in June and decided to organize it, come what may, without restricting it by the program or the regulations of the Third International. In September 1920, during the Congress of the Peoples of the East, the organizational committee of the party assembled in Baku. It was composed of several members—whose names cannot be mentioned at present in view of the conditions prevailing in the USSR—and also Validov and Dzhanizakov. An outline of the new program was elaborated in twenty-seven points. The composition of the committee was then modified once more; Dzhanizakov no longer appeared in it, and it now included Abdulhamid Arifov, military commissar of the Soviet Republic of Bukhara. The committee, whose purpose was organizational work, adopted during its sessions of 7 to 10 January 1921 in Bukhara, the name of "Turkestan Sosialistlar Tüdesi" (abbreviated to "Tüde"), meaning Group (or Circle) of Turkestan Socialists. The enlarged council of Tüde, including Validov, Arifov, and representatives of autochthonous socialists of the republics of Kirghizia (Kazakistan) and Khoresm (Khiva), met in Bukhara on 15 to 18 April of the same year. The twenty-seven points of the projected program were then reduced to nine. At the beginning of 1926 there was a session of the party council, during which the name "Tüde" was changed to *Sosialist ERK Firkasi* ("Socialist Party of Turkestan ERK"). The nine-point program was confirmed during the sessions of 8 to 9 January. It runs as follows:

Program of the Socialist
Party of Turkestan ERK

Theoretical Part

In spite of the present feeble development of industry, the working class in the cities of Turkestan is daily increasing. It can defend its class interests against local and foreign exploiters and play a dominant part in the economic construction of the country only if it is organized into professional unions and into an independent workers' party. The efficiency of such a party is subject to the condition that it will not remain a closed professional organization of the working class but will promote cooperation between workers and peasants (*dehkans*) based on their common interests. A solid alliance between workers and peasants in Turkestan is based on the fact that the destiny of the great majority of the *dehkans* working for the textile factories is closely linked with that of the workers in the same factories. While European workers are struggling for the ownership of the means of production, the workers of Turkestan and cotton producers are equally interested in the development of a nationalized textile industry in Turkestan. The Turkestani worker and the peasant producer of cotton would represent (if a common political organization were established among them) a social and political force more important than the peasantry engaged in production of cereals. ERK aims to be a political organization uniting the classes of the revolutionary workers and of the *dehkans* in Turkestan.

Socialism will free the oppressed and enslaved classes of Asia, including those of Turkestan, from the darkness of the withdrawn East into the enlightened arena of contemporary life, from the domain of superstition into that of reality, from ethnicotribal limitations into international class strife. Socialism will teach them to cooperate and communicate with other nations. It will transform the economic conceptions of the working class of Turkestan, composed in the main of peasants, now entangled in the quagmire of the obscure life of the *kishlak* and in the enclosed semireligious corporations of city craftsmen; it will force them to face the problems of the world economy pertaining to the reconstruction of the economic life of humanity on a new basis. The educational influence of socialism in Turkestan will be enormous, however backward the country may be. The socialist party, based on economic and class principles and working for the propagation of socialism, will likewise contribute to the organization of other political parties in the East solely on an economic basis, so that religious and personal elements will play no part in the structure of political parties. Schools and national education, likewise, will be based only on vital economic principles.

Turkestan, dominated at present by an imperialistic power, cannot develop economically as it should, taking into consideration the geographical and natural conditions of the country. So long as it is being ruled by conquerors with whom the native population is forced to coexist, it will be forced to live in a constant state of warfare. It is a known fact that Russians in Turkestan are the conquering people and that Russian colonial policy, different for instance from that of the British in India, aims at a total and complete russification of the conquered regions. Russian imperialism aims at a specific object: to implant itself irretrievably in Turkestan, which is to be transformed into a Russian region; to replace the native majority of the population by Russian immigrants from European Russia; and to make Turkestan a base for future pilfering conquests in Central, Southern, and Eastern Asia. Russian imperialism is striving toward this goal by different measures, for instance by armed extermination and by plunder of the natives in different regions, their land being seized as a reprisal for the revolts often caused by the activity or the provocation of the imperialists themselves. Economic measures, such as extortion of land and water, are constantly and systematically applied. The richest, the most fertile, and the most densely populated valleys of Southern Turkestan are being pitilessly devastated; the native elements who had worked on this land for centuries are being deprived of it and replaced by armies of new colonists from Russia, unfamiliar with the agricultural technique of intensive irrigation. Sedentary or semisedentary natives of Northern Turkestan are losing their fertile, cultivated lands; the Kazak-Kirghiz, who had already transferred to sedentarism, are being driven into the desert. Construction of new major canals for the use of factories (for instance, those of textiles) or mills, such as metallurgical works, are allowed exclusively in the interest of Russian implantation. The culture of cotton, which in certain regions is at present the most profitable crop, is also used as a tool of enslavement of the native population. The cultivation of cotton is compulsory and is accompanied by restrictions on the culture of cereals and rice, which is not allowed even in cases where it would have favored the expansion of industrial plants. The object of this restriction is to ensure complete dependence of the local population on Russia as regards their daily bread. And yet at times Russia is unable to supply Turkestan with a sufficient quantity of bread. This happened, for instance, in 1917–18 when nearly two million Turkestani died of hunger. Tractors and other modern agricultural machinery are supplied in the first place to Russian immigrants. The indigenous *kishlak* is dependent on Russian settlements for his water supply and agricultural equipment.

Such measures naturally result in a certain mistrust or even hostility of the native workers toward the novelties introduced by Russians. The conquerors, in turn, monopolize information on the conditions prevailing in their colonies and systematically implant in the consciousness of educated societies of other nations the notion that they took over in Central Asia a virgin land, peopled by savage natives similar to the redskins, who are opposed to all innovation in the economic domain, and that they had to enforce culture in this region, that the natives are doomed to "natural disappearance" and that they will be replaced by the "legal owners" of the land (the colonists, who will "legally" assimilate them), and that the Russians are transforming this wild country into an America. In the meantime, the natives of Turkestan have no chance to export their products on the world market, or to establish contact with the rest of the world, and thus they have no means to explain to cultured people—and even less to their own workers—that industry and the improved techniques and equipment of agricultural economy are offered to them in the guise of death. The truth is that the natives have never opposed innovations in national economy. On the contrary, being representatives of a much older and incomparably higher rural culture than the Russians, they, from the beginning of the occupation, sent to the Russian authorities demands to repair the old irrigational canals and build new ones (for instance, in the lower part of Sir Darya), to ensure the preservation of "Saksaül forests" in the region of moving sands, and to build bridges, and so on. But these demands were never met. Russian economic policy resulted in wars and revolts but never enlisted the enthusiasm of the natives, whereas the productivity in all the countries, colonies included, now depends on the consciousness and the interest of the workers involved.

In view of the foregoing, the foremost task of ERK is the economic revival of Turkestan, to be attained by involving in it the interest of the native population. This can be achieved by opening the access to Turkestan to all the peoples and by linking the country by railway with its neighbors in Asia, namely with India, Iran, and China, thus liberating its markets from the monopoly of the Russian railways. It is only thus that Turkestan will be able to probe the as yet unknown and unused treasures hidden in its underground, and develop its internal economic resources; only then will it be able to make use of its system of great rivers, build major canals, expand its irrigational system, enlisting the technical and material resources of all the cultured nations. It will then be able to encourage the nomads of the steppes to adopt the sedentarian way of life in the irrigated areas and to attract kindred and economically equal people, thus increasing the density of its population. Finally, only when there will be nonmonopolized freedom of communication with other people will Turkestan be able to ensure its workers of salaries on the same level as those of workers in other countries. The integration of the economic life of Turkestan into this natural current depends entirely on its political independence. The imperialistic yoke of the enslaving power, which weighs on all the classes of the native population, prevents the class differentiation in a country which is already economically backward. The working class of Turkestan, even under the present circumstances, has proved that it is destined to be an important factor in the cultural and economic revival of the country and that it is capable of generating real national-social workers. However, the development of city life, of industry, and of a native workers' class to the level on which it could acquire an even more significant and dominating position in the political life of Turkestan depends entirely on the political independence of the country, which would ultimately allow it to utilize its own raw materials and cotton and exploit its metallurgical resources. It will thus become again what it has been in the past, a producer of textiles and metal products.

The conquerors of Turkestan, to ensure their everlasting domination, have taken many other measures besides those already mentioned. Thus, natives are excluded from military training; remainders of antiquated feudalism are maintained, as are foundations of the old familial and patriarchal system; tribal conflicts are artificially provoked for the benefit of the political goals of the Russians; development of a strong and viable Turkestani culture on a modern basis is thwarted; century-long cultural development of the country as a whole is replaced by a nonviable tribal tradition which within the plans of the conqueror is to be used as a stepping-stone to the full assimilation of the natives; professional and technical knowledge is monopolized by the dominating nation; and the native population has no opportunity to receive education in other European countries and to become acquainted with other forms of culture higher than that of its enslavers; rather it is the culture of the dominating nation which is constantly being glorified. However, whatever measures it takes, the imperialistic state will never succeed in russifying Turkestan or completely assimilating the native population. The only result of these measures is a waste of energy and strength of the natives in a struggle against the harmful and murderous measures taken by the imperialists. This energy and strength could have been profitably utilized for the positive work of cultural development, which is so necessary and so precious; only political independence will eliminate this waste.

The independence of Turkestan and the conquest by the workers of the leading role in the political life of the country can be obtained either by peaceful work among the population, or by revolutionary means. The independence of Turkestan is an ideal common to all the classes of the oppressed nation, and therefore a temporary union of all classes and their solidarity in the struggle against the oppressors is absolutely essential. However, even at this stage and while accepting a temporary union in a common strife for a common object, the workers cannot renounce their class profile. The native bourgeois intelligentsia can no longer lead the popular masses, leaving aside the economic questions and replacing them by slogans common to the nation as a whole. On the contrary, the bourgeoisie of colonial and semicolonial countries is acquiring a clear class conscience and is openly engaging in the defense of its interests. The small bourgeois democratic groups of Azerbaidzhan, Turkestan, and certain other Asiatic countries, which up to now were dispersed and hesitated between socialists and genuine bourgeoisie, have started in the years following the revolution to organize themselves as a class. Some of these groups openly express in their propaganda literature the necessity to develop national capitalism. These facts which are an undisputable and characteristic symptom of the cultural development of these countries make it an absolute necessity for the representatives of the workers of Turkestan, for the young people and the members of the native intelligentsia who had, during the revolution, assimilated the ideas of socialism to organize themselves into a socialist party.

The political parties of the nonsocialist native intelligentsia can work only among the bourgeoisie of their nation. In their struggle for the independence of the colony they can obtain no support from a strong international union. On the other hand, the revolutionary socialists, who consider that the objectives of complete liberty and independence of the oppressed peoples can be achieved through the victory of socialism in the whole world and the formation of an international federation of socialist societies, are supported by the international union of political forces fighting against capitalism and imperialism throughout the world. Therefore the party of the working class and of the socialists of the colonial countries (in spite of their present weakness due to the general backwardness of the country) bear a great responsibility for the political fate of these countries. It is only by the medium of these socialist parties that the struggle for the independence of the colonies and of the oppressed nations is raised to the level of the common struggle of all the oppressed elements and of the world proletariat. In the meantime, the socialist parties of the colonies and of the oppressed peoples must draw conclusions from the experience of the Russian Revolution. This revolution proved the following:

1. A proletariat of an imperialistic nation cannot easily renounce opinions and attitudes toward colonies and peoples formerly oppressed by their own bourgeoisie, opinions and attitudes which that same bourgeoisie implanted in the minds of proletarians. According to that opinion, it is only by systematic violence that certain products and raw materials can be obtained from colonies and goods manufactured in a designated metropolis. In spite of the official recognition of the rights of the colonies, the generation of proletarians who inherited the power from the bourgeoisie does not differ in any way from its forerunners. The result is that native workers consider the socialists of the metropolis as hypocritical oppressors, of even a worse kind than the bourgeoisie, utilizing the slogan of the liberation of the colonies as a means of propaganda for their own profit in the colonies of their competitors, other imperialistic states.

2. While socialism is being constructed in only one country, the socialists of the metropolis trust only the centralizing elements of the imperialistic nation insofar as colonies are concerned, and the native proletariat is viewed with suspicion because of the decentralizing tendencies ascribed to it. The allegiance to socialism of native proletarians is evaluated only by their submission to the dominating nation as a whole. The socialists of the metropolis of the present generation are experts at hiding their suspicions of the native proletarians and socialists under slogans such as "a unique front against world imperialism." Long years of experience of "proletarian colonial policy" showed that the latter has done nothing but improve on the former system of transplantation and assimilation of the population. It has merely hastened the process by applying "new revolutionary" methods and by supporting the mainstays of feudalism and tribal organization, which are considered as a "counterpoison" to the union of natives around the national culture, the only viable one but deemed undesirable by the "proletariat in command." This proves beyond any doubt that the attitude of *trust* or *mistrust* is determined in every given case solely by a categorical decision of a certain proletarian generation of an imperialistic nation to maintain its domination in colonies

and to finalize the enterprise of assimilation and economic absorption. It is precisely for this reason that the social-communists of the metropolis do not tolerate the existence of distinct national social-communist parties or the formation of national factions within the common communist party which must remain unique, monolithic, and Russian.

These conclusions drawn from the Russian Revolution prove without a possibility of doubt that the proletariat of the metropolis and of the colonies can come to an understanding only in the presence of and with the intervention of a third element—a strong Socialist International, morally and materially independent from the proletariat of the nation that dominates a colony.

Beyond any doubt, the relations of the proletariat of the oppressing and of the oppressed nations, respectively, will follow the same pattern in other colonies as well, for instance, in those of Asia, Africa, and Australia. The best, the sincerest, and the staunchest socialists, upholding the freedom of colonies and of the nations, will remain, as in Russia, a feeble minority, deprived of a possibility to influence the masses.

The party ERK believes that the Socialist International is destined to become a decisive political force and will represent efficiently the interests of the oppressed on the condition that it takes as a basis of its organization the classification of humanity not by states or countries but by nationalities. Then a proper place and a real significance will be reserved within the Socialist International for the representatives of socialist parties of oppressed populations and colonies and the part played within this framework by ERK will be just as useful as theirs.

The party believes that it is destined to become the strongest and the most closely united political organization of Turkestan; it will attract the mature and the revolutionary elements among the working *dehkans,* and thus both the workers and the *dehkans* will be represented by it in the family of international socialism.

Text of the Program of
the ERK Party Based on
the Conclusions Outlined
Above

The following principles should be put into practice in the economic domain:

1. Land, waterways, and forests belong to the people as a whole. Their free use is granted to them without any retribution.

2. The mining industry and the exploitation of the underground and of the railways are to be completely nationalized and their management must be

completely in the hands of the government of Turkestan; the nationalization of other branches of industry is to be executed in accordance with the needs of the quickest economic development of the country and the improvement of the material situation of the workers.

3. Collective principles in rural economy must be maintained; with this objective in view, the work of irrigation and of the indigenous system of collective *hashar,* that of communal work for the installation of *ariks,* the maintainance and the management of the irrigational system and other elements of unification of the agricultural economy of Turkestan, must be considered as the most suitable basis for the organization of native social life on new socialist principles and for the general implantation of collectivism. The construction of new, large, modern canals, of sluice gates of the same type to regulate the systems of large rivers, the erection of country-wide hydroelectrical stations in the mountains of Turkestan and their management must place the collectivism and the constructive work by common effort at the foundation of the national economy of the country.

4. A worldwide effort must be made to industrialize the rural economy, to develop intensive agriculture throughout Turkestan, to check the offensive Russian expansive dry farming in favor of the fertilizing irrigational system, especially in the northern parts of the country (in Kazakistan).

5. The newly irrigated lands must be repopulated by native nomads and involuntary nomads.

6. Further immigration of Russians must be stopped and the density of the population in cities and in newly irrigated regions must be increased by implanting immigrants akin to the Turkestani and in general belonging to nonimperialistic nationalities of Asia and Europe such as Tatars, Persians, Indians, nonimperialistic peoples of Eastern Europe, and so on.

7. A unique income tax must be established by the parliament.

8. All forms of cooperation must be developed and State credit banks established.

9. Gradual transfer must be made to the modern type of urban construction; indigenous towns planned according to the European model; domestic water supply and canalization installed; system of communications and of transport in indigenous towns developed according to the new plans, thus liquidating the distinction between European and indigenous towns.

The following measures are needed for the settlement of the problem of the working class:

1. Professional and labor organizations existing in all of the civilized countries—professional unions, workers' funds, conciliation boards, life insurance, and so on—must be created throughout Turkestan. They must be

endowed with full rights and entitled to defend the interests of the working class. Measures must be taken to enable the indigenous workers to acquire in professional schools and courses the necessary knowledge of modern professional methods so that the Turkestani worker might settle his own problems without the assistance of "organizers and instructors" who enslave the country.

2. The workers' problems must be settled and the worker's life in State-managed factories must be improved to the degree where it will serve as a model for private enterprise.

The ERK party will struggle for the full independence of Turkestan and for its manifestation on the international arena as an independent, self-governing force as becomes its geographical position and the natural and economic peculiarities of Central Asia.

The form of governmental authority in Turkestan, once it is freed from the yoke of foreign imperialists and from that of feudals and of the clergy within the country, will be a democratic republic. The source of authority will be a parliament elected by a system of secret, equal, and direct vote; the rural and urban administrations are to be organized on the basis of the same principles. The democratic regime and the free elections in Turkestan, which are free from the tradition of bourgeois leadership, must be preserved from the pressure of capitalists and the bourgeoisie and must ensure the emergence of fresh popular forces from the ranks of the most oppressed and the least cultured classes of population.

The party will strive to attain independence and people's power by legal and peaceful means. Nevertheless, since the people can conquer power and retain it only if it possesses a national army, the party will promote the call for obligatory military service and generalized military training. On the other hand, even during foreign occupation the party will give its support to the struggle against the monopoly of high command by the imperialistic nation and will oppose the departure of native military detachments from the limits of Turkestan and the breaking up of the native army into small units incorporated within the great military detachments of the imperialists.

The national question in Turkestan in general and the problem of national minorities in particular must be settled by means of generalization of the democratic electoral rights for all the nationalities and by putting at their disposal the opportunity to utilize the State schools and other public institutions as well as the natural resources of the country, land, and water and to benefit from the governmental measures as regards the organization of social work and the fight against unemployment in proportion to the quantitative importance of every nationality involved. The party will also fight against feudalism and its inheritance and the tribal principles which were always used as weapons by the imperialists; it will give its support to measures for reinforcing the unique national Turkestani culture for ethnic groups belonging to the race predominating in the country which did not yet succeed—or did not endeavor—to give status to their specific national culture. The creation of a unique and modern system of laws and jurisdiction, over and above the customary and religious tribal jurisdictions, will also contribute to the liquidation of tribal traditions and inequalities.

Public education in Turkestan must aim first of all at the most rapid material and spiritual progress of the population; at the reinforcement of the people's power and at the liberation of the natives from the chains of financial-industrial and technical monopoly based on knowledge, such as railways, the telegraph, the telephone, tramways, electrostations, and so on, centralized in the hands of the immigrants of the imperialistic nation (who, moreover, are destined to remain permanently as citizens in the independent Turkestan). Education must also aim at the radical annihilation of all the traces of class and caste inequalities and at the creation of a new, democratic popular culture, instead of the existing institutions of feudalism. Systems of workers' schools and general, free primary education must be organized, and, finally, the Turkestani must be given the opportunity to become directly acquainted with the genuine culture of Europe in the schools of civilized nations. Such are the basic requirements of the party as regards public education. The organs of national education paid by the government must be proportionately used by all nationalities and classes. The inertia and the indifference of the more backward classes of the population must not allow their part of national education to be placed at the disposal of the richer, more energetic, and better advised classes. At the same time, when elaborating and distributing proportionally the budget of national education, the party will take into consideration the fact that in the past the interests of education for the most backward classes and the workers were ignored and will pay special attention to catching up with what these classes and nationalities had thus formerly lost.

In matters of religion the principle of full freedom of conscience is to be applied. Religion is to be considered as a private matter for every citizen and the church must be absolutely separated from the government. The government's task is only to see that religious cult should be observed without prejudicing social order and to avoid religious propaganda which might be used with some political object so that religion would not appear as a weapon in the hands of internal and external enemies of progress and national independence of Turkestan.

The ERK party believes that the struggle of the working classes of colonial people against capitalism and imperialism will end only in conditions of international solidarity. For this reason it will endeavor to coordinate all of its activity with the international movement of liberation and will enter into a Socialist International which truly will be able to ensure the coordination of the struggle of the oppressed classes of capitalistic countries with the revolutionary movements of liberation of small and colonial peoples.

Appendix F

Demographics of Soviet Muslim Nationalities

Nationalities	1926	1959	Increase 1926– 59 (%)	1970	Increase 1959– 70 (%)
Total Population of the USSR	147,005,000	208,827,000	42	241,720,000	16
Great-Russians	77,732,000	114,114,000	47	129,015,000	13
Total Muslims	17,292,000	24,380,000	41	35,232,000	45
Uzbeks } Uighurs }	3,988,000[1]	6,015,000 95,000	53	9,195,000 173,000	53 82[2]
Tatars[3] } Azeris[3] }	4,899,000	4,968,000 2,940,000	61	5,931,000 4,380,000	19 49
Kazakhs } Kirghiz }	4,579,000	3,622,000 969,000	.26[4]	5,299,000 1,452,000	46 50
Tadzhiks[5]	980,000	1,397,000	42	2,136,000	53
Turkmens	766,000	1,002,000	31[6]	1,525,000	52
Daghestani peoples	642,000	945,000	47	1,365,000	44
Avars	167,000	270,000	62	396,000	47
Lezghins	134,000	223,000	66	324,000	45
Darghins	126,000	158,000	25	231,000	46

Nationalities	1926	1959	Increase 1926– 59 (%)	1970	Increase 1959– 70 (%)
Kumyks	95,000	135,000	42	189,000	40
Laks	40,000	64,000	60	85,000	33
Tabasarans	28,000	35,000	25	55,000	57
Nogays	36,000	39,000	8	52,000	33
Rutuls	13,000	6,732	−48[7]	12,000	79[7]
Tsakhurs	3,300	7,321	121	11,000	50
Aguls	...	6,709	...	9,000	34
Bashkirs	983,000	989,000	.6[8]	1,240,000	25
Chechens	318,000	419,000	31[9]	613,000	46
Ossetians[10]	272,000	413,000	52	488,000	18
Kabardians	140,000	204,000	46	280,000	37
Karakalpaks	126,000	173,000	37	236,000	36
Ingushes	74,000	106,000	43[9]	158,000	55
Karachais }	186,000[11]	81,000	−33[12]	113,000	40
Balkars }		42,000		59,000	40
Adyghes.		80,000		100,000	25
Cherkess	79,000	30,000	64	40,000	33
Abazas		20,000		25,000	25
Kurds[13]	69,000	59,000	−14[14]	89,000	51
Abkhaz[15]	57,000	65,000	14	83,000	28
Dungans	14,600	22,000	50	39,000	77[16]
Iranians[17]	51,000	21,000	−59[14]	28,000	33
Baluchis	7,800	8,000	2.5	13,000	62
Afghans	1,900	2,000	5.2	4,000	100
Talyshes	77,000	...[18]	...	...[18]	...
Tats	29,000	11,000	−62[14]	...[18]	...
Arabs	...	8,000	...	...[19]	...

NOTE: In 1926, Muslims represented 11.76 percent of the total population of the USSR; in 1959 their relative importance dropped to 11.67 percent (because of the brutal liquidation of the nomads). In 1970, they represented 14.57 percent.

The projection of Muslim population in the near future (next twenty-seven years) may be placed within the following limits:

Maximum growth corresponding to the 45 percent increase for the eleven years between the last two census periods (1959 to 1970). If this growth is maintained, in 2003 the Muslims of the Soviet Union will number 110,379,000, which would represent *grosso modo* 30 percent of the total population of the USSR.

Minimum growth of the Muslim population corresponding to 20 percent for eleven years (present-day growth of the Volga Tatar nation). This would represent in 2003 a total of 61,000,000, or 16 percent of the total population of the USSR.

It is reasonable to accept that by the turn of our century, total Muslim populations will represent around eighty-five million souls—which would make the USSR the third Muslim power in the world, behind Indonesia and Pakistan.

[1]Includes some smaller Turkic groups listed in 1925 as separate nationalities: Kuramas, Ferghana Turks, Kashgarlyks, Sarts, Taranchis, and so on.

[2]The exceptional increase of the Uighurs is due mainly to immigration from Sinkiang in the late 1950s.

[3]Includes the Crimean Tatars (200,000) and some smaller Volga Turkic groups listed in 1925 as separate nationalities: Mishars, Kriashens, Teptiars, Nagaybaks, and so on.

[4]The Kazakhs lost almost a million souls during the forced sedentarization of the nomad tribes in the 1930s.

[5]Includes the Pamirian peoples (100,000?).

[6]The relatively low increase of the Turkmens between 1926 and 1959 may be explained by the forced sedentarization of the nomad tribes in the 1930s.

[7]The decrease of the Rutuls between 1929 and 1959, their exceptional increase after 1959, and the important increase of the Tsakhurs between 1926 and 1959 may be explained only by the twists in the census practices of Daghestan.

[8]The small increase of the Bashkirs between 1926 and 1959 may be explained by the sedentarization of the seminomadic Southern Bashkir tribes and also by the assimilation of the Northern Bashkirs by the Tatars.

[9]In spite of their deportation in 1943, the Chechens and the Ingushes had between 1926 and 1959 a relatively high increase, mainly because of their extremely high fertility rate.

[10]Only partly Muslim. The majority (Western Ossetians ''Iron'' tribes) is Christian Orthodox. Only a minority (Eastern Ossetian, Digor tribes) is Muslim.

[11]Includes, in 1926, the Kumyks and the Nogays (partly).

[12]The decrease is due to the deportation of the Karachais and the Balkars in 1943.

[13]Includes the Yezidis (devil worshippers), some 15,000 listed as a separate nationality in 1926.

[14]The decrease of the Kurds, Iranians, and Tats is due to their assimilation by the Azeris or by the Uzbeks (Iranians). In 1926 the Jewish and the Christian Tats were listed together with the Jewish Tats. In 1959, the Jewish Tats were listed as ''Jews'' and the Christian Tats as ''Armenians.''

[15]Only partly Muslim. The majority are Christian Orthodox of the Georgian rite.

[16]The exceptional increase of the Dungans (Chinese Muslims) is certainly due to immigration from China.

[17]Under this term are listed recent migrant colonies from Iran in the Caucasus and an old colony (eighteenth century) around Khiva and Bukhara.

[18]Assimilated by and listed as Azeris.

[19]Assimilated by and listed as Uzbeks.

Appendix G

Chronology, 1917-28

1917
(New Style=Gregorian)

12–15 March	"February" Revolution. Establishment of the Provisional Government.
17 March	Formation of the Ukrainian Central Rada in Kiev.
11 May	Foundation of Milli Shura (Muslim Central Council) in Moscow.
14 May	Opening of the First All-Russian Muslim Congress in Moscow.
23 June	Foundation of the Kazan Muslim Socialist Committee with Mulla-Nur Vahitov as chairman. First "Universal" of the Ukrainian Central Rada.
4 July	Foundation of the Harbi Shura (Muslim Military Council) in Kazan. Establishment of Milli Idare (Muslim National Directory) in Ufa.
7 November	Bolshevik coups in Petrograd and in Kazan.
8–12 November	Bolshevik and Rada coup in Kiev.
7–14 November	Bolshevik and Left Socialist Revolutionary coup in Tashkent.

16 November	First Kazan Revkom of fourteen members, all of whom are Russians.
24 November	Establishment of the Transcaucasian Commissariat dominated by the Mensheviks.
28 November	Third Regional Congress of the Soviets in Tashkent. Election of a Turksovnarkom of fifteen members, all of whom are Russians. Convocation of the Millet Mejlisi (Muslim National Assembly) in Ufa.
6 December	Finland proclaims its independence.
11 December	Lithuania proclaims its independence. Opening of the Fourth Regional Muslim Congress, called by the Central Muslim Council, in Kokand.
17 December	Bolshevik ultimatum to the Ukrainian Rada.
18 December	Opening of the All-Kirghiz (Kazakh) Congress in Orenburg. Proclamation of Kazakh autonomy (26 December) and of two governments, Eastern Kazakhstan (Bukeykhanov) and Western Kazakhstan (Dosmohmmedov).
19 December	Opening of the First All-Ukrainian Congress of Soviets in Kiev.
20 December	Opening of the All-Bashkir *kurultay* in Orenburg. Zeki Validov proclaims Bashkir autonomy.
27 December	Opening of the Belorussian National Congress in Minsk. Sverdlov declares (at the cession of the Central Committee of the Russian Socialist Democratic Workers party) that "the creation of a separate Ukrainian Communist party, whatever it might be called, whatever programs it might adopt, we consider undesirable."

1918

12 January	Latvia proclaims its independence.
18 January	Offensive of Red troops against Kiev.
21 January	Red troops take Orenburg. Dutov flees. Opening of the Second Muslim Military Congress dominated by the nationalists in Kazan.
22 January	Fourth Universal of the Rada proclaiming Ukrainian independence.
27 January	The Sebastopol Revkom liquidates the Crimean Tatar *kurultay* in Simferopol. Execution of the Tatar national leaders. Establishment of the first Soviet regime, which is strongly antinative, in Crimea.

1 February	Sovnarkom creates the Central Muslim Committee (Muskom) by decree. Soviet power reestablished in the Kazakh steppes.
8 February	Red Army takes Kiev.
19 February	Russian Red troops from Tashkent take Kokand. Slaughter of the Muslims. The survivors join the Basmachis.
24 February	Estonia proclaims its independence.
3 March	German Army takes Kiev.
4 March	Creation of the Kazan Muskom.
14 March	Russian Red troops of Tashkent unsuccessfully assault Bukhara.
16 March	Bolsheviks disband the Second Muslim Military Congress in Kazan.
21 March	Conference of Muslim Workers of Russia in Moscow. Foundation of the "Muslim Socialist-Communist party of Russia."
23 March	Creation of the Tatar-Bashkir Republic by decree of the Narkomnatz.
28 March	Liquidation of the "Trans-Bulak Republic." Last attempt of the Tatar nationalists to preserve their autonomy.
1 April	Soviet regime established in Daghestan. German troops occupy Crimea. End of the Soviet regime in Crimea and beginning of regime of General Sulkevich.
2 April	Bolshevik-Dashnak coup in Baku creates the "Commune of Baku."
8 April	Liquidation of the Muslim Harbi Shura.
12 April	Liquidation of the Milli Shura and of the Millet Mejlisi.
16 April	Bashkir national leaders join Ataman Dutov and raise a Bashkir army.
22 April	Transcaucasian Federative Republic proclaims its independence.
25 April	German authorities disband the Ukrainian Central Rada. Liquidation of all Muslim national institutions, Milli Shura, Ikomus, Millet-Mejlisi. Taganrog Conference of the Ukrainian Communist party. German troops reach Georgia.
2 May	Decree of the Narkomnats entrusting the organization of the Muslim Red Army to the Central Muskom.
25 May	Beginning of the revolt of the Czech legions along the Trans-Siberian railway.
26 May	Georgia proclaims its independence.
28 May	Armenia and Azerbaidzhan proclaim their independence.

June	Victory of the Counterrevolution in the Middle Volga. Komuch in Samare. Sultan Galiev becomes the representative of the RCP (b) in the Central Muskom. Turkish Army marching toward Baku occupies the region of Gandzha. Rebellion of the Ural and the Orenburg cossacks against the Soviet regime.
17–23 June	Leaders of the Central Muskom organize the First Conference of Muslim Communists in Kazan. Foundation of the "Russian party of Muslim Communists (Bolsheviks)." The Muskom becomes its regional organ.
July	Russian counterrevolutionary forces (Right SR and Mensheviks), aided by the British, seize power in Ashkhabad and remain in power until August 1919.
4 July	Ataman Dutov takes Orenburg.
10 July	Ratification of the first constitution of the RSFSR by the Fifth All-Russian Congress of Soviets.
20 July	Liquidation of the Commune of Baku by the right-wing Socialist Revolutionaries, the Mensheviks, and the Dashnaks. Flight of the Baku commissars.
August	General Dunsterville's force occupies Baku; beginning of British administration in Baku. Muslim regiments placed under the general command of the Red Army and incorporated into larger Russian units. General Malleson's troops move into Trans-Caspian region and occupy Ashkhabad. Abortive Communist uprising in the Ukraine. Imam Najmuddin of Gotzo and Sheikh Uzun Haji establish a theocratical power in the mountainous Daghestan.
2 August	Decree of the Narkomnats creates a Peasants and Workers Muslim Red Army which is controlled by the Muslim Military Collegium (Sultan Galiev, chairman).
6 August	Czech legionnaires take Kazan. Mulla-Nur Vahitov taken prisoner and executed.
September	General Bicherakhov's forces destroy Soviet power in Daghestan.
10 September	Red Army recaptures Kazan.
15 September	Turkish Army occupies Baku.
23 September	Left-wing counterrevolutionary forces (Dutov, Komuch, Alash-Orda, Bashkirs, and so on) proclaim the "provisional government of Russia" in Ufa.
November	German troops evacuate Crimea and General Sulkevich resigns. Government of Solomon Krym in Crimea.

5 November	First All-Russian Congress of Muslim Communists. End of Muslim Communist autonomy.
11 November	End of World War I.
18 November	Admiral Kolchak liquidates the "provisional government of Russia."
30 November	Turkish troops evacuate Baku. British forces under General Thomson occupy Baku.
14 December	Ukrainian troops of the Directory occupy Kiev.
15 December	British occupation of Batum.
31 December	Red Army takes Ufa, the Bashkir capital.

1919

January	Conflict between the Ukrainian Directory and the Red Army.
22 January	Red Army recaptures Orenburg.
23 January	Kolchak arrests Bashkir officers.
26 January	Kolchak disbands Bashkir units which have been fighting on his side.
31 January	Secret meeting of Bashkir leaders with Soviet representatives.
February	Creation of the Turkish Socialist party in Istanbul.
6 February	Red Army captures Kiev. Sovnarkom grants amnesty to all Bashkirs who promise to abandon Kolchak.
19 February	Zeki Validov signs a preliminary agreement with the Soviet government which creates the provisional government of Bashkiria.
22 February	Bashkir troops go over to the Red side.
4 March	Kolchak's second offensive on the Eastern front.
18–23 March	Eighth Congress of the RCP (b).
April	Second occupation of Crimea by Soviet units from the Ukraine. Overthrow of the government of Solomon Krym in Crimea. Left wing Milli Firqa cooperates with the Bolsheviks. First Jewish Red units ("Borochov units") founded in Minsk.
28 April	Beginning of the second major Red counteroffensive on the Eastern front.
June	Denikin troops occupy Crimea. Alash Orda goes over to the Red side. Baytursun, Jangildin, Lenin, and Stalin sign an agreement creating a Kirrevkom.
July	Mustafa Subhi organizes a Communist group with Turkish PW. Red Army recaptures Ekaterinberg.

August	Conference of Jewish Communist groups in Gomel. Foundation of the "Jewish Communist party—Poale Zion." Evacuation of Baku by British troops. Formation of National Azerbaidzhan government under the chairmanship of Khan Khoyski.
September	Big offensive of Denikin's armies against Moscow. Foundation of the "Socialist party of Workers and Peasants of Turkey" in Istanbul.
2 October	Dissolution of the Central Committee of the CP (b) of the Ukraine.
14 October	Denikin's armies occupy Orel.
20 October	Red Army retakes Orel. Turning point in the Civil War. Unfinished articles of Sultan Galiev appear in *Zhizn' Natsional' nostei* on social revolution and the East.
November	Red Army breaks through to Central Asia and links with Tashkent's soviet; Türkkommissiya in Tashkent. Alash Orda recognizes Soviet power. Beginning of the conquest of Siberia by the Red Army.
14 November	Red Army captures Omsk.
21 November	Preparatory Conference to the Second Congress of Communist Organizations of the Peoples of the East. Lenin definitively rejects the project of the Tatar-Bashkir Republic.
22 November–3 December	Second Congress of the Communist Organizations of the Peoples of the East. First attack against national communism by Stalin.

1920

January	Third Conference of Muslim Communist party of Turkestan. Turar Ryskulov demands the creation of "Turkic Communist party." Collapse of Denikin's forces. Sultan Galiev becomes member of the Collegium of the Narkomnatz.
5 January	Red Army captures Irkutsk.
12–18 January	Fifth Regional Conference of the Communist party of Turkestan. Report by Turar Ryskulov on the national communist sections.
February	Official establishment of the Communist party of Azerbaidzhan. Creation of the Caucasian Bureau of the RCP (b) (Kavbüro).
20 February	Red Army captures Khiva.
21 February	Decree of the Central Committee of the RCP (b) on "the

work with the Muslims.''

8 March	Central Committee of the RCP (b) declares that the Communist party of Turkestan is a simple regional organization of the RCP (b). Fourth Conference of the Communist party of the Ukraine. Purge of its Central Committee.
April	Invasion of Daghestan by the Red Army.
25 April	Outbreak of the Soviet-Polish War.
27 April	Invasion of Azerbaidzhan by the Eleventh Red Army. Conquest of Baku.
28 April	Ordzhonikidze and Kirov, chairman and vice-chairman of the Kavbüro, arrive in Baku.
May	Mustafa Subhi and his Turkish Communist party move to Baku. Secret meeting of national communist leaders in Moscow; foundation of the clandestine Ittihad ve Tarakki.
6 May	Polish Armies occupy Kiev.
7 May	Signing of the Soviet-Georgian Treaty.
22 May	Decree of the Sovnarkom on Bashkir autonomy; outbreak of Bashkir rebellion. Zeki Validov flees to Turkestan.
25 May	Outbreak of rebellion in Gandzha.
27 May	Foundation of the autonomous Tatar SSR Republic.
31 May	Red Army recaptures Gandzha.
June	Adalet party moves from Baku to Ghilan. Foundation of the Turkish Communist party in Ankara.
4 June	Kuchik Khan proclaims the Soviet Socialist Republic of Ghilan.
20 June	First Congress of the Communist party of Iran in Resht.
July	Second Congress of the Komintern in Moscow. Bashkiria reconquered by the Red Army. Georgian government occupies Batum.
August	Outbreak of rebellion in Daghestan under the leadership of the Naqshebandi brotherhood.
26 August	Foundation of the Kirghiz (Kazakhstan) Soviet Socialist Republic.
September	First Congress of the Turkish Communist Organization. Foundation of the Communist party of Turkey with Mustafa Subhi as chairman. Congress of the Peoples of the East in Baku.
2 September	Red Army captures Bukhara.
12–18 September	First All-Russian Conference of Young Communists of the East with Sultan Galiev as chairman. Foundation of an autonomous Central Committee of Eastern Komsomol.

13 September	Agreement between Soviet Russia and the Khorezm Peoples' Republic.
October	Red Army conquers Crimea. End of Wrangel.
30 October	Turkish Army seizes Kars.
11 November	Young Bukharians and the Communist party of Bukhara blend together in a Bukharian Communist party with Fayzullah Khojaev as chairman.
29 November	Bolshevik ultimatum to Armenia. Beginning of the conquest of Armenia by the Red Army. Foundation of the Soviet Socialist Republic of Daghestan.
2 December	Treaty of Erevan signed by Soviet authorities and the Armenian National Government. Formation of Soviet Armenia.

1921

January	In Bukhara the clandestine Ittihad ve Tarakki becomes the Socialist party of Turkestan, which later, in 1926, will become the underground Socialist ERK party.
10 January	Conference of the Turkic Peoples' Communists of the RSFSR in Moscow. New attack of Stalin against nationalism, "the obstacle to the development of Communism in the East."
20 January	Foundation of the ASSR of Daghestan.
28 January	Mustafa Subhi and other Turkish Communist leaders killed in Trabzon.
10 February	Rebellion engineered by the Kavbüro in the Borchalo region (Georgia).
11 February	Invasion of Georgia by the Red Army.
16 February	Outbreak of rebellion in Armenia.
25 February	Red Army captures Tiflis. Treaty of friendship between RSFSR and Iran.
28 February	Treaty of friendship between RSFSR and Afghanistan.
March	Kronstadt Rebellion.
4 March	Agreement between Soviet Russia and the Bukharian Peoples' Republic.
11 March	Turkish Army occupies the city of Batum.
16 March	Treaty of friendship between RSFSR and Turkey.
18 March	Georgian government capitulates to the Red Army.
19 March	Red Army and Georgian units recapture Batum.

April	Tenth Congress of the RCP (b). First important attack against pan-Islamism and pan-Turkism.
24 April	Sultan Galiev criticizes Soviet policy in Crimea.
May	Daghestani revolt crushed by the Red Army.
18 October	Foundation of the ASSR of Crimea.
November	Enver Pasha joins the Bashmachis.
14–23 December	Sultan Galiev's article in *Zhizn' Natsional'nostei* on the religious propaganda among the Muslims.

1922

16 January	Foundation of the Kabarda-Balkar Autonomous Region.
February	Bukharian Communist party is absorbed by the RCP (b).
12 March	Formation of the Soviet Trans-Caucasian Federation.
4 August	Death of Enver Pasha.
October	Resignation of the Central Committee of the Communist party of Georgia.
December	Purge of the Communist party of Turkestan.
30–31 December	Lenin's letters on the national question.

1923

17–25 April	Twelfth Congress of the RCP (b).
25 May	First official attack against Sultan Galiev in the Tatar newspaper *Eshche* of Kazan. Sultan Galiev already arrested.
9–12 June	Fourth Conference of the Central Committee of the RCP (b) with the Responsible Workers of the National Republics and Regions condemnation of Sultan Galiev. Sultan Galiev liberated and sent to Georgia.

1924

21 January	Death of Lenin.
31 January	Ratification of the Constitution of the USSR by the Second All-Union Congress of Soviets.

1926

Spring	Removal of Shumsky from his position as the Ukrainian *narkom* for education.

1927

20–29 November	Tenth Congress of the Communist party of the Ukraine. Shumsky and Khvylovy accused of nationalism.

1928

7 May	Execution of Veli Ibrahimov.
26 June	Liquidation of Poale Zion.
17 July– 1 September	Sixth Congress of Komintern.
November	Second arrest of Sultan Galiev.
December	Beginning of the great purge in the Muslim republics.

Appendix H

Biographies

Akchokrakly, Osman (18?–1936?), Crimean Tatar, son of a nobleman of Baghchesaray, historian, archeologist, and writer. A radical nationalist and pan-Islamist, Akchokrakly contributed to the *Terjüman* of Gasprinski and to the periodicals published by Abdurrashid Ibragimov. After February 1917, he played a major role in the political life of Crimea; he was a member of the Milli Firqa party and leader of its right wing. After the establishment of the Soviet regime, he remained in Crimea as a professor of history at the Pedagogical Institute and as one of the main ideological leaders of Crimean nationalism. He disappeared during a purge in 1936.

Al-Afghani, Jemaleddin (1838–97), an Islamic religious thinker, political theorist, and agitator. Despite his name, al-Afghani was of Persian origin and the son of a family of the Hanafi school in Kabul. He followed the usual Muslim pattern of university studies at Kabul, and then traveled widely throughout the Islamic world and Europe as an exponent of militantly anti-Western pan-Islamism. He supported movements for constitutional liberties and fought for liberation from foreign control (Egypt and Persia). He attacked Muslim rulers who opposed reform or did not show enough resistance to European encroachments. He even envisaged the possibility of political assassination. His ultimate object was to unite Muslim states (including Shiite Persia) into a single caliphate, able to repulse European interference and recreate the glory of Islam.

In 1884 al-Afghani was in Paris and published the first issue of the journal *al-Urwa al-Wuthqa* (The Indissoluble Link) which was edited by Muhammad Abduh. This journal was the organ of a secret Muslim society of the same name, which financed it.

In 1886 al-Afghani went to Russia where he established important political contacts and on behalf of Russian Muslims obtained the czar's permission to have the Koran and religious books published. He stayed there until 1889.

Al-Afghani lived out his days in Constantinople at the court of the sultan, Abd al-Hamid. The sultan offered him the post of *shaykh al-Islam*, but al-Afghani refused, He died on 9 March 1897 from cancer. Rumor had it that Abul-Huda, the leading religious dignitary at the court, ordered the doctor only to pretend to treat him, or even poisoned him.

Azizbekov, Meshadi (Aziz bey oglu) (1876–1918), Azeri, son of a wealthy nobleman, graduate of the Institute of Technology of St. Petersburg. Azizbekov was a member of the Russian Social Democratic Workers' party, since 1904 one of the leaders of the Hümmet, and, in 1917, member of the Central Committee of Hümmet. In April 1908 he was vice-chairman of the Sovnarkom of the Baku Commune. In September 1918, he was shot by the Whites, along with other "Baku commissars."

Bauer, Otto (1882–1938), Austrian politician and socialist theoretician. As leader of the left wing of the Social Democrats, Bauer was considered the leading exponent of the "Austro-Marxist" school. He held political office only once, briefly, as foreign minister from 1918 to 1919. He was editor of the socialist newspaper *Arbeiter-Zeitung*.

Bauer was a leading opponent of the Anschluss and was forced in 1936 to flee to Paris, where he died. His ideas on the national problem complementing those of Renner, with whom he collaborated in expounding the theories of national communism, are found in several works, notably *Die Nationalitaetenfrage und die Sozialdemocratie* (1907) and *Der Weg zum Sozialismus* (1919).

Baytursun, Ahmed (1873–1937), Kazakh, born to an aristocratic family of the Argyn tribe of the Turgay region, poet, educator, and political leader. Baytursun studied in the Pedagogical Institute of Orenburg and was a teacher in various Kazakh schools. In 1909, he was expelled from the steppe region by czarist authorities for revolutionary activity. A radical nationalist, Baytursun was one of the founders of the Alash Orda party in 1917. During the revolution he was, with Bukeykhanov, one of the leaders of the Kazakh national movement. During the Civil War he switched from a moderate socialist position favorable to the Komuch to acceptance of the Soviet regime (*see* Bukeykhanov). He became a member of the RCP (b) in 1920, and until his purge he was one of the leading figures of the cultural and educational life of Kazakhstan. Until 1929 he was the chairman of the Scientific Commission of the Peoples' Commissariat for Education of the Kazakh Republic.

Together with other former leaders of Alash Orda (Bukeykhanov, Dulatov, and so on), Baytursun has never been rehabilitated and is still considered an archenemy in Soviet historiography.

Bigi, Musa Jarullah (1875–1949), Tatar, religious thinker, and publicist, son of a Tatar *mullah* of Rostov on the Don. Bigi was educated in the "Gölboyu" *medresseh* of Kazan, and traveled extensively to study in Bukhara, Medina, Cairo, Istanbul, and finally in the University of St. Petersburg. On his return to Russia in 1904, he cooperated with the radical pan-Islamist philosopher, Abdurrashid Ibragimov, and became the editor of many *jadid* periodicals, including the famous *Vaqt* of Orenburg, and *Ülfet* and *Tilmiz* of St. Petersburg. The only activity, however, which captivated him entirely was his research and writing on Islamic theology. He was appointed *imam* of the St. Petersburg mosque in 1910.

Bigi devoted his life to reconciling Islam with modern progress and was considered a controversial and daring, though perfectly orthodox, theologian. In 1915, Bigi wrote an article in which he deplored the indifferent attitude of the Russian government toward the Tatars and their religion despite the loyalty which the latter had proved as soldiers of the czarist army.

Bigi remained in Soviet Russia after the revolution, defending Islam against antireligious attacks. In the beginning he considered Islam compatible with communism, but later he lost his faith and emigrated. His travels took him to India, Egypt, Finland, and finally to Turkey, where he died in 1949.

Bigi did not believe in blind adherence to religion, but in a conscious and active participation in it. He himself worked on a Tatar translation of the Koran.

Borochov, Ber (1881–1917), Jewish Socialist leader, born in the village of Zolotonski in the Ukraine. As a result of pogroms, his parents moved after a few months to Poltava. In 1900 Borochov joined the Russian Social-Democrat party and was active as a local organizer and propagandist. He searched for a solution to the national question which the Party ignored. Borochov's doubts led to his expulsion from the Party in May 1901. He became more involved in Zionism.

Borochov joined the Poale Zion party in November 1905. At that time the burning issue was Palestine versus Uganda. His opposition to any other territory than Palestine found expression in his essay, "To the Question of Zion and Territory."

At the Poltava Conference (November 1905), Borochov helped to formulate the Poale Zion program. The young party could not unite all the different elements. Only after many splits in December 1906, did the first convention of the "Proletarians Palestinias Poale-Zion" take place.

During 1905–6 Borochov edited the Russian party organ, *Yevreskaia Rabotchaia Chronika*. At the same time he wrote one of his most famous articles, "The National Question and the Class Struggle."

On 3 January 1906, he was arrested. In prison he came in touch with Ukrainian socialists, many of whom accepted his national theory. After a short time he escaped and settled in Minsk and in 1907 left Russia. He helped found the World Confederation of Poale Zion in Vienna. From 1907 to 1910 he was the editor of the Party organ, *Das freie Wort*.

With the outbreak of World War I, Borochov left for America where he became the editor of *Der Yiddisher Kamfer*. Borochov was against the pro-ally sentiment that dominated the Party during the war.

The February Revolution in 1917 caused Borochov's return to Russia. In Moscow he attended the Third All-Russian Poale Zion convention. The Party selected him as one of its delegates to the Conference of Nationalities. He died in Kiev on 7 December 1917.

Bubi, Abdullah (Bobinski), Tatar, born in the village of Izh-Bobino in the Viatka region to the family of a *mudarris*. Bubi was educated in the *medresseh* of his father and in the secondary school of Istanbul. After lengthy travels in the Middle East he became the director of his father's *medresseh*. A brilliant and radical *jadid* reformer and a follower of Gasprinski and al-Afghani, he tried very successfully to conciliate reformed Islam with modern progress. His village school rapidly became one of the most sophisticated and the most progressive Muslim education institutions in the entire Muslim world. He invited foreign teachers, mainly Turks, and imported schoolbooks from abroad. He was a devoted nationalist, pan-Turk, and pan-Islamist who had radical opinions and who strongly opposed Russian pressure. Bubi was often arrested for propagating pro-Turkish ideas. In 1911 his *medresseh* was shut down and he was exiled to Siberia. After 1919, he stayed in Soviet

Russia, but we do not know what happened to him. Bubi was one of the most daring Muslim theologians of the early twentieth century.

Bukeykhanov, Ali Khan (1869–1932), Kazakh, a scion of princely family (princes of the Bukey Horde) and a descendant of Genghis Khan; born in Samara; graduate of the Institute of Forestry in Omsk; official in the czarist administration in the steppe region (present-day Kazakhstan); and later executive in the Agricultural Bank of Samara. Bukeykhanov was, with Baytursun and Dulatov, the leading figure of the Kazakh national movement. He was an associate of the Russian Constitutional Democratic party and he was a deputy in the First and in the Second Duma. More radical than the Russian Kadets and strongly opposed to the cultural russification of the nomads, Bukeykhanov was not opposed, in the beginning at least, to the czarist regime. However, after 1916 and the Great Revolt of the nomads against the Russians, he moved to the Left. In 1917, he was one of the founders of the national party, Alash Orda, which was politically situated between the Constitutional Democrats and the right-wing Socialist Revolutionaries. In July 1917, the provisional government nominated Bukeykhanov as the head of the administration of the Turgay region. In December 1917, he was the president of the Alash Orda "government" of Eastern Kazakhstan in Semipalatinsk. During the Civil War, Bukeykhanov at first favored the Komuch, then tried unsuccessfully to collaborate with Kolchak, and finally, in despair, went over to the Soviets in November 1919. He became a member of the RCP (b) in 1920. During the Soviet regime he led the right wing of the Communist party of Kazakhstan, but remained a devoted nationalist. Until his purge, he dominated the cultural life of Kazakhstan as an historian of the nomads and as the greatest specialist of their epic folklore.

Bunyat Zade, Dadash (1888–1938), Azeri, born in a merchant family; worked as a teacher and joined the RSDWP in 1908. He participated in revolutionary democratic activity in Tehran and Tabriz (1908–9). Back in Russia he edited some socialist newspapers (*Ary* and *Baku Hayaty*) and was arrested many times by czarist police. In 1917–18, he was the director of the Secretariat of the Central Committee of the Hümmet party. During the Baku Commune (spring 1918), he was the special delegate of the Baku Sovnarkom for the fight against counterrevolutionaries. In February, he became a member of the Central Committee of the PC of Azerbaidzhan; in 1929, *narkom* for Education of Azerbaidzhan; and in 1930, president of the Sovnarkom of the same republic. Liquidated together with other leaders of the Hümmet in 1938, he was rehabilitated in 1956.

Burundukov, Mikdad (18?–1928), Tatar, comrade of Sultan Galiev, member of the RCP (b) since 1917. In September 1918, he was one of the leaders of the Central Bureau of the Communist Organization of the Peoples of the East; in November 1919, he chaired the Conference of Muslim Communists of the city of Kazan. In 1920 he became the Peoples' Commissar for National Education in the Tatar Republic, a position in which he was able to protect and patronize the leading prerevolutionary progressive bourgeois *jadid* writers, who perpetuated a pan-Turkic ideology well into the late twenties. As a prominent member of the nationalist right-wing faction of the Tatar Communist party, Burundukov was purged and condemned for "counterrevolutionary" plotting in 1928.

Dulatov, Mir-Yakub (1885–1937), Kazakh of the Argyn tribe, member of the clanic nomad aristocracy, studied at the Galiyeh *medresseh* of Ufa and at the Russian-Kazakh school. Dulatov was one of the founders of Alash Orda and one of the best Kazakh poets and writers. Violently anti-Russian and a radical nationalist, he followed the other leaders of Alash Orda and, in 1919, joined the RCP (b). He remained, however, a devoted nationalist, and between 1920 and 1936 he deeply influenced the entire new generation of Kazakh intellectuals. Accused of "nationalism," he disappeared during a purge in 1937.

Efendiev, Sultan Mejid (1887–1938), Azeri Communist leader, son of a nobleman of Shemakha; studied in the Russian-Tatar School in Baku and graduated from the Faculty of Medicine of Kazan; member of the Russian SDWP in 1904 and one of the founders of the Hümmet. Efendiev took an active part in the Civil War; in 1918–20, he was commissar for Muslim affairs of Transcaucasia of the Narkomnats (1919) and chairman of the Revkom of the province of Gendzhe (1920).

In May 1921 he was the *narkom* for Agriculture and he later was *narkom* for the Rabkrin of Azerbaidzhan. From 1920 he was a member of the CC of the Communist party of Azerbaidzhan. In 1924, he served as chairman of the Control Commission of the Communist party of Azerbaidzhan, and from 1931 to 1937, he was chairman of the CEC of Azerbaidzhan.

In spite of the fact that Efendiev had always been a staunch supporter of Stalin, he was, together with the vast majority of Caucasian Communists, condemned and executed in 1938 as a "bourgeois-nationalist." He was rehabilitated in 1956.

Efendiev-Samurskii, Najmuddin, Daghestani, leader of the CP of Daghestan, first secretary of the Daghestani Obkom of the RCP (b), and RCP (b) member since 1917. He played an important role in the revolution and the Civil War in the Northern Caucasus and was a member of the Narkomnats. He was the author of a book, *Daghestan*, published in 1924, in which he strongly opposed the introduction of the Russian language into Daghestan and favored the use of Azeri Turkic. Accused of nationalism and pan-Turkism, Efendiev-Samurskii disappeared during the Stalinist purges of the 1930s.

Fitrat, Abdurrauf, Uzbek, modernist and nationalist writer and philosopher, born in Bukhara, studied in a *medresseh* of that city, and graduated from the University of Istanbul, where he became influenced by the Young Turks' nationalist ideology. Back in Turkestan he became one of the leaders of the *jadidist* movement and one of the founders of the Young Bukharian group. He edited or took part in the editing of many *jadid* periodicals in Tashkent and Samarkand together with his comrades, Mahmud Behbudi and Münevver Kari. After 1918, he remained a radical nationalist. In 1923, he became the minister of foreign affairs of the Peoples' Republic of Bukhara, in spite of his violent hatred of the Russians. In 1924, he became a professor in the universities of Tashkent and Samarkand. He was arrested in 1938 for "nationalism." His final fate is unknown.

Gaspraly, Ismail bey (Gasprinski) (1851–1914), Crimean Tatar, reformer, publicist, and philosopher, born in the village of Gaspra, son of an impoverished nobleman. He studied in the local *mektep* and in the "Cadet Corps" in Moscow, where he was exposed (through the Katkov family) to slavophile ideas. Later he traveled to France (1871–75) and Turkey (1875–77), where he imbibed French liberalism and Young Turk ideology. In 1877, back in Crimea, he became the mayor of Baghchesaray (1877–82). In 1882, he founded a modernist-*jadid medresseh* and launched his famous newspaper, *Terjüman* (The Interpreter), which became one of the greatest Muslim newspapers and for which he devised a simplified Turkic language that was supposed to be understood "from the Bosphorus to the Chinese borders."

Gasprinski was the first exponent of pan-Turkism among Russian Muslims, but he rejected its most violent anti-Western manifestations. He was a thoroughly modernized and innovative educator, whose new school at Baghchesaray became a model for *jadid* establishments throughout Russia and the rest of the Islamic world. His ideas on the socioeconomic, political, and religious rejuvenation of the Islamic world were presented in many writings, most forcefully in his *Terjüman*. He played a leading role in the three Muslim congresses of 1905–6.

Gasprinski was the leading figure in the Muslim liberal national movement.

He advocated the cooperation between the Muslim world and Russian liberals. After 1908, his prestige began to lose its hold over the younger generations of Muslim intellectuals, who had lost all hope to cooperate with Russian liberals and were turning themselves toward socialism.

Ibragimov, Abdurrashid (18?–1944), Siberian Tatar (Bukharlyk), trained in Medina. On his return to Russia he became a *mullah* and in 1893 was elected *kadi* to the Spiritual Muslim Assembly of Orenburg. Later he traveled to Egypt, where he collaborated on some radical pan-Islamic periodicals, and to Turkey, where in 1895 he published his *Cholpan Yulduzy* (Morning Star), a violent anti-Russian attack.

Back to Russia in 1904, he remained politically very active. A radical *jadid* and a devoted pan-Islamist, he was the closest follower of Jemaleddin al-Afghani among Russian Muslims. He was a fanatical adversary of the czarist establishment and of Muslim conservatives, whom he accused of compromising with Russian power, and of the Socialists, whom he called "humbugs and brats." Between 1906 and 1907 he published many periodicals, *Ülfet*, *Nejat* (Tatar), *Al-Tilmiz* (Arabic), *Sirke* (Kazakh). He was instrumental in the convening of the three Muslim congresses of 1905–6 and in the founding of the *Ittifaq al-Müslimin*. In 1910, he left Russia, traveling extensively in Japan, India, Turkey, and Germany, continually involved in pan-Islamic and pan-Turkic activities and collaborating on many important periodicals, in particular *Türk Yurdu* and *Türk Sözü* of Istanbul (1913). During World War I, he was in Berlin and in Vienna, organizing Russian Muslim prisoners. He died in Japan.

Ibragimov, Galimjan (1887–1938), Tatar, writer and political leader, son of a *mullah* of the village Sultanmuratovo, "government" of Ufa, studied in the *medresseh* "Galiyeh" of Ufa, where he became one of the leaders of the revolutionary "Islah" movement. A radical nationalist in the beginning, he became affiliated in 1905 with the left wing of the Russian Socialist Revolutionary group in Ufa. He was a deputy (SR membership) to the Constituent Assembly and to the Third Pan-Russian Congress of the Soviets. In 1918 Stalin invited him to direct the Central Commissariat for Muslim Affairs (with Mulla-Nur Vahitov and Sherif Manatov). A member of the RCP (b) since 1918, between 1920 and 1929 he was the chairman of the Academic Center of the Narkom for the Education of the Tatar Republic. Ibragimov dominated entirely Tatar Soviet literature and historical science. He published numerous novels, historical essays, and political pamphlets. A lifelong admirer and disciple of Nasyri, Ibragimov wrote two essays for the commemorative volume, published in 1922, on the twentieth anniversary of Nasyri's death.

Even after he joined the RCP (b), Ibragimov remained a staunch nationalist. He opposed russification, and at the First Congress of Turkology in Baku he was almost alone in defending the Arabic alphabet for the Muslim languages and opposing the introduction of the Latin alphabet. In 1927 he published a pamphlet, "Which Way Will Tatar Culture Go?" (Tatar medeniyetine nindi yol blän barajaq?), which was a violent attack against Russification and a passionate defense of the Tatar culture. As he had stated in 1911 in the pages of *Shura*, "We are Tatars. Our language is Tatar. Our literature is Tatar, all we do is Tatar, and our future culture will be Tatar." In 1927 Ibragimov advocated the tatarization of the language, the government, the party apparatus, and intellectual cadres as the only alternative to russification imposed under the guise of proletarian internationalism. This pamphlet was condemned as "nationalist" by a decision of the Tatar Obkom on 14 June 1927.

Ibragimov was never a follower of Sultan Galiev, but he also championed the spiritual unity of the Muslim Turkic peoples of the USSR. Arrested for "nationalism" in 1937, Ibragimov died in prison in January 1938. He was rehabilitated after 1954.

Ibrahimov, Veli (?–1928), Crimean Tatar, son of a poor artisan, typograph worker in the *Terjüman* typography, collaborator of Ismail Gasprinski. He was a member of the Cultural Tatar Society of Simferopol before 1914, and after February 1917 a member and leader of the left wing of Milli Firqa and a member of the RCP (b) in 1919. He was one of the organizers of the underground Bolshevik in Crimea during the regime of Denikin and Wrangel. After 1920, he was chairman of the Central Executive Committee and president of the Sovnarkom of the ASSR of Crimea. Accused of "Sultangalievism," he was arrested (probably in 1927) and executed in May 1928.

Ikramov, Akmal (1898–1938), Uzbek, born at Tashkent, son of a wealthy peasant, educated in a Tashkent *mektep*. He joined the Communist party in February 1918 in Tashkent and worked in Ferghana, Tashkent, and Namangan. In 1919 he was deputy chairman of the Namangan Revkom, and in 1920 secretary of the Syr Darya and Ferghana Obkom. In 1921–22 he was secretary of the Central Committee of the Communist party of Turkestan.

In 1922, he studied at the Sverdkov University in Moscow. Back in Central Asia, Ikramov was elected secretary of the Central Committee of the Uzbekistan Communist party at the First Congress of the Uzbekistan Communist party in March 1923. In 1925 he became secretary of the Tashkent Gorkom and in 1929, first secretary of the Central Committee of the Uzbekistan Communist party. He occupied this post until his arrest in 1937.

During 1925–34 he was a candidate member and in 1934 a full member of the All-Union Central Committee of the RCP (b). During 1931–34 he was also secretary of the Central Asian Bureau of the Central Committee of the RCP (b).

In the 1930s he was also a member of the CEC of the USSR and a candidate member of its presidium.

Arrested in 1937, Ikramov was tried and executed along with Khojaev, Bukharin, and others. In 1964 he was officially rehabilitated.

Iskhaki, Mohammed Ayaz (1878–1954), Tatar, writer and political leader, one of the most active and influential among the leaders of the Muslim national movement, born in the village of Evshirma, "government" of Kazan, in the family of a *mullah,* studied in the *medresseh* of Chistopol (1890) and of Kazan (1893), and graduated in 1899 in the Russian-Tatar school of Kazan. Iskhaki took an active part in the "Islahist" movement. In 1905 he was the leader of the radical left wing of the national movement and one of the organizers of the Tangchylar group, which was inspired by the ideology of the Russian Socialist Revolutionaries. Violently anti-Russian, Iskhaki was arrested many times and deported to Siberia and Arkhangelsk.

A key figure in the First All-Russian Muslim Congress in May 1917, Iskhaki was president of the Executive Committee of the National Muslim Council (Milli Shura), established in Moscow in 1917. After the October Revolution he became a resolute enemy of the new regime and emigrated first to Japan and then to France, Germany, and Turkey. In emigration he remained an adversary of the Soviets. He played an important role in the Muslim Congress of Jerusalem in 1931 and was an active member of the "Prometée" Group in Paris and published many periodicals, *Milli Yol* (Istanbul), *Yaña Milli Yol* (Istanbul), and *Milli Bayrak* (Mukden).

Iskhaki was one of the outstanding Tatar *jadid* writers. He died in Ankara.

Kazakov, Iskhak (1876–1937), Tatar, son of a Kazan merchant, graduated from the Pedagogical School of Kazan, worked as a teacher of the Russian language in the Tatar *medressehs*. Kazakov was arrested for "revolutionary activity" in 1911. In 1917, he was a member of the First and Second All-Russian Muslim congresses, and since 21 February 1918, a member of the RCP (b). He collaborated with the Central Muskom of the Narkomnats. In

1920, he was a member of the Revkom and of the presidium of the CEC of Tatarstan, vice-chairman of the Tatar Sovnarkom, and a member of the Bureau of the Obkom of Tatarstan. He was a fervent follower of Sultan Galiev. Kazakov was arrested after 1930 and liquidated in 1937.

Khojaev, Fayzullah (1896–1938), Uzbek, born in Bukhara in a family of a wealthy merchant (his father was the head of the biggest fur-trading firm), educated in a Russian school in Moscow where he joined the *jadid* movement. In 1917 he joined the underground Central Committee of the Young Bukharian party in that city. In April 1917, being the leader of the left wing of the Party, Khojaev was condemned to death by the emir and fled to Tashkent, where he was active in the Bolshevik takeover.

In the spring of 1918 he went to Moscow, and in 1919 served as the representative of the Young Bukharian party in the office of Turkestan. Back in Tashkent in September 1919, he took an active part the next summer in organizing the uprising of the Young Bukharians against the emir. After the conquest of Bukhara by the Red Army, he became the chairman of the Council of Peoples' Commissars and the commissar (*nazir*) for foreign affairs of the new Bukharian Peoples' Soviet Republic (until 1924). He became a member of the Communist party when, in September 1920, the Young Bukharians decided to dissolve themselves and join the Bukharian Communist party. Khojaev became a member of the Central Committee of the BCP.

In the following years Khojaev took an active part in the fight against the Basmachis. In 1922 he was in Moscow as a member of the Central Asian Bureau of the Central Committee of the RCP (b). Between 1924 and 1938, he was chairman of the Sovnarkom of Uzbekistan and a member of the Central Committee of the Communist party of Uzbekistan. In May 1927 he was elected one of the chairmen of the presidium of the CEC of the USSR.

Arrested in 1937, he was executed together with Bukharin, Rykov, and others in March of 1938. He was rehabilitated in the 1960s.

Kulahmetov, Gafur (1881–1918), Tatar, poet, associate of Husein Yamashev, born in Penza in a family of a wealthy industrialist; graduated from the Russian-Tatar School of Kazan. Kulahmetov joined the RSDWP around 1905 and in 1906, the short-lived Muslim social group, Berek ("Unity"), which had an ideology closely related to the Russian SRs: "freedom for the people and land for the peasants." In 1907 he collaborated with Yamashev to create the Bolshevik Tatar newspaper, *Ural*. He played no role during the Revolution of 1917, probably because he was ill. Kulahmetov was a convinced Bolshevik, one of the few who openly professed atheism.

Manatov, Sherif (?–?), Bashkir, son of an *imam*, studied in St. Petersburg (Polytechnical Institute) and in Istanbul. A nationalist in the beginning, Manatov emigrated in 1912 to Turkey and Switzerland. Back in Russia in 1917, he started as an extreme right-winger of the Bashkir national movement. In August of 1917, he was vice-chairman of the Thirtieth Bashkir Congress in Orenburg. In late 1917, he did an about-face and went over to the Bolshevik side. Stalin rewarded him with one of the vice-chairmanships of the Central Commissariat for Muslim Affairs set up in January 1918. In July 1918, he joined Zeki Validov in the National Bashkir Organization, but did not participate actively in political life. In 1919, he was sent (probably by Stalin) to Turkey, where he helped to found the Turkish Communist party in Ankara. Expelled by Kemal, he went back to Bashkiria. His fate after 1920 is unknown.

Mansurov, Burhan (18?–1937), Tatar, companion of Sultan Galiev. He was a member of the Muslim Socialist Committee of Kazan in 1917, member of the RCP (b) in early 1918(?), member of the Central Committee of the Muslim Communist (Bolshevik) party in June of 1918, and in 1919 a member of the Central Bureau of the Communist Organizations of the Peoples of the East. In 1920, he was the chairman of the Central Executive Committee of the Tatar Republic. In disgrace after Sultan Galiev's trial in 1928, he was, until his final purge in 1937, chairman of the Tatar Union of Militant Godless.

Marjani, Shihabeddin (1818–99), Tatar, religious reformer, historian, and teacher. Marjani wrote both Tatar and Arabic. He advocated the study of Western social and natural sciences and languages, and introduced the study of Russian to his *medresseh*. He successfully fought the medieval scholastic philosophy, condemned the *taqlid*—the blind imitation of the authority, implying an uncritical acceptance of traditional interpretation of the Koranic law. He also advocated universal *ijtihad*, individual interpretation of the Koranic law. Marjani is rightfully considered as the father of Tatar reformism.

Mdivani, Budu (?–1937), Georgian Old Bolshevik and former president of the Sovnarkom of the Georgian Soviet Socialist Republic. He was the leader of the Georgian Communist party and a member of the Kavbüro in 1920. He opposed Stalin at the Twelfth Congress of the RCP (b) in 1923 and, in turn, was denounced as a "Trotskyite" in 1929. During the Piatrakov trial he was accused of planning a terrorist act against Yezhov and Beria. He was condemned as a "traitor," "British agent," and so on by the Georgian Supreme Court on 10–12 July 1937, and was executed.

Lavrentii Beria described Mdivani and other Old Bolsheviks in the following passage of *K Voprosu ob istorii bolshevistskikh organizatsii v Zakavkaze* (Moscow, 1948, p. 256):

In the years 1927 to 1935, national deviationism, having fused with counter-revolutionary Trotskyism, grew into an agency for fascism and turned into an unprincipled and cynical gang of spies, saboteurs, diversionists, agents, and murderers, a wild gang of mortal enemies of the working class. In 1936, a Trotskyite Center for spying, sabotage, and terrorism was discovered, which included B. Mdivani, M. Okudzhava, M. Toroshelidze, O. Gikladze, N. Kiknadze, and others.

Muzaffar, Hanafi, pseudonym of Hanafi Kaibyshev, a Tatar radical intellectual, Muslim, and nationalist. He joined the Bolsheviks in 1918. In 1918–20 he collaborated with Sultan Galiev on the Narkomnatz and was one of the chief editors of its official organ, *Cholpan*, together with other Tatar national communists, such as the historian Fatyh Saif Kazanly, and others.

His work, *Din ve Millet Mese'leri* (Religious and National Problems), written in Kazan in 1922, is considered by some Soviet historians (for instance by Arsharuni and Gabidullin, *Ocherki Panislamizma i Panturkizma v Rossii* [Moscow, 1931, pp. 77–81]) as the doctrinal basis of Muslim national communism. It has never been published.

Narimanov, Nariman bey (1870–1933), Azeri, born in Tbilisi in a family of a wealthy nobleman, studied in Gori and graduated from the Medical Faculty of Odessa in 1902. Narimanov entered the RSDWP in 1905, the same year he was one of the founders of the Hümmet party; and in 1906, he contributed to the creation of the Persian Social-Democratic group in Baku. In March 1917, he became the president of Hümmet and in June 1916 a member of the Baku Committee of the RSDWP. In April of 1918 he was a member of the Sovnarkom of the Soviet Republic of Azerbaidzhan and a member of the Central Committee of the Communist party of Azerbaidzhan. After 1922 he was one of the presidents of the CEC of the USSR and a member-candidate of the Central Committee of the RCP (b). In spite of his brilliant career in the Communist party, Narimanov remained a dubious communist with a tendency toward Azeri nationalism. He died happily in his bed, but was unmasked as a "peoples' enemy" and a "bourgeois nationalist" after his death, together with all other former members of Hümmet who joined the Russian Communist party in 1920. After Beria's liquidation, Narimanov was entirely rehabilitated.

Orakhelashvili, Mamia (1883–1937), Georgian, born in the village of Sakara of the *gubernia* of Kutaisi in the family of a landlord, attended a high school in Kutaisi, the medical faculty of Kharkov University, and the Petersburg Military-Medical Academy. In 1903 Orakhelashvili joined the RSDWP. He took an active part in the revolutionary events of 1905 in Petersburg. In 1906, he was in Paris and Geneva; between 1906 and 1914 he was arrested many times.

In 1917, he was the chairman of the Vladikavkaz soviet, and between 1918 and 1920 he worked in Georgia in the underground Bolshevik organization. Arrested by the Georgian government and released in 1920, he became chairman of the Central Committee of the Georgian Communist party. In 1921–27 he was chairman of the Georgian Revkom, and in December 1926 first secretary of the Transcaucasian Kraikom of the RCP (b). In 1930 he came to Moscow as a member of the editorial board of *Pravda*. Between 1932 and 1937 he was deputy director of the Marx-Engels Institute in Moscow. He was arrested in 1936, liquidated in 1937, and rehabilitated in 1963.

Pokrovski, Mikhail Nikolaevich (1868–1932), Soviet Marxist historian, author of many works on Russian history, the most important being the four-volume *Russkaia Istoria s Drevneishikh Vremen* (A History of Russia from the Earliest Times), and the two-volume *Ocherki Istorii Russkoi Kul' tury* (A History of Russian Culture). Pokrovski's strict Marxist approach to Russian history was condemned by Stalin in 1934 and 1936.

Rasul Zade, Mehmed Emin (1884–1954), Azeri, born in the family of a nobleman. He began his political career as a member of the RSDWP. In 1908 he emigrated to Persia and took an active part in the revolutionary movement in Tehran, where in 1908–10 he published the famous radical newspaper, *Iran-e Nou*. Expelled from Persia on the demand of the Russian Embassy in Tehran, he took refuge in Turkey where his political ideology moved from socialism to pan-Turkism and he cooperated with the *Türk Yurdu*. In 1913 Rasul Zade went back to Russia and became one of the leaders of the Musavat party. In 1917 he became president of the Party and took a major role in the All-Russian Muslim Congress of May 1917. On 20 May 1918, he was elected chairman of the National Committee of the Azerbaidzhani Republic. In April 1920 he was captured by the Red Army in Baku and transferred to Moscow. He succeeded in emigrating abroad in 1922, and he lived in Germany, Poland, Rumania, and finally in Turkey.

Renner, Karl (1870–1950), Austrian politician and statesman. As leader of the right wing of the Social Democrat party, Renner advocated a federated Austro-Hungarian Empire. He was chancellor of the first Austrian Republic from 1918 to 1920, and then retired from politics until 1930, when he became president of the National Assembly. He was briefly chancellor of the second Austrian Republic in 1945, and then was president from 1945 until his death. His earlier works, written under various pseudonyms, influenced later national communist theoreticians. They include *Staat und Nation* (1899), *Der Kampf der Oesterreichischen Nationen um den Staat* (1902), and *Gundlagen und Entwicklungs Ziele der Oesterreichischer-Ungarischer Monarchie* (1905).

Ryskulov, Turar (1894–1938), Kazakh, political leader and historian, born in the Semirechie, in a wealthy nomadic family. Ryskulov joined the national Kazakh movement before World War I and took an active part in the great uprising of the nomadic tribes in 1916. Arrested and jailed in 1916, he joined the Communist party in September 1917, but remained a nationalist. In 1918, he was chairman of the local soviet of Dzhambul (Aulie-Ata) and a member of the Turkestan CEC and the *narkom* of health of the Turkestan Republic. In 1919–20, he was a member of the Kraikom of the Communist party of Turkestan, deputy chairman of the CEC of the Turkestan Republic, and in 1920, chairman of the same CEC.

At this time he was one of the leading Muslim communists. It was in 1920 that he asked for the formation of a "Turkic Communist party," a national Muslim army, the expatriation of Russian colonizers, and the creation of a Great Turkic Republic in Central Asia. In spite of his "deviation," he was not purged, but was recalled to Moscow in 1921 where he became a member of the collegium of the Narkomnats. In 1923–24 back in Central Asia he became chairman of the Sovnarkom of the Turkestan Republic, member of the Central Asia Bureau of the Central Committee of the RCP (b), and member of the Central Committee of the Turkestan Communist party. In 1923, at the Twelfth Congress, he was elected a candidate-member of the Central Committee of the RCP (b).

After 1923, his career "goes downward." In 1925 he was Komintern representative in Mongolia, a rather modest position, and from 1926–37, in semidisgrace, he was the head of the press department of the Caucasian Regional Commission of the RCP (b). He also lectured at the KUTVa in Moscow. Arrested in 1937 he was executed on 9 or 10 February 1938, together with some other communist leaders, including G. M. Musabekov, candidate-member of the Central Committee of the RCP (b) and chairman of the Sovnarkom of Azerbaidzhan. Ryskulov was posthumously rehabilitated after the Twentieth Party Congress.

Said Galiev, Sahibgiray (1894–1939), Tatar, born in Ufa, son of a worker. In 1916 Said Galiev was an officer in the Infantry Regiment in the city of Ekaterinburg (Sverdlovsk). In March of 1917 he joined the RCP (b) and became a member of the soviet of Ekaterinburg and chairman of the soviet of the garrison of the same town; in November, he became commissar for Muslim affairs of the Forty-Seventh Brigade of the Infantry. In February 1918 he was elected commissar for nationality problems of the Kazan Soviet. Said Galiev played an important role in the Kazan Muskom and was chairman of the Central Bureau of the Communist Organization of the Peoples of the East (November 1919). He was also chairman of the Tatar Revkom (1920) and in September 1920, president of the Sovnarkom of Tatarstan. From 1921 he was president of the Sovnarkom of the Crimean Tatar Republic. Said Galiev was also a member of the CEC of the RSFSR and a member of the Russian delegation at the Third Congress of the Komintern. He belonged to the "left," orthodox Bolshevik and pro-Russian wing of Tatar communism and opposed Sultan Galiev. In spite of his loyalty to the establishment, he was arrested in 1938 and executed in 1939.

Skrypnik, Mykola (1872–1933), Ukrainian Old Bolshevik, born at Sloboda Yasinovataia, Ekaterinoslav *gubernia*, son of a railroad official, educated in a technical school at Izum. Skrypnik joined the RSDWP in 1897. In 1900 he was a student of the Petersburg Technological Institute; in 1901 he was arrested and once again in 1902. Skrypnik was exiled to Siberia, but escaped and worked along the Volga and in the Ukraine. He was arrested again in 1904, but escaped once again. In 1905 he was the secretary of the Petersburg committee of the RSDWP. During World War I he worked in Petrograd.

In December 1917 he was sent to the Ukraine. In March 1918 he was elected chairman of the Soviet government of the Ukraine. From December 1918 he was a member of the CC of the Ukrainian CP. Skrypnik took an active part in the Civil War. In 1918 he was member of the All-Russian Cheka. In early 1919 he was a member of the Narkom of State Control of the Ukraine, in 1921 of the Narkom of Internal Affairs, between 1922 and 1927 of the Narkom of Justice of the Ukraine, and between 1927 and 1933 of the Narkom of Education. Between 1925 and 1933 he was a member of the Politburo of the CC of the CP of the Ukraine.

Skrypnik was the recognized leader of the "national" wing of the Ukrainian Communist party. He committed suicide on 7 July 1933.

Subhi, Mustafa (1883–1921), Turk, born in Giresun (Turkey) in the family of an Ottoman civil servant, graduated from the law faculty in Istanbul and the Ecole des Sciences Politiques in Paris. He returned to Turkey after the Young Turk Revolution and worked in Istanbul as a journalist and a professor in the Pedagogical Institute. In 1910 he was a member of the Osmanlı Sosiyalist Firkası. He was arrested for revolutionary activity in 1913 and expelled from the country in 1914. He went to Russia, was interned during the war, and deported, first to Kaluga and then to the Urals. In 1915 he became a member of the RWSD party. On 25 July 1918 he organized the first communist group of Turkish PW and published *Yeni Dünya*, first in Moscow, then in Simferopol.

Subhi was editor of the official organ of the Central Muskom, *Chulpan*, in 1918–20, along with Mulla-Nur Vahitov, Sultan Galiev, and Galimjan Ibragimov. In 1919 he was a delegate to the First Congress of the Komintern and an organizer of the First Congress of the Communist Turkish Organization (former Turkish PW) in Baku in September 1920, where the official Turkish CP was founded. Subhi became its first president. Subhi was an important member of the Narkomnats and the organizer and chairman of the important Turkish section. Among other tasks, he translated into Turkish many classical works of Marxism-Leninism. On 28 January 1921, Subhi and the entire leadership of the Turkish CP were sent home to Turkey by boat. On their arrival, they were killed by Turkish police in the port of Trabzon. The Soviet government did not protest.

Sultan Galiev, Mir-Said (1880–1939?), Tatar, leader of the national communist Muslim movement, born in the village of Kyrmyskaly in a family of a Tatar teacher, studied in the Russian-Tatar teachers' school of Kazan. He began his active life as a journalist, collaborating with many liberal nationalist and radical nationalist periodicals of Kazan, St. Petersburg, Baku, and Orenburg. He took part in the First All-Russian Muslim Congress of May 1917 in Kazan and in July 1917 became one of the leading members of the Muslim Socialist Committee of Kazan. In November 1917 he entered the RCP (b) and, because of his exceptional gifts for organization, rapidly became the highest-ranking Muslim in the CP hierarchy—member of the Central Muslim Commissariat, chairman of the Muslim Military Collegium, member of the Little Collegium of the Narkomnats, editor of the *Zhizn Natsional'nostei*, the official organ of the Narkomnats, and member of the Central Executive Committee of the Tatar Republic.

He was arrested for the first time in May 1923 and excluded from the CP for "nationalist deviation." Liberated soon after, he worked successfully in Georgia and in Moscow. Arrested for the second time in 1928, he was tried and condemned to ten years of hard labor in the Solovki camp. All traces of him disappear around 1939.

Tan Malaka, Indonesian Communist leader, born in Sumatra. Tan Malaka began his political career as a member of the "national party," Sarekat Islam. In October 1921, he, together with his wife, Semzun, led the "Communist faction" at the Sixth Congress of Sarekat Islam. After he was expelled from Sarekat Islam in December 1921, he created a "Red Sarekat Islam" called Sarekat Rakjat ("People's Association"). In 1922, in Moscow, Tan Malaka attended the KUTVa and was present at the Fourth Komintern Congress. In the same year Tan Malaka was elected chairman of the official PKI (Partai Komunis Indonesia). In 1923, the Dutch authorities banished him from Indonesia. For several years (1923–28), he shuttled between Moscow and Manila as the agent of the Komintern for Southeast Asia and Australia with headquarters in Manila. In 1926 he opposed as premature and nonrealistic the Communist uprising organized by the PKI. At the Sixth Congress of the Komintern Bukharin accused Tan Malaka of being a "Trotskyite" while Tan Malaka broke with Stalin, whom he accused of supporting anti-Islamic policies. Tan Malaka thus embarked on a path leading toward national communism.

In 1927 he created an undergound Marxist-Leninist party, PARI (Partai Republik Indonesia), a rival of PKI. PARI, headquartered in Bangkok, was a typical national communist organization with strong "pan-Asian" bias.

Before World War II, Tan Malaka became a partisan of pro-Japanese orientation. In 1942, he returned to Indonesia to work with Japanese authorities. After 1945, he became once more the leading figure of the Indonesian Left and he propagated theories which represented a perfect blending of nationalism, Marxism, and Islam.

Arrested and imprisoned between 1946 and 1948, Tan Malaka created in 1948 a new Left party, Murba ("Proletariat"), and launched a guerrilla war. He was arrested and executed on 16 April 1949.

Teregulov, Ömer, Tatar, born in the village of Kargaly, "government" of Ufa, in the family of an impoverished nobleman. Teregulov graduated together with other radical Tatar militants (Yamashev, Kulahmetov) from the

Russian-Tatar school in Kazan, which had been a breeding ground of Muslim revolutionaries in the early twentieth century. Teregulov joined the RSDWP around 1905 and cooperated with Yamashev to create the Bolshevik periodical, *Ural*. In October 1917, he abandoned the Bolshevik camp and fought against them during the Civil War. He emigrated to China and died in Turkey.

Tuktar, Fuad (18?–1938), Tatar, born in the village of Morasa, "government" of Kazan, studied in the Kazan Russian-Tatar school where he met Ayaz Iskhaki and acquired socialist ideas. He was trained as a lawyer and graduated from the Law Faculty of the University of Kazan. Tuktar was deputy at the Second Duma, where he chaired the Muslim Labor Group (of SR trend). In 1917, he was president of the Muslim Military Council (Harbi Shura) of Petrograd and was active in the Second Pan-Russian Muslim Congress held in Kazan in February 1918. In that same year, along with Iskhaki and other Tatar SRs, he turned against the Soviets and emigrated to Turkey. He died in Ankara.

Uzun Haji, Chechen, sheikh of the Naqshebandi *tariqa.* An active adversary of Russian power in the Northern Caucasus, Uzun Haji was arrested and deported to Siberia by the czarist police. Liberated in 1917, he came back to the Northern Caucasus and rapidly became the leading *mürshid* of the Naqshebandi. In 1917 he became the aide in office of Najmuddin of Gotzo, who was elected *imam* of Daghestan and of the mountain region.

Uzun Haji was a pure conservative. His favorite slogan, which he often put into practice, was, "I am weaving a rope with which to hang the students, the engineers, the intellectuals, and, more generally, all those who write from left to right" (that is, all those who accept Russian influence).

Between 1917 and 1921, Uzun Haji enjoyed an immense prestige and popularity among the Caucasian mountaineers. His fanatical religious followers fought on all fronts, against the White Armies of Denikin, against the Reds, and also against the more moderate members of Uzun Haji's own religion. After the conquest of Daghestan by the Red Army, Uzun Haji (nearly ninety years old), together with Najmuddin of Gotzo, led, in September 1920, the great revolt of Daghestani and Chechen mountaineers against Soviet power—one of the most terrible challenges the Red Army ever faced in the Muslim borderlands. Uzun Haji died during the revolt, which was crushed by the Red Army in the summer of 1921.

It was Uzun Haji who, according to Samurskii, "more completely than any other leader gave expression to the spirit and aims of the Daghestani

'clericals.' It was he who most accurately expounded the teaching be-
queathed by Shamil. . . . Internally he sought to set up a petty 'caliphate
of the Caucasus,' a theocracy based on democratic equality for all true
believers. In his foreign policy he was inspired by an irreconcilable hatred
of everything Russian and a passionate striving for complete independence from the infidels and a union with Turkey, the country which he
envisioned as destined to hold hegemony over all Muslim lands'' (cf. W.
E. D. Allen and Paul Muratoff, *Caucasian Battlefields: A History of the
Wars on the Turco-Caucasian Border, 1828–1921.* [Cambridge: Cambridge University Press, 1953]).

Vahitov, Mulla-Nur (1885–1918), Tatar, born in Kungur, province of Ufa, in
the family of a Tatar merchant. Vahitov studied in the Russian gymnasium of
Kazan (1907) and in the Polytechnical Institute of St. Petersburg (from 1910
on) where he encountered Russian Marxists. Expelled from the Institute for
his revolutionary ideas in 1911, he entered the Psycho-Neurological Institute
of St. Petersburg, but in 1912 was expelled for the same reasons. In February
1917 he worked as an engineer in Kazan. In March of the same year he
created, with Sultan Galiev and some other radical nationalists, the Muslim
Socialist Committee of Kazan. In October 1917, he fought with the Bolsheviks and in December 1917 joined the RCP (b). In January 1918, he was
put in charge of the Central Muslim Commissariat by Stalin and was also
made the chairman of the Muslim Military Collegium of the Peoples' Commissariat for War (Narkomvoen). In August of 1918 Vahitov led a Tatar-
Bashkir battalion against the Whites on the Eastern front. He was captured by
the Czechs in the struggle for Kazan and executed on 19 August 1918.

Yamashev, Husein (1882–1912), Tatar poet and revolutionary leader, born in
Kazan in the family of a merchant, studied in the *medresseh* ''Muham-
mediyeh'' and in the Russian-Tatar school in Kazan (1904), and graduated
from the University of Kazan (1911). Yamashev joined the Russian SDWP as
early as 1903. He was one of the first SD Tatars and one of the very few real
Marxist-Bolshevik Muslims. In January 1907, together with another Tatar
writer, Gafur Kulahmetov, he founded in Orenburg the newspaper, *Ural*,
which was the only real pre-1917 Bolshevik Muslim periodical.

   Ural was closed in April of the same year and the Tatar Bolshevik group
(the ''Uralchylar'') was dispersed by the police. Yamashev died in 1912.

   He is the author of many revolutionary poems and of translations into Tatar
of some manifestos of the RSDWP.

Zeki Validov, Ahmed (Zeki Velidi Togan) (1890–1969), Bashkir, political
leader and historian, born in an aristocratic feudal family of the Southern

Urals (village of Kuzen), son of an *imam*, studied in the *medresseh* of Kasymiyeh (Kazan) and graduated from the University of Kazan. In 1909, he was a professor of history at the University of Kazan. In May 1917 he took an active part in the First All-Russian Muslim Congress as the leader of the Bashkir national movement. He held a variety of offices, president of the Bashkir Shura, president of the Bashkir government (1918), and head of the Bashkir Army during the Civil War. When the Bashkirs, disgusted with Kolchak's antiminority policy, went over to the side of the Bolsheviks, Zeki Validov became the chairman of the Bashrevkom; and in 1919–20, he was war commissar of the Soviet Socialist Republic of Bashkiria. In 1919, he represented the RCP (b) at the First Congress of the Komintern, but in June 1920, he was the first of the Muslim leaders to understand that no cooperation was possible with the Bolsheviks. Together with some of his Bashkir comrades of the Bashrevkom, he fled to Turkestan and joined the Basmachis. In 1922, he left Turkestan for Afghanistan and then Turkey. In emigration he remained a brilliant scholar and held the position of director of historical studies at the University of Istanbul.

Appendix I

Political Parties

Adalet ("Justice"). Political group of communistic trend which was founded in Baku in 1916 by some Iranian revolutionaries from Tabriz and Tehran. It was based on another Iranian political association, Ejtemayun Amiyun, which had been formed in Baku in 1905. The leaders of Adalet were arrested by the Russian police in 1913, but in 1917 the group reappeared with the help of Hümmet. Like Hümmet, Adalet came under the control of the Central Committee of the Russian Social Democratic Workers party (of Bolshevik trend). Its leaders were Asadullah Kafar Zade and Haidar Khan Amuoglu. In June of 1920 Adalet moved from Baku to Resht and on 20 June 1920, Adalet transformed itself into the Communist party of Persia.

Alash Orda (*Alash* is the name of the mystical ancestor of the people of Kazakh; it is also their *uran* or war cry. *Alash Orda* means the "horde or the nation of Alash"). Alash Orda was a liberal nationalist Kazakh political party founded in March 1917 by a group of moderate intellectuals—Ali Khan Bukeykhanov, Ahmed Baytursun, Mir-Yakub Dulatov, and H. Dosmohammedov; the ethnographer, Mohammezhan Tynyshbaev; and Abdül Hamid Zhuzhdybaev, Öldes Omerov, and others. The program of the party (in the beginning, close to the Russian KD party) was a blending of moderate Menshevik and Social Revolutionary ideas. Indifferent to religion and to pan-

Turkism, Alash Orda was concerned mainly with the formation and the protection of the Kazakh nation. In 1917, Alash Orda completely dominated the political life of the steppes. In December 1917, its leaders (all of them from the upper class) joined counterrevolutionary forces (the Komuch, the Orenburg cossaks, the Bashkirs of Zeki Validov). On 10 December 1917, the party proclaimed the autonomy of the steppes with two governments, one for the western area at the village of Zhambeitu, chaired by H. Dosmohammedov, and the other for eastern Kazakhstan in Semiplatinsk, chaired by Bukeykhanov. Both were strongly anticommunist, but Kolchak's policy against minorities obliged the leaders of Alash Orda to switch to the Left. On 10 November 1919, Alash Orda recognized Soviet power and its leaders entered the RCP (b). Until their purge and physical liquidation in the 1930s, these leaders formed the right, nationalist wing of the Communist party of Kazakhstan.

Basmachi is a term for the loosely organized, popular, anti-Soviet, counterrevolutionary uprising of the Muslim population, both sedentary and nomadic, of Central Asia. (In Uzbek, *basmach* means "brigand.") The term described many independent movements in several regions: the Ferghana Valley (the main theater of the uprisings); the eastern and southern areas of the former emirate of Bukhara (especially among the nomadic Lokay tribe); and the northern area of the Turkmen steppes. The movement, led by local chieftains (the *kurbashy*), erupted in 1918, and continued sporadically and in varying degrees of intensity until at least 1930 and in some areas until 1936.

In conjunction with the uprising of the Daghestani-Chechen mountaineers in 1920–22, the Bashmachi movement was certainly the most dangerous popular, mass, anti-Soviet movement.

Berek ("Unity"). Berek was a Tatar, revolutionary, political group founded in Kazan in the spring of 1906 and dispersed by the police in September of the same year. Its program was not very coherent, having been inspired by both the Russian Social Democratic party and the Socialist Revolutionaries. Its slogan was "liberty for the people, land for the peasants." The group edited two newspapers, *Azat* ("Free") and *Azat Khalyk* ("Free People"). The leaders of Berek formed a curious conglomerate. Side by side with authentic Tatar Bolsheviks (Husein Yamashev, Gafur Kulahmetov) stood radical pan-Islamists. The president of the group was a *mullah mudarris*, Abdullah Apanay, the *imam* of a Kazan mosque, and a member of the Central Committee of Ittifaq al-Müslimin.

Borotbist (from Ukrainian *borotba,* "fight"). Borotbist was the name of the official organ of a Ukrainian revolutionary party founded during the Civil War on the foundation of the old Ukrainian Socialist Revolutionary party. In the spring of 1918, the left wing of the Ukrainian Socialist Revolutionary party obtained the majority in the Central Committee and excluded the right wing from the party. After March 1919, the party changed its name from Ukrainian Socialist Revolutionary party to "Ukrainian party of the Socialist Revolutionaries—Communists—Borotbists." In the summer of 1919 this party merged with the left wing of the "Independent Ukrainian Social-Democrats (Menshevik)" and changed its name once more to the "Ukrainian Communist party (Borotbists)."

The new party, in spite of its socialist color, remained deeply nationalist. Its strength came from the western Ukrainian peasantry and from the poor elements of the cities. The program of the party contained the following issues: the creation of a separate Ukrainian army, the autonomy of the Ukrainian economy, the use of the Ukrainian language, and so on.

During the Civil War, the Borotbists fought on the side of the Bolsheviks at the same time they were trying to establish their control over the Ukrainian masses.

In early 1920, the Borotbists tried in vain to be accepted as an independent party by the Komintern, and refused to recognize the authority of the Ukrainian Communist party. However, in March 1920, the Borotbists decided to dissolve their party and, following the decision of the Fourth Conference of the Communist Party (Bolshevik) of the Ukraine, they were admitted individually as members of the Communist party (Bolshevik) of the Ukraine.

Bund. This was a Jewish Social-Democratic union which arose in October 1897 in the western provinces of Russia. At the First Party Congress of the RSDWP in 1898, Bund joined the Party as an autonomous organization, "independent only in questions concerning the special Jewish proletariat." At its Fourth Congress (1901), Bund raised the question of the need to reorganize the Party on the basis of federations. At the Second Congress of the RSDWP (1903), Bund put forward the demand for the national division of the proletariat. Bund demanded that it be recognized as the only representative of Jewish workers in Russia, and that it be granted a special place in the Party. The Second Congress of the RSDWP emphatically voted down Bund's organizational nationalism, and Bund left the Party.

During the Revolution of 1905, Bund took a Menshevik position. In 1906 at the Fourth ("United") Congress of the RSDWP, Bund again joined the RSDWP. At the Ninth Conference of 1912, Bund sanctioned union with the

Mensheviks. At the Sixth (Prague) All-Party Conference of the RSDWP (1912), Bund was expelled from the Party.

At the end of 1918, leftist groups began forming within Bund. This led to its split. At its Twelfth Conference (1920), Bund's left wing accepted the program of the RCP (b); its right wing left the conference. In 1921 some of its members were accepted into the Bolshevik party. The majority of these new adherents were later liquidated.

Dumachylar ("Those of the Duma"). This Muslim political group was founded in April 1907 by a group of the Muslim Labor faction of the Second Duma (Müsülmanlarynyng Hizmet Taifesi). Its founders and members were former militants of the "Islah" movement and members of the Tangychylar party. These members included five Tatars—Hadi Atlasy (a *mullah* of Bugul'ma), Abdullah Najmuddin (a *mullah* of Simbirsk), Habiburrahman Masudov of Yelabuzh, Arif Badamsin (a merchant from Chistopol), Kalimulla Hasanov (a *mudarris* of Ufa); and one Azeri—Zeynal Zeynalov, a worker of Baku, a member of the Hümmet, and a future RCP (b) member. The group published a newspaper, *Duma*, in St. Petersburg (six issues in all). Dumachylar was strongly influenced by the program of the Russian Trudoviki and by the ideology of the Social Revolutionaries. The group disappeared after the end of the Second Duma.

ERK ("Will"). The ERK was a Muslim, underground, socialist, but anti-Russian political organization. The idea of such a party appeared simultaneously but independently in the spring of 1919 in Bashkiria and in Tashkent. In November 1919 some Muslim socialist leaders from Tashkent, Bukhara, Kazakhstan, and Bashkiria met in Moscow and decided to unite their efforts in order to found one Muslim socialist party. They drafted a program of twelve points. In the spring of 1920, when it became obvious that the RCP (b) would never tolerate a Muslim socialist party as an autonomous member of the Komintern, the same leaders decided to found their own party, completely independent from both the RCP (b) and the Komintern. During the Congress of Baku in September 1920, the same leaders drafted a statute of the Party. Only three founders of the clandestine group can be positively identified: Zeki Validov (the Bashkir leader), Abdul Hamid Arifov (the war commissar of the Government of the Bukharian Republic in September 1920), and Janizakov of Turkestan. It is probable that the Kazakh leaders, Baytursun and Bukeykhanov, and possibly the Uzbeks, Fayzullah Khojaev and Osman Khojaev (commissar for the finances of the Bukharian government), were also among the founders. In January 1921, in Bukhara, it was decided to change the name to Türkistan Sosialistlar Tüdesi ("Group of Turkestan Socialists"). In April of the same year a secret congress of the party held in Bukhara reduced the program of the party to nine points. In early 1926 the name was changed once more to Türkistan Soçialist ERK Firkasy ("Turkistan Socialist Party-ERK"). But, it is not known if this decision was made in the territory of Soviet Central Asia or abroad, where some of the leaders of ERK already had emigrated.

Harbi Shura ("Military Council"). A Muslim board created by the Second All-Russian Muslim Congress at Kazan in July 1917 in order to raise Muslim military units headquartered in Kazan. Its chairman was a Bashkir, Lt. Iliyas Alkin, who later fought on the side of the Komuch against the Reds; he then joined the Bashkir forces of Zeki Validov, and finally became a member of the Bashrevkom. In 1920, when Zeki Validov escaped to Central Asia, Alkin continued to cooperate with the Soviet regime.

Harbi Shura controlled Muslim (mainly Tatar) military units (which remained neutral in the battles of October). It was disbanded on 26 March 1918, by the Narkomnatz.

Hümmet ("Endeavor"). The party's complete name was "Muslim Social Democratic party—Hümmet." Hümmet was an Azerbaidzhan political party created in 1904 as a circle for the study of socialism. It was attached to the Russian Social-Democrat Workers' party of Baku (of Bolshevik trend), and its adherents were mainly young intellectuals of bourgeois or aristocratic origin, plus some stray workers. All of the members were Muslim. In 1906 it became a separate political party and was officially recognized at the Sixth Congress of the Russian Social Democratic Workers' Party, despite the strong opposition of some Social Democratic leaders. They suspected—and with good reason—that Hümmet represented a kind of "Muslim Bund." In 1906, some members of Hümmet took part in the revolutionary movement in Persia. From 1907 until 1917, Hümmet was a semiclandestine organization. Its founders included Nariman Narimanov, Meshadi Azizbekov (executed by the Whites in 1918 along with other "Baku commissars"), Sultan Mejid Efendiev, Isa Ashurbeyli (a millionaire industrialist), and Dadash Bunyat Zade. In 1917, Hümmet resurfaced and played a major role in the Commune of Baku in the spring of 1918, but in 1919–20 it became semiclandestine once more. In April 1920, after the conquest of Azerbaidzhan by the Red Army, it transformed itself into the Communist party of Azerbaidzhan. Its leaders, even after they became leaders of the new Communist party, remained dubious communists. They were marked by psychological scars of the period when the

Hümmet was vacillating between nationalism and Marxism. In 1937–38 all of the surviving, former leaders of Hümmet disappeared in the bloody purges.

Islah (In Arabic, "reform"; the full name of the group was *Islah Komitesi* or "Committee for Reform").This Tatar political group was created in 1905 by young radical intellectuals. The founders were all former militants who had participated in the revolutionary unrest of 1905 of the students of the Tatar *medressehs* of Kazan, Ufa, Orenburg, and Troitsk. The ideology of the group remained vague. It represented the radical left wing of *jadid* reformism; it was violently anticonservative, anticlerical, and anti-Russian. The ideology was nationalist and strongly influenced by the ideology of direct action (going as far as supporting terrorism) of the Russian Social Revolutionaries and of the anarchists. The group also accepted a certain number of socialist slogans. There was no united program and no party discipline; the members were united only by their romantic radicalism. After 1917, some joined the RCP (b) and others fled Soviet power. Nonetheless, Islah was definitely the nursery of the greatest Tatar political leaders. The most outstanding Muslim prerevolutionary intellectuals were adherents of Islah: Galimjan Ibragimov, the poet Abdullah Tukay, the writer Fatyh Amirkhan, and the future Tangchylar—Ayaz Iskhaki, Fuad Tuktar, and Abdullah Devletshin.

Ittifaq al-Müslimin ("Muslim Union," also known as Rusiya Müsülmanlarynyng Ittifaqy or "Union of Muslims of Russia"). Ittifaq al-Müslimin was a great all-Muslim political party created in January 1906, at the Second All-Russian Muslim Congress in St. Petersburg. In principle the party was open to all Muslims of the Russian Empire; in practice it was dominated by Volga Tatars, along with some Crimeans and Azerbaidzhanis. Its leaders—the members of the Central Committee—all belonged to the upper level of Muslim society. The Central Committee was comprised of eleven Volga Tatars—Abdurrashid Ibragimov, Yusuf Akchura (son of a wealthy merchant and member of the Russian KD party), Seyid Giray Alkin (nobleman and lawyer), Abdullah Apanay (*mudarris*), Galimjan Barudi (*mufti* of St. Petersburg), Sadri Maksudi (wealthy lawyer of Kazan), Shah-Haydar Syrtlanov (nobleman and landlord), Musa Jarullah Bigi, Abdullah Bubi, Selim Giray Janturin (nobleman and landlord), Hadi Maksudi (member of a wealthy merchant family); one Azeri—Ali Mardan Topchibashy (wealthy industrialist); two Crimean Tatars—Ismail Gasprinski and Mustafa Davidovich (mayor of Baghchesaray); and one Kazakh—Shahmardan Koshchegulov.

Ittifaq followed rather closely the political programs of the KD party. It was moderately pan-Islamic and pan-Turkic and moderately opposed to czarism. Its leaders hoped that a fruitful cooperation was possible between liberal Muslims and the liberal Russian bourgeoisie. Ittifaq sent twenty-five members to the First Duma, twenty-nine to the Second Duma (where they formed a Muslim faction allied to the KD), ten to the Third Duma, and only seven to the Fourth Duma. Not one of its demands was accepted, and in 1908, at the time of Stolypin's policy against minorities, Ittifaq's Central Committee decided to disband. Some of its leaders emigrated to Turkey (Y. Akchura); some abandoned political life; and others switched to the Left (A. Apanay).

Ittihad ve Taraqqi ("Union and Progress"), a clandestine political group founded in Moscow in the late 1920s by some Muslim national communist leaders: Sultan Galiev (Tatar), Zeki Validov (Bashkir), Najmuddin Khojaev (Uzbek), Ahmed Baytursun (Kazakh), and others whose names are not known.

According to Soviet literature (which is not always reliable), the aims of this group were as follows: (1) to introduce Turkic nationalist militants into the Communist party and into the Soviet apparatus; (2) to obtain control of the educational network of the Muslim republics; (3) to establish contacts with counterrevolutionary organizations and movements, especially with the Basmachis. The final goal was the "destruction of the Soviet (that means Russian) regime and the foundation of a "pan-Turkic bourgeois state."

Jengelis ("Of the Jungle"). A Persian, pan-Islamic, anti-Western, antifeudalist, and anti-Kajor guerrilla movement centered in the densely wooded mountains (jungle) of the province of Ghilan in northern Iran. Its leadership was made up of radical bourgeois intellectuals and conservative religious elements. At the head of the movement were the Muslim cleric (*mullah*), Mirza Kuchik Khan; a radical intellectual from Tehran, Ehsanullah Khan; and a few other men who were either merchants or petty landed gentry.

The movement began before 1914 and received a new impetus in 1917 when the Germans and Turks gave it funds and arms. It received an even greater impetus in 1917 when the Russian army in Iran collapsed. In 1918, the movement expanded to the neighboring Caspian provinces of Mazanderan and Astarabad and northward toward the Russian border. In July 1918, British troops under General Dunsterville passed through Ghilan on their way to Baku; and in August 1918, an agreement was made between the British and Kuchik Khan, whose authority in Ghilan was recognized.

In the summer of 1919, the government of Tehran launched a big offensive against the Jengelis. Persian troops took Resht, but the guerrilla fighters escaped to the densely wooded mountains of Southern Ghilan. The defeat convinced Kuchik Khan of the necessity to look for allies.

On 18 May 1920, a Red flotilla under the command of Admiral Raskol'nikov appeared before the port of Enzeli. The British troops retreated from Ghilan; Resht was occupied by Red soldiers; and Kuchik Khan and the Red commander proclaimed the "Soviet Socialist Republic of Ghilan," with Kuchik Khan as president. An enthusiastic telegram was sent to Lenin (text in Abikh: "Natsionalnoe i Revoliutsionnoe Dvizhenie v Persii Vospominanie Ekhsan-Ully Khana," *Novyi Vostok*, vol. 30; English translation in G. Lenczowski, *Russia and the West in Iran, 1918–1948* [Ithaca, N.Y.: Cornell University Press, 1949], p. 57).

With the Red fleet, the leaders of the former Adalet party arrived in Ghilan and founded the Communist party of Iran under the chairmanship of Haydar Khan Amuoglu. The new Communist party of Iran cooperated with the Jengelis. However, the unholy alliance between devoted Marxists and radical religious nationalists was short-lived.

In the spring of 1921, however, Soviet government seemed to be playing the Jengeli card. A regular division of the Red Army (purely Russian) landed in Enzeli, supposedly to help the Jengelis in their offensive against Tehran, which had been launched in July 1921.

But in September 1921, Soviet troops suddenly withdrew. At the same time differences between Kuchik Khan and his Communist allies gave birth to an open schism. Kuchik Khan slaughtered the entire Central Committee of the Communist party of Iran, including Haydar Khan Amuoglu. In October 1921, Iranian troops launched their counteroffensive and the Jengeli movement collapsed. Kuchik Khan fled northward and froze to death in the mountains of Talysh. His head was brought to Tehran.

Millet Melisi. See Milli Idare.

Milli Firqa ("National Party"). This Crimean Tatar National party was founded in July 1917 by a group of young intellectuals educated in Turkey or in Western Europe. These intellectuals were more radical than the elder generation of Crimean nationalists who had followed the liberal pan-Turkism of Ismail Gasprinski. The program of the party was tinted with socialism and its nationalism was radical and revolutionary. However, there was no official affiliation to any Russian socialist organization. The party was not a monolithic body, and soon it split into two factions. The leaders of the relatively moderate faction were Hasan Sabri Ayvaz (a former colleague of Gasprinski and former chief editor of the *Terjüman*), Ahmed Özenbashly,

Ali Bodaninsky (a left-wing Social Revolutionary who was killed in 1920 while fighting on the side of the Red Army), and Halil Chapchakchy. The more radical faction (minoritarian) was closer to the Bolshevik platform, but remained within the limits of nationalism and of Islam. Among its leaders were Mehmed Koja Vezhdi (*mudarris*), Abdulhakim Hilmi Arif Zade (historian and writer), Veli Ibrahimov (the future president of the Communist party of Crimea), and the writers Batyr Aytuvgan and Mustafa Berke.

During the Civil War, which was particularly bloody in Crimea, Milli Firqa was constantly switching from one trend to the other and did not play any important role until June 1919 when Denikin occupied Crimea. Because of its anti-Tatar position, the left-wing members of Milli Firqa went underground and collaborated with the Bolsheviks. After October 1920, when Crimea was finally occupied by the Red Army, the left-wing members of Milli Firqa joined the RCP (b).

Milli Idare ("Muslim National Board"), a Muslim organization formed in Ufa by the decision of the Second All-Muslim Congress at Kazan on 17 July 1917. Its goal was to give effect to the national extraterritorial cultural autonomy of the Turks and Tatars of Russia and Siberia which had been proclaimed at the Second Congress at Kazan. Its second goal was to pave the way for a Muslim National Assembly (Millet Mejlisi), which met for the first time at Ufa on 20 November 1917. The chairman of Milli Idare was the liberal Tatar, Sadri Maksudi. Milli Idare was disbanded on 12 April 1918 by a decision of the Narkomnatz.

Milli Shura ("National Council"). This Muslim central agency was responsible for coordinating joint political action with headquarters at Moscow. It was chaired by the Ossetian Menshevik Ahmed Tsalikov. Milli Shura was created by the First All-Russian Muslim Congress of 1 May 1917, in Kazan. Its executive committee (Ikomus) was established in Petrograd and was chaired by the Tatar Socialist Revolutionary, Ayaz Iskhaki. Milli Shura was disbanded by a decision of the Narkomnats on 12 April 1918.

Musavat ("Equality"). This Azerbaidzhani political party was created in 1911 in the city of Elizavetpol' (Gendzhe, now called Kirovograd) by a group of young Muslim intellectuals with socialistic and nationalistic leanings. Some of them were, since 1905, members of the Russian Social Democratic Workers' party. Members of the Central Committee of Musavat included Mehmet Emin Rasul Zade, Gholam Reza Sherif Zade, Abbas Kuli Kerim Zade, and Kerbelai Veli Mikhal Zade. Between 1911 and 1917 this influential party inclined toward the right, away from socialism and toward nationalism. In 1917, Musavat defended autonomist (not yet separatist) positions. Rasul Zade, as leader of Musavat, imposed his views concerning the autonomy of Muslim areas within a Russian federation on the members of the First All-Russian Muslim Congress of May 1917 in Moscow. In 1918, however, the leaders of Musavat became partisans of total independence for Azerbaidzhan. On 20 June 1917, Musavat absorbed the smaller and more conservative party, the Turk Federalist party (created in April 1917, by some intellectuals and landlords). The expanded organization took the name of Turk Federalist party—Musavat. Mehmet Emin Rasul Zade became its president. During the period of the Independent Azerbaidzhani Republic (November 1918 to April 1920), the Musavat party completely dominated Azerbaidzhani political life. Its ideology remained a blending of moderate socialism (of Menshevik trend) and of local nationalism (different from Tatar pan-Turkic nationalism).

Müsülmanlarynyng Hizmet Taifesi ("Muslim Labor Faction"). A Muslim group of the Second Duma, formed by six members (five Tatars and one Azeri, *see* Dumachylar) of Socialist background who withdrew from the *Ittifaq al-Müslimin* and adopted the program of the Russian Trudoviki (Socialist Revolutionary) faction, it disappeared with the Second Duma.

Petrashevtzy. This radical revolutionary Russian group was founded in St. Petersburg in 1845 by Mikhail Butashevich-Petrashevskii (1821–66). Members of this group were arrested in 1849 and deported to Siberia and to the Kazakh steppes. In Vernyi (now Alma-Ata), Turgay, and Semipalatinsk they met some radical Kazakh intellectuals. Their influence on the infant Kazakh national movement was important.

Shura-yi Islamiyeh ("Muslim Council"). This nationalist Turkestani political association was very hostile to Russia but moderate in its social demands. It was created in April 1917 in Tashkent, and in the fall of the same year it blended with the more conservative association, Ulema Jamiyeti ("The Ulema Association"). Both parties opposed the Soviet of Tashkent and supported the short-lived and unfortunate attempt to create an independent Muslim government in Kokand which ended in the slaughter of the natives by the Russian troops of the Tashkent soviet on 19 February 1918.

Tangchylar ("Those of Tang"). This Tatar political group was created in Kazan in the spring of 1906 by a group of former militants of the Islah movement, Ayaz Iskhaki, Fuad Tuktar, Shakir Mohammedyarov, and Abdullah Devletshin. The party was organically independent, but it followed rather closely the program, ideology, and methods of the Russian Socialist Revolutionaries. In May of 1906, the group edited a newspaper, *Tang Yulduzy* (Morning Star), which disappeared after its sixty-third issue of September 1906. It was one of the most violently radical Tatar periodicals.

The Tangchylar party was dispersed by the police in 1907; its leaders (arrested many times by the czarist authorities before 1914) became staunch adversaries of the Soviet regime in 1917. Most of them emigrated to Turkey during the Civil War.

Uralchylar ("Those of Ural"). This small Tatar Social Democratic Party was created in January 1907 in Orenburg by two members of the Russian Social Democratic Workers' party of Kazan—Husein Yamashev and Galimjan Seyfuddinov—with the permission and the help of the Russian Social Democratic Workers' party of Orenburg and Ufa and with the personal blessing of Lenin (in Switzerland at the time). The party edited a weekly newspaper, *Ural*, which closely followed the platform of the Russian Social Democratic Workers' party (Bolshevik). It was the only authentic Marxist Muslim political group. It was strongly opposed to any manifestation of Tatar nationalism, but the distinction between Bolshevik and Menshevik tendencies was still vague. In April 1907, the group was dispersed by the police and *Ural* disappeared after the thirty-first issue (27 April 1907). Among its other leaders were Gafur Kulahmetov and Ömer Teregulov. The latter will join the anti-Soviet camp during the Civil War.

Üsh-Zhüz ("The Three Hordes"). This Kazakh political group was created in 1913 in the region of the Syr-Darya (southern Kazakhstan). It was led by petty bourgeois intellectuals and clerics, deeply influenced in the beginning by Bukhariot ideas, and very conservative and pan-Islamist. After 1914, Üsh-Zhüz began to penetrate to the northern areas of the steppe region (Turgay, Semirechie, and Omsk). During World War I it became more radical and more anti-Russian. In 1916, its leaders were sympathetic to the great revolt of the nomadic tribes. In 1917, it switched to the left and accepted Social Democratic ideas. In November 1917, it became a regular party with headquarters in Omsk. It remained radical pan-Islamist, but became strongly influenced by the Bolsheviks. During the Civil War, its members (not very numerous) fought on the side of the Red Army against Kolchak and against Alash Orda. Its official periodical, *Üsh-Zhüz* (published in 1918–19, first in Tashkent, then in Petropavlovsk), presented a curious and perfectly illogical blending of pan-Islamism and bolshevism. It was both violently hostile to the presence of Russian colonists in Kazakh lands and enthusiastically pan-Islamist and pro-Bolshevik. Its leaders joined the RCP (b) in 1919–20, but remained third-class individuals.

Vaisites ("God's Regiment of Vaisov"). Vaisites (Vaisovtzy in Russian) was a mystic Sufi brotherhood and a dissident branch of the great Naqshebandi *tariqa* which was founded in Kazan in 1862 by Bahauddin Vaisov. Its members were mainly Tatar artisans, craftsmen, and small merchants. Its doctrine, heretical from the standpoint of orthodox Muslims, was a curious blending of puritan reformism of the Wahhabi type, of Tolstoyism, and, later, of Socialism (of Socialist Revolutionary trend). The Vaisites were not only strongly nationalistic and anti-Russian, but they were also hostile to all other Muslims whom they treated as heretics. The founder, Bahauddin, was arrested by the Russians and died in a psychiatric hospital. His son, Iran Vaisov, after many arrests, became the leader of the *tariqa* and proved more radical than his father. He was a partisan of direct action against his Russian and Tatar enemies. In September of 1917, the Bolsheviks of Kazan armed the Vaisites and in October they became the only Tatar group to fight alongside the Russian workers and soldiers. In February 1918, the Vaisites fought once more on the side of the Russian Baltic sailors against their Tatar compatriots when the Tatars tried to create an independent Muslim government in the Transbulak part of the city of Kazan. Iran Vaisov was killed in the battle. Soviet historians are extremely embarrassed about the Vaisites and are at a loss to explain this unholy cooperation of the Bolsheviks with a mystical puritan Muslim group.

Young Bukharians ("Yeni Bukharlylar"). The Young Bukharians were a secret society founded in 1909 in Bukhara by a group of young radical *jadid* Turkestani intellectuals, some of whom had been educated in Istanbul. Among the leaders figured Abdurrauf Fitrat; Abdul Kadir Muhitdinov (president of the Peoples' Republic of Bukhara in 1920, later a member of the Central Committee of the Communist Party of Tajikstan, and finally purged for nationalism in 1937); Fayzullah Khojaev; Akmal Ikramov; the *mufti* Mahmud Behbudi of Samarkand (the leader of *jadid* reformism in Central Asia, later executed by the emir of Bukhara in March 1919); Münevver Kari (Abdurrashidov) (the greatest prerevolutionary Turkestani writer, publicist, *jadid*, and pan-Islamist); and many others.

The ideology and the political program of the Young Bukharians were not clearly defined. It was more pan-Islamic than pan-Turkic; it was a blending of Tatar radical reformism and of the ideology of the Young Turks with a violently revolutionary emphasis. The influence of Russian socialism was, at least in the beginning, weak.

In March 1918, the Young Bukharians tried to seize power in Bukhara with the help of a Soviet expedition launched from Tashkent. The endeavor failed and the Young Bukharians had to flee the emirate to Tashkent. In May of 1920, the second attempt was successful. The Red Army took Bukhara and the Young Bukharians formed the first government of the Peoples' Republic of Bukhara.

In 1923, the major part of the Young Bukharians were admitted into the Communist party of Uzbekistan and until 1936–37 remained its leaders.

Appendix J

Glossary

Agitprop	Agitation and Propaganda Department
Alpamysh	Uzbek epic poem which recounts the wars of the Turkic Kungrat tribe against the Buddhist Kalmyks
Aqsaqal	In Turkish, this means "white beard" or "elder"
CC	Central Committee (of the CP)
CCC	Central Control Committee
CEC	Central Executive Committee
CP	Communist party
CPSU	*See* RSDWP
Dar ul Islam	Literally, the House of Islam, that is, all Muslim lands, as opposed to the Dar ul-Harb, the House of War, which includes all non-Islamic lands
Dede Korkut	Turkic epic cycle common to the Azeris and the Turkmens, which recounts the history of the Oghuz, the ancestors of the Seljuk Turks
Gorkom	City Committee
Gubernia	Province in the Czarist Empire
Ijtihad	The doctrine condoning individual interpretation of the sacred law, the Shariy'at, by qualified doctors of law, termed *mujtahids*

Islah	Reform
Jadid and Jadidism	From the Arabic *jadid* or "new"; a loose term used to designate the ideology of late nineteenth-century modernists and reformers (*jadids*); they opposed *qadym* and *qadymists*
Jihad	Religiously sanctioned warfare aimed at the expansion and defense of the Dar ul-Islam
KUTVa	Kommunisticheskii Universitet Trudiashchikhsie Vostoka= Communist University of the Workers of the East, in Moscow
Kolkhoz	Collective farm
Komintern	Communist International
Krai	Territorial unit of the RSFSR; generally more important than the *oblast* (region); as a rule a *krai* contains one or more small national units (autonomous region or national district)
Kraikom	Territorial Committee
Kulak	From the Russian, meaning "fist"; a wealthy peasant, supposedly an oppressor of poor peasants
Manas	Kirghiz epic cycle which recounts the history of the wars waged by the Turkic tribes against the Buddhist Kalmyks in the seventeenth and eighteenth centuries
Medresseh	Muslim high school
Mektep	Muslim elementary school
Miras	In Arabic, "patrimony"
Mudarris	Professor in a *medresseh*
Mullah	Title of respect given to members of the religious hierarchy; synonymous with *cleric*
Narkom	*Narodnyi Kommissar*=Peoples' commissar
Narkomindel	Peoples' Commissariat for Foreign Affairs
Narkomnats	Peoples' Commissariat for the Affairs of the Nationalities
Narkomvoen	Peoples' Commissariat for War
Obkom	Regional Committee
Oblast	Region, an administrative unit within a Soviet republic; corresponds more or less to the old *gubernia*
Qadymist	From the Arabic *qadim* ("ancient"); designates the representatives of the conservative trend in Russian Islam before 1917; they opposed *jadid*
Raikom	District Committee
Raion	District, an administrative unit; a subdivision of an *oblast*; corresponds to the *uezd*

RCP (b)	*See* RSDWP
Revkom	Revolutionary Military Committee
Revvoensovet	Military revolutionary council
RSDWP	Russian Social Democrat Workers' party, founded at a congress in Minsk in March 1898. At its Second Congress (July–August 1903, Brussels–London), it split into Bolshevik and Menshevik factions. At its Sixth Conference (Prague, January 1912), the Bolshevik faction became a separate party, which at the Seventh Conference (Petrograd, May 1917) took the name of Russian Social Democrat Workers' party (Bolsheviks)=RSDWP (b). At its Seventh Congress (Petrograd, March 1918), it changed its name to the Russian Communist party (Bolshevik)=RCP (b). At the Fourteenth Congress (Moscow, December 1925), the name was changed once more to the All-Union Communist party (Bolshevik). In October 1952, at the Nineteenth Congress, a new name was adopted: Communist party of the Soviet Union=CPSU
RSDWP (b)	*See* RSDWP
Shakird	Student in a *medresseh*
Shariy'at	Koranic law
Shiism	Form of Islam prevalent today primarily in Iran and contiguous regions (Azerbaidzhan). Its principal differences with orthodox Sunni Islam revolve around the rejection of the first three caliphs
Soviet	Council
Sovnarkom	Council of People's Commissars
Sufism	From the Arabic *al-suf* (wool); a mystical doctrine of Sunni Islam based on initiation and leading to the personal union with God. See *Tariqa*
Sunni	From the Arabic *sunna* or "tradition"; the main orthodox form of Islam prevalent in the Arab and Turkic world; Soviet Muslims (with the exceptions of the Shii Azeris) are Sunni
Taqiyyah	Legal right of dissimulation, which permits a Shiite to deny his religious affiliation
Taqlid	Literally, "imitation," implying an uncritical acceptance of traditional interpretations of the Shariy'at
Tariqa	In Arabic, "the Way"; Sufi brotherhood
Uezd	Small territorial unit in the Czarist Empire

Umma   Arabic word used to denote the Islamic community of faith

Vakufs   Islamic religious endowments primarily intended to support educational philanthropies and pious establishments

Notes

Chapter 1

1. Kommunisticheskaia Partiia Azerbaidzhana, Institut Istorii Partii, *Bol'-sheviki v bor'be za pobedu Sotsialisticheskoi Revoliutsii v Azerbaidzhane–Dokumenty i Materialy 1917–1918* (Baku, 1957), p. 24.

Chapter 2

1. S. M. Dimanshtein, *Revoliutsiia i National'nyi Vopros* (Moscow, 1930), 3:288.

2. Kolesov in *Nasha Gazeta* (Tashkent), 23 November 1917, quoted by G. Safarov, *Kolonial'naia Revoliutsiia—Opyt Turkestana* (Moscow, 1921), p. 70.

3. M. S. Sultan Galiev, "Tatary i Revoliutsiia," *Zhizn' Natsional'nostei,* 21(122), 1921.

4. Ahmed Baytursun, "Kirgizy i Revoliutsiia," *Zhizn' Natsional'nostei,* 29(36), 1919.

5. Hanafi Muzaffar, *Din ve Millet Mese'leri* (Religious and National Problems) (Kazan, 1922), unpublished but used by most national communists. Quoted in A. Arsharuni and Kh. Gabidullin, *Ocherki Panislamizma i Panturkizma v Rossii* (Moscow, 1931), pp. 77–81.

6. Ibid.

7. Ibid.

8. Ahmed Baytursun in *Narodnoe Khoziaistvo Kazakhstana* (Alma-Ata, 1931), p. 26.

9. Interview in *Bombay Chronicle,* 1 August 1925, quoted in A. Baıtal-Taymas, *Musa Jarullah Bigi* (Istanbul, 1958), p. 23.

Chapter 3

1. Maxime Rodinson, *Marxisme et Monde Musulman* (Paris, 1972), p. 48.

2. A typical example is the Bashkir Sherif Manatov. Before the revolution he was a strongly religious, right-wing nationalist, heading the conservative faction at the Bashkir Congress at Orenburg in December 1917. By January 1918, he had become vice-chairman of the Soviets' Central Commissariat for Muslim Affairs and a loyal and unquestioning supporter of Stalin.

3. Ahmed Zeki Validov, for example, the most important leader of nationalist Bashkir forces, cooperated with Stalin in 1919 and 1920, serving as president of the Bashkir Revolutionary Committee (Bashrevkom) and war commissar of the Bashkir Soviet Republic. He even represented the RCP (b) at the First Congress of the Third International. In June 1920, he fled with his supporters to Turkestan, where he joined the anti-Soviet Basmachi guerillas. Eventually, he emigrated to Afghanistan and Turkey.

4. Sultan Galiev at the Regional Congress of the Kazan Organization of the RCP (b), March 1918; quoted in A. Arsharni and Kh. Gabidullin, *Ocherki Panislamizma i Pantiurkizma v Rossii* (Moscow, 1931), p. 78.

5. Report at the fourth plenum of the Tatar Obkom of the RCP (b), Kazan, 15 September 1927; quoted in L. Rubinstein, *V bor'be za Leninskuiu Natsional'nuiu Politiku* (Kazan, 1930), p. 24.

6. Report at the Conference of the Tatar Obkom, June 1926; quoted by L. Rubinstein, *V bor'be za Leninskuiu Natsional'nuiu Politiku,* p. 120. Veli Iskhakov at this time was vice-president of the Gasplan of the Tatar Republic.

7. In *Yeni Dünya* (Simferopol), 12 November 1922, official organ of the Turkish Communist party; quoted by A. K. Bochagov, *Milli Firqa* (Simferopol, 1930), pp. 83–84.

8. Quoted in *Kontrrivolütsiyon Soltangäliefcheleke Karshy* (Kazan, 1929), p. 38.

9. Report at the Ninth Conference of the Tatar *obkom,* Kazan, 1923; quoted by L. Rubinstein, *V bor'be za Leninskuiu Natsional'nuiu Politiku,* p. 15.

10. Quoted by T. Davletshin, *Sovietskii Tatarstan* (London, 1974), p. 143.

11. Program of the ERK party; manuscript in possession of the authors. See appendix E.

12. "The Jewish workers support Marxism and fight for the socialist revolution because of their honest belief that the new order will solve their national

and economic problems. For this reason, we want to join the Third International" (Truband in *Undzer Welt* [Kharkov], 8 January 1922, quoted by Baruch Gurewitz, "National Communism in the Soviet Union, 1918–1928" [Ph.D. diss., University of Rochester, 1973], p. 101).

13. For instance, Karl Grassis, one of the leaders of the Kazan Obkom in *K Natsional'nomu Voprosu* (Kazan, 1918).

14. Cited by Z. I. Gimranov, at the Ninth Conference of the Tatar Obkom, 1923, and published in *Stenograficheskii otchot 9oi oblstnoi Konferentsii Tatarskoi organizatsii RKP (b)* (Kazan, 1924), p. 130.

15. Quoted in a report presented by Razumov at the Fifteenth Conference of the Tatar Obkom, 1930; and published in *VKP(b)-nyng XVnie Tatarstan Ölke Konfierensiäse otchoty* (Kazan, 1930) (in Tatar).

16. The ERK Party Program; see appendix E.

17. Quoted by Tobolev in *Kontrrivolütsiyon . . .*, p. 14.

18. *Premier Congrès des Peuples d'Orient, Baku 1920, Compte rendu Stenographique* (French translation) (Petrograd, 1921).

19. In *Kontrrivolütsiyon . . .* , p. 13.

20. See appendix C.

21. L. Rubinstein, *V bor'be za Leninskuiu Natsional'nuiu Politiku*, pp. 37–39.

22. *Zhizn' Natsional'nostei*, 39(47), 1919.

23. Ibid.

24. *Zhizn' Natsional'nostei*, 38(46), 1919.

25. *Zhizn' Natsional'nostei*, 42(50), 1919.

26. In the *Premier Congrès des Peuples de l'Orient*.

27. Enbaev, "Natsional'naia politika RKP (b)," *Izvestiia Tatarskogo Tsentral'nogo Ispolnitel'nogo Komiteta* (Kazan, 1922).

28. *Premier Congrès des Peuples de l'Orient.*

29. *Zhizn' Natsional'nostei*, 27(81), 1920.

30. Sultan Galiev, "K ob'iavleniu Azerbaidzhanskoi Sovetskoi Respubliki," *Zhizn' National'nostei*, 18(70), 1920.

31. *Zhizn' Natsional'nostei*, 1(58), 1920.

32. *Zhizn' Natsional'nostei*, 18 December 1918.

33. Sultan Galiev, "Tatarskaia Autonomnaia Respublika," *Zhizn' Natsional'nostei*, 1923, p. 25.

34. In a letter of Narimanov, quoted in *Bor'ba za pobedu sovetskoi vlasti v Azerbaidzhane 1918–1920* (Baku, 1967), p. 20.

35. G. Galoian, *Rabochie dvizhenie i natsional'nyi vopros v Zakavkaze* (Erevan, 1969), p. 314.

36. *Daghestan* (Moscow, 1924), pp. 117–18.

37. *Premier Congrès des Peuples de l'Orient.*

38. Ibid., pp. 172–73.

39. Ibid., p. 146.

40. Tobolev, in *Kontrrivolütsiyon*, p. 13.

41. A. Arsharuni in Kh. Gabidullin, *Ocherki Panislamizma i Pantiurkizma v Rossii* (Moscow, 1931), p. 89.

42. Tobolev in *Kontrrivolütsiyon*, p. 14.

43. In the Ukraine and in Georgia, for example, the fight for local autonomy generally was between local factions of Ukrainians and Georgians, some of whom were allied from the start with the Russian Communist party.

44. L. Rubinstein, *V bor' be za Leninskuiu Natsional' nuiu Politiku*, p. 52.

45. Muhariamov, *Oktiabr' i Natsional'nyi Vopros v Tatarii (Oktiabr' 1917– Iul'1918)* (Kazan, 1958), p. 242.

46. Almost at the same time, in April 1918, at the Taganrog Conference of the Ukrainian Communist party, the partisans of Ukrainian autonomy led by Mykola Skrypnik introduced a motion according to which the UCP (b) was to have its own Central Committee, and the connection between the UCP (b) and the RCP (b) was to be maintained only through an international commission of the Komintern. This motion was accepted by the conference.

47. In July 1918, the Central Committee of the RCP (b) established in Moscow a Ukrainian Communist party "as an integral and subordinate part of the RCP (b) and subject to its supervision."

48. *Istoriia Kommunisticheskikh Organizatsii Srednei Azii* (Tashkent, 1967), pp. 382–86.

49. *Izvestiia Ts. Kom. RKP (b)*, 2 March 1920.

50. *Istoriia Kommunisticheskikh Organizatsii Srednei Azii*, p. 426. The official *Ocherki Istorii Kommunisticheskoi Partii Kazakhstana* (Alma Ata, 1963), p. 202, describes Ryskolov's national program as follows:

    1. Formation of a Muslim Turkestani army; 2. Formation of a Turkic CP; 3. Expulsion of Russian and other "European" colonizers from Turkestan or at least limitation of their rights in using the land; 4. Creation of a federal union of all Turkic-Muslim territories of the Soviet Union, free of both West European capitalism and Soviet Russian imperialism.

51. The final liquidation of the autonomy of Ukrainian Communism took place at the same time. In March 1920, at the Fourth Conference of the CP (b) of the Ukraine in Kiev, the Central Committee of the RCP (b), intervening directly in Ukrainian affairs, dissolved the Ukrainian Central Committee and invited the Ukrainian Communists to "purge their Party of the petty bourgeois intellectual and semi-intellectual elements." This attack concerned, of course, the national communists.

52. Quoted by R. Nafigov, "Dieatel'nost' Tsentral'nogo Musul'manskogo kommissariata pri Narodnom Kommissariate po delam Natsional'nostei v 1918 godu," *Sovetskoe Vostokovedenie* (Moscow, 1958), pp. 105, 116.

53. Sultan Galiev, "Tatary i Oktiabr'skaia Revoliutsiia," *Zhizn' Natsional'-nostei*, 21(122), 1921.

54. *Kommunisticheskaia Partiia Sovetskogo Soiuza v rezoliutsiiakh i resheniiakh S'ezdov, Konferentsii i Plenymov Ts K. 1898–1960* (Moscow, 1954), 1:473.

55. Kharutdinov, "Organizatsiia i propaganiistskaia rabota tsentral'nogo Tataro-Bashkirskogo Kommissariata v zashchitu zavoevannii Velikoi Oktiab'skoi Sotsialisticheskoi Revolutsii," in *Deiatel'nost' Partiinoi Organizatsii Tatarii po Osushchestvleniu Leninskoi idei stroitel'stva sotsialisticheskogo Obschchestva* (Kazan, 1971), p. 48.

56. The attempt by the Jewish National Communist party to create purely Jewish military units parallels Sultan Galiev's attempt to create a Muslim Red Army. While the Bolsheviks encouraged Jews to join the regular units of the Red Army, the leaders of Poale Zion supported the idea of separate Jewish units in the Red Army which would become the vanguard of the Jewish social revolution. In the spring of 1919, the first Jewish Red units, named "Borochov units," were created in Minsk. This same year, leaders of Poale Zion were discussing the possibility of moving Jewish Red units from the Ukraine and Belorussia through the Black Sea and the Mediterranean "to bring the Socialist Revolution to Palestine and from there to the entire Middle East" (cf. Baruch Gurewitz, *National Communism in the Soviet Union*, p. 95).

57. Richard Pipes, *The Formation of the Soviet Union* (Cambridge, Mass., 1957), pp. 37–38, gives the best translation of Stalin's definition of a nation: a "historically evolved, stable community arising on the foundation of a common language, territory, economic life and psychological makeup, manifested in a community of culture."

58. Said Galiev, "Polozhenie o Tataro-Bashkirskoi Respublike," *Zhizn' Natsional'nostei*, 4(61), 1920.

59. See appendix E.

Chapter 4

1. Both German and Japanese authorities, in fact, have devoted some attention to this subject, although their interests generally tend to be more military than scholarly. Gerhard von Mende's *Der Nationale Kampf der Russlands in Turken* (Berlin, 1936) remains one of the best treatments of Islam in the USSR.

2. A number of Soviet periodicals, such as *Revolutsiia i Natsional'nosti* (Moscow, 1928–38), have gone largely unplumbed for the light which they shed on this crucial period.

3. L. Rubinstein, *V bor'be za leninskuiu Natsional'nuiu Politiku* (Kazan, 1930), p. 8.

4. V. I. Lenin, "The Socialist Revolution and the Right of Nations to Self-Determination," in *Collected Works*, English edition (Moscow, 1964), 22:146.

234 Notes to Pages 74–91

5. V. I. Lenin, "On the National Pride of the Great Russians," in *Collected Works*, English edition (Moscow, 1964), 21:105.

6. S. Dimanshtein, "Metody Revoliutsionnoi i Kommunisticheskoi propagandy na Vostoke," *Zhizn' Natsional' nostei*, 8(14), 1922.

7. Demetrio Boersner, *The Bolsheviks and the National and Colonial Questions (1917–1928)* (Geneva-Paris: 1957), p. 139.

8. Ibid., p. 137.

9. *Pravda*, 12 January 1921.

10. *Dvenadtsatyi S'ezd RKP (b)—Stenograficheskii Otchot* (Moscow, 1968), pp. 479–95—Stalin's report on the "national movement."

11. Ibid., pp. 591–94.

12. Ibid., pp. 598–601.

13. See appendix D.

14. Ibid.

15. Text in *Revoliutsiia i Natsional' nostei*, 11(1933):107–8.

16. Ibid.

17. *Pravda Vostoka* (Tashkent), 18 December 1934.

18. Robert C. Tucker and Stephen F. Cohn, eds., *The Great Purge Trial: Transcript of the Moscow Trial of Anti-Soviet Bloc of Rightists and Trotskyites* (New York, 1965), pp. 297, 305.

19. Ibid., p. 181.

20. Between February 1917 and the end of 1920, 258 newspapers were published in Russia/RSFSR in various "Muslim" languages. In this number, 139 were in Kazan Tatar. The Uzbek press came in second with 39 titles, followed by Kazakh with 37, and Crimean Tatar with 21. In 1935, Kazan Tatar had lost its preeminent position; it occupied second place with 203 titles. Uzbek took first place with 234. In 1960 Kazan Tatar, with 78 titles, occupied fourth place behind Kazakh (144), Uzbek (112), and Azeri (84) (cf. A. Bennigsen and Ch. Lemercier-Quelquejay, *La Presse et le Mouvement National chez les Musulmans de Russie avant 1920* [Paris, 1964], pp. 283–84).

21. Z. Muhsinov, "Dom Tatarskoi Kul'tury," in *Ocherki izucheniia mestnogo kraia* (Kazan, 1930), pp. 9–10. See also, Ayşe-Azade Rorlich, "Which Way Will Tatar Culture Go? A Controversial Essay by Galimdzhan Ibragimov," *Cahier du Monde Russe et Sovietique* 15 (1975): 363–91.

22. *Kontrrivolütsiyon Soltangäliefcheleke Karshy* (Kazan, 1930), pp. 32–33.

23. In 1933, Mykola Skrypnik, the leading Ukrainian national communist, committed suicide. After his death, the official *Pravda* (8 July 1933) explained his crimes in the following way:

> Comrade Skrypnik fell victim to the bourgeois-nationalist elements who, disguised as formal members of the Party, gained his confidence and exploited his name for their anti-Soviet, nationalist pur-

poses. Having become entangled with them, comrade Skrypnik committed a series of political errors and on realizing this he could not find the courage to overcome them in a Bolshevik manner and thus resorted to the act of suicide.

A more specific list of accusations appeared in the Party newspaper *Kommunist* (172, 1933):

1. He exaggerated the importance of the national problem, assigning to it an independent role and denying its dependence on the dictatorship of the proletariat.
2. He substituted the struggle against imperialist chauvinism for the struggle against two fronts in the realization of the nationality policy.
3. He regarded cultural construction as limited only by the national development.
4. He was also responsible for the introduction of forced Ukrainization in schools.
5. His attitude was harmfully nationalist on the questions of terminology and orthography which were leading to a break between the Ukrainian toiling masses and the language and culture of the toiling masses of Russia.

These accusations are almost identical with those launched at the same time against other national communists.

24. Abbas Baghirov, first secretary of the Central Committee of the Azerbaidzhani Communist party, in *Bakinskii Rabochi,* 8 December 1938. Baghirov himself was liquidated after Stalin's death as one of "Beria's henchmen," and Narimanov was posthumously rehabilitated.

Chapter 5

1. Maxime Rodinson, *Marxisme du Monde Musulman* (Paris, 1972), pp. 385–86.

2. Jamal Kamol, "Samarqandu Bukhara bu ... ," *Sharq Yulduzi* (Tashkent, 1969), 9:117; English translation by James Critchlow, "Signs of Emerging Nationalism in the Moslem Soviet Republics," in Norton T. Dodge, ed., *The Soviets in Asia* (Mechanicsville, Md., 1972), p. 19. The title of the Uzbek poem is inspired by the first verse of the very famous *ghazel* of Hafez:

   Agar ân Tork-e Shirazî . . .
   be-däst äräd del-e märä
   be häl-e hinduyesh bakhshäm Samarqand-o Bokhara-ro . . .

3. See Alexandre Bennigsen, "The Crisis of the Turkic National Epics, 1951–1952: Local Nationalism or Proletarian Internationalism?" *Canadian Slavonic Papers* 17 (1975): 463–74.

4. J. Critchlow, "Signs of Emerging Nationalism ... ," pp. 18–19.

5. M. Rodinson, *Marxisme du Monde Musulman,* p. 386.

6. See appendix F for a complete breakdown of Muslim ethnic groups in

terms of their percentage and numerical increase, 1959–70.

7. J. Critchlow, "Signs of Emerging Nationalism . . . ," p. 23.

8. Ibid., p. 27.

9. Ibid., pp. 24–26.

10. See Alexandre Bennigsen and S. Enders Wimbush, "Muslim Religious Dissent in the U.S.S.R.," in Richard T. DeGeorge and James P. Scanlan, eds., *Marxism and Religion in Eastern Europe* (Dordrecht, Holland and Boston, 1975), pp. 133–46.

11. See Tura Kamal, "Renewed Criticism of Sultan-Galievism," *Radio Liberty Research*, 19 March 1976; "The October Revolution and its falsifiers," *Sovet Mektebe*, vol. 11, 1975; and "Sultan Galiev and his Bourgeois Defenders," *Tatarstan Kommunisty*, vol. 1, 1975.

12. Arnold C. Brackman, *Indonesian Communism: A History* (New York, 1963), p. 27.

13. Ibid.

14. Alexandre Bennigsen and Chantal Lemercier Quelquejay, *Les Mouvements Nationaux chez les Musulmans de Russie: Le Sultan-Galievisme à Kazan* (Paris-La Haye, 1960).

15. *Newsweek*, 13 January 1964, p. 28.

16. Mao Tse-tung, "On New Democracy," in *Mao Tse-Tung: Selected Works* (New York: International Publishers, 1954), 3:153–54.

17. José Carlos Mariátegui, "Aniversario y balance," *Amauta*, vol. 17, 1928; quoted in Robert Paris, "José Carlos Mariátegui et le modèle du 'communisme inca,'" *Annales* 5 (1966): 1072.

18. Robert Paris in his preface to the French translation of José Carlos Mariátegui's *Siete ensayos de interpretacion de la realidad peruana* (Lima, 1958); translated by Roland Migrot and entitled *Sept Essais d'Interpretation de la Réalité Peruvienne* (Paris, 1968), p. 20.

19. José Carlos Mariátegui, "Intermezzo polemico," *Mundial*, 25 February 1927; quoted in R. Paris, *Annales*, p. 1072.

20. José Carlos Mariátegui, "El problema indigena," in *Bajo la bandera de la C. S. L. A.* (Montevideo, 1930); quoted in R. Paris, *Annales*, p. 1072.

21. Mao Tse-tung, "The Chinese Revolution and the Chinese Communist Party," in K. Fan, ed., *Post-revolutionary writings of Mao Tse-tung and Lin-Piao* (Garden City, N.Y., 1972), p. 374.

22. Lin Piao, "Long Live the Victory of the Peoples' War," in *Post-revolutionary writings* . . . , p. 377.

23. Ibid., p. 396.

24. Ibid., p. 409.

25. Ibid., p. 377.

26. *Conference of Heads of State and Governments of Nonaligned Countries: Cairo, 5–10 October 1964* (Cairo, 1964), p. 113.

27. *Newsweek,* 3 January 1964, p. 28.

28. Muammar al-Qaqhdhæafæ1, *Fī al-Nazarīyah al-thālithah* (The Third Theory) (Benghazi, 1974).

29. M. Rodinson, *Marxisme et Monde Musulman,* p. 326.

30. Quoted ibid., p. 387.

31. M. N. Roy, *Memoirs* (Bombay, 1964), p. 379.

32. M. Rodinson, *Marxisme et Monde Musulman,* p. 387.

Chapter 6

1. Ali Shari'yati, *Intizar, Madhab-e I'teraz* (Expectancy—Religion of Protest) (Tehran, 1350/1971).

2. *Revolution et Travail,* no. 73, 20 January 1965.

3. Speech of 28 February 1965, in David Ottaway and Marina Ottaway, *Algeria: The Politics of a Socialist Revolution* (Berkeley, Calif., 1970).

4. Hsiao Lou, "Five Years of Continual Backsliding: From the Soviet Revisionists' 24th Congress to their 25th Congress," *Peking Review,* 27 February 1976.

5. See, for example, the following *Peking Review* articles: "The New Tsars: Common Enemy of the People of All Nationalities in the Soviet Union" (4 July 1969); "Soviet Social-Imperialism Pursues a Policy of National Oppression" (28 May 1976). The Soviets launch a vigorous counterattack against these Chinese charges, including several books about how bad things are for China's minorities. See, for instance, M. I. Sladkovskii, ed., *Velikoderzhavnaia politika maoistov v natsional'nykh raionakh KNR* (Moscow, 1975).

6. I. R. Shaferevich, "Obosoblenie ili sblizhenie? (Natsional'nyi vopros v SSSR)," *Iz Pod Glyb* (Paris, 1974), p. 97.

7. Alexander Solzhenitsyn, "Raskaianie i samogranichenie kak kategorii natsional'noi zhizni," ibid., p. 141.

8. Albert Memmi, *The Colonizer and the Colonized* (New York, 1965), pp. 132–33.

Bibliography

Agabekov, George. *OGPU: The Russian Secret Terror*. New York: Brentano's, 1931.

Alba, Victor. *Historia del Communismo en America latina*. Mexico City: 1954.

Alikberov, G. A. "Bor'ba za Sovetskuiu Vlast' v Dagestane." In *Uchenye Zapiski Instituta Istorii, Iazyku i Literatury imeni G. Tsadasy*. Makhatch-Kala: 1960, vol. 8.

Allen, William E. D., and Muratoff, Paul. *Caucasian Battlefields: A History of the Wars on the Turco-Caucasian Border, 1828–1921*. Cambridge: Cambridge University Press, 1953.

Allworth, Edward, ed. *Central Asia: A Century of Russian Rule*. New York: Columbia University Press, 1967.

————. *The Nationality Question in Central Asia*. New York: F. Praeger, 1973.

————. *Uzbek Literary Politics*. New York: Humanities Press, 1964.

Al-Qadhdhāfi, Mu'ammar. *Al-Islām fi muwājahat al-'asr watahaddiyātih*. Cairo: Dār al-fikr al-'arabi, 1972.

————. *Al-Thawrah al-Sha 'bīyah*. Beirut: 1974.

————. *Fī al-Nazarīyah al-thālithah*. Bengazi: 1974.

————. *Qissat al-thawrah*. Beirut: Dar al-'awdah, 1974.

Antonius, G. *The Arab Awakening*. London: H. Hamilton, 1938.

Arkomed, S. T. *Materialy po Istorii Otpadeniia Zakavkazia ot Rossii*. Tiflis: 1923.

Armstrong, John. *The Politics of Totalitarianism*. New York: 1961.

Arsharuni, A. "Antireligioznaia propaganda na Sovetskom Vostoke." In *Kommunisticheskaia Revoliutsiia*. Moscow: 1929.

———. "Ideologiia Sultangalievshchiny," 1930.

Arsharuni, A., and Gabidullin, Kh. *Ocherki Panilamizma i Pantiurkizma v Rossii*. Moscow: Bezbozhnik, 1931.

Arzhanov. "Burzhuaznyi Natsionalizm-Orudie Podgotovki antisovetskikh interventov." *Revoliutsiia i Natsional'nosti* 8 (1934): 22–32.

Ashirov, Nugman. *Evoliutsiia Islama v SSSR*. Moscow: 1972.

———. *Islam i Natsii*. Moscow: Politizdat, 1975.

Ashurov, G., and Ismailova, R. "Leninskaia Natsional'naia Politika K.P.S.S. i ee Falsifikatory." *Izvestiia A.N. Tadzhikskoi SSSR—Otdelenie Obshchestvennykh Nauk* 2 (1973): 71–77.

Atnagulov, Salah. *Bashkiriia*. Moscow: 1925.

———. "Soltangaliefchelkeneng Tarikhi Tamyrlary" (The Historical Roots of Sultangalievism). In *Kontrrivolutsion Soltangaliefsheleke karshy*. Kazan: 1930, pp. 35–40.

Avtorkhanov, Abdurrahman. *K osnovnym Voprosam Istorii Chechni*. Groznyi: 1930.

——— *Revoliutsiia i Kontrrevoliutsiia v Chechne*. Groznyi: 1933.

———. *Stalin and the Soviet Communist Party*. London–New York: F. Praeger, 1959.

Aydemir, Şevket Süreyya. *Suyu arayan Adam*. 2d ed. Istanbul: 1965.

Bacon, Elizabeth E. *Central Asians under Russian Rule: A Study in Culture Change*. Ithaca: Cornell University Press, 1966.

Bagirov, M. D. *Iz Istorii Bol'shevistskoi Organizatsii Baku i Azerbaidzhana*. Moscow: 1946.

Bagramov, E. *Natsional'nyi Vopros i burzhuaznaia Ideologiia*. Moscow: 1966.

Baibulatov, J. *Chagataizm-Pantiurkizm v uzbekskoi Literature*. Moscow-Tashkent: 1932.

Baichurin, G. "Piatnadtsat' let ordenonosnoi Tatarskoi Avtonomnoi Respubliki." *Revoliutsiia i Natsional'nosti* 6 (1935): 31–36.

Bammate, Haidar. *The Caucasian Problem*. Bern: 1919.

Banani, Amin. *The Modernization of Iran, 1921–1941*. Stanford: Stanford

University Press, 1961.

Battal-Taymas, Abdulla. *Kazan Türkleri-Tarikhi ve Siyasi Görüşler*. Istanbul: 1925.

——. *Musa Carullah Bigi*. Istanbul: 1958.

——. *Rus Ihtilâlinden Hatıralar*. Istanbul: 1947.

Baudin, Louis. *L'Empire Socialiste des Incas*. Paris: 1968.

——. "Siete ensayos de interpretación de la realidad peruana, par José Carlos Mariátegui." *Revue de l'Amerique Latine* 19 (1930): 550–65.

Bauer, Otto. "Nationalitetenfrage und die Sozialdemokratie." In *Marx-Studien: II*. Vienna: 1907.

Beilin, A. "Byt' bditel'nym i zorkim." *Revoliutsiia i Natsional'nosti* 9 (1936): 12–21.

Belen'kii, S., and Manvelov, A. *Revoliutsiia 1917 v Azerbaidzhana*. Baku: 1927.

Bennigsen, Alexandre. "Sultan Galiev, the USSR and the Colonial Revolution." In *Middle East in Transition*, edited by W. Z. Laqueur. New York: F. Praeger, 1958, pp. 398–415.

——. "The Crisis of the Turkic National Epics: 1951–1952: Local Nationalism or Internationalism?" *Canadian Slavic Papers* 18 (1975): 463–75.

Bennigsen, Alexandre, and Lemercier-Quelquejay, Chantal. *Islam in the Soviet Union*. New York–London: Pall-Mall–F. Praeger, 1967.

Bennigsen, Alexandre, and Quelquejay, Chantal. "Der Sultangalievismus und die nationalistischen Abweichungen in der Tatarischen Autonomen Sowjetrepublic." *Forschungen zur Osteuropaische Geschichte* 8 (1959): 323–96.

——. *Les Mouvements Nationaux chez les Musulmans de Russie: I. Le "Sultangalievisme" au Tatarstan*. Paris–La Haye: Mouton, 1960.

——. *The Evolution of the Muslim Nationalities of the USSR and their Linguistic Problems*. London: Central Asian Research Center, 1961.

Bennigsen, Alexandre, and Wimbush, S. Enders. "Muslim Religious Dissent in the USSR." In *Marxism and Religion in Eastern Europe*, edited by Richard T. DeGeorge and James P. Scanlan. Dordrecht-Boston: R. Reidel, 1975, pp. 133–46.

Benzing, J. *Turkestan*. Berlin: 1943.

Beria, Lavrentii. *K Voprosu ob Istorii bol'shevitskikh Organizatsii v Zakavkaze*. Moscow: 1948.

Berkes, Niyazi. *The Development of Secularism in Turkey*. Montreal: McGill University Press, 1964.

Bigi, Musa İarullah. *Eslahat Esaslary* (The Basis of the Reform). Petrograd: 1915–17.

Bikbaev, N. "Bor'ba s Validovshchinoi v Bashkirii." *Revoliutsiia i Natsional'nosti* 4 (1935): 88–94.

Binder, Leonard. *Iran: Political Development in a Changing Society.* Berkeley–Los Angeles: University of California Press, 1962.

Biulleten' Chetvertogo S'ezda Sovetov Tatarskoi Sotsialisticheskoi Sovetskoi Respubliki, 17–24 Dekabria 1923 goda. Kazan: Tatizdat, 1923.

Bloom, S. F. *The World of Nations: A Study of the National Implications in the Work of Karl Marx.* New York: Columbia University Press, 1941.

Bochagov, A. K. *Milli Firka.* Simferopol: 1930.

Bochkov, A. I. *Tri Goda Sovetskoi Vlasti v Kazani (1917–1920).* Kazan: 1921.

Boersner, Demetrio. *The Bolsheviks and the National and Colonial Question (1917–1928).* Geneva-Droz-Paris: Minard, 1957.

"Bol'sheviki Tatarii v Bor'be za Razgrom Kolchaka." *Istoricheskii Arkhiv* 5 (1958): 99–122.

Bor'ba za Kazan'—Sbornik Materialov o Chekho-Uchredilovskoi Interventsii v 1918 godu. Kazan: Tatizdat, 1924.

Bor'ba za Pobedu sovetskoi Vlasti v Azerbaidzhane—1918–1920— Dokumenty i Materialy. Baku: 1967.

Bor'ba za Ustanovlenie i Uprochnenie sovetskoi Vlasti v Dagestane—1917– 1920—Sbornik Dokumentov i Materialov. Moscow: Academy of Science, 1958.

Borisenko, I. *Sovetskie Respubliki na severnom Kavkaze v 1918 godu.* Rostov on the Don: 1930.

Borozdin, I. N. "Sovremennyi Tatarstan." *Novyi Vostok* 10–11 (1925): 118–37.

Borys, Jurii. *The Russian Communist Party and the Sovietization of Ukraine.* Stockholm: 1960.

Bozhko, F. *Oktaibr'skaia Revoliutsiia v Srednei Azii.* Tashkent: 1932.

Brackman, Arnold C. *Indonesian Communism: A History.* New York: F. Praeger, 1963.

Brainin, S., and Shapiro, Sh. *Ocherki po Istorii Alash-Ordy.* Alma-Ata: Kazkraiizdat, 1935.

———. *Pervye Shagi Sovetov v Semirech'i.* Alma-Ata–Moscow: 1934.

Braker, Hans. *Kommunismus und Weltreligionen Asiens, zur Religions und Asienpolitik der Sowjetunion.* 2 vols. *Kommunismus und Islam.* Tübingen: J. C. B. Mohr, 1969–71.

Brand, Conrad; Schwartz, Benjamin; and Fairbank, John K. *A Documentary History of Chinese Communism*. London: Allen and Unwin, 1952.

Brzezinski, Zbigniew. *The Permanent Purge*. Cambridge, Mass.: 1956.

Bubenov, M., and Valeev, A. *Osvobozhdenie Kazani ot Belo-Interventov v 1918 godu*. Kazan: 1939.

Bunegin, M. *Revoliutsiia i grazhdanskaia Voina v Krymu*. Simferopol: 1927.

Burmistrova, T. Iu. *Teoriia sotsialisticheskoi Natsii*. Leningrad: Leningrad University Press, 1970.

Bütün Russia Müsülmanlarynyng 1917-nchi iylda, 1–11 Maida Meskvede bulgan umumi Isiezdining Protokollary (Protocols of the Pan-Russian Congress of the Muslims in Moscow, 1–11 May 1917). Petrograd: 1917.

Capanoğlu, Munir Süleyman. *Türkiyede Sosyalizm Haraketleri ve Sosyalist Hilmi*. Istanbul: 1964.

Carr, E. H. *Socialism in One Country*. 3 vols. London: 1958–64.

Carrère d'Encaussee, Helène. *Reforme et Revolution chez les Musulmans de l'Empire Russe-Bukhara, 1867–1924*. Paris: A. Colin, 1966.

Castagné, Joseph. "Le Bolchevisme et l'Islam." *Revue du Monde Musulman*, vol. 51, 1922.

———. *Le Turkestan depuis la Revolution russe (1917–1921)*. Paris: 1922.

Cerrahoğlu, A. *Islâmiyet ve Osmanli Sosyalistleri; Islâmiyet ve yöncü Sosyalistler*. Istanbul: 1964.

———. *Türkiyede Sosyalizm*. 2 vols. Istanbul: 1965–66.

Chanyshev, Iakub. "Soltangäliefchelkeneng jimerelie" (The Destruction of Sultangalievism). In *Kontrrivolutsion Soltangaliefsheleke karshy*. Kazan: 1930, pp. 51–55.

Chokaev, Mustafa. "The Basmaji Movement in Turkestan." *Asiatic Review* 24 (1928): 273–88.

Chokay, Mustafa. *Turkestan pod Vlast'iu Sovetov*. Paris: 1935.

Coates, W. P. *Soviets in Central Asia*. London: Lawrence and Wishart, 1951.

Colotti-Pischel, Enrica, and Robertazzi, Chiara. *L'Internationale Communiste et les Problemes Coloniaux, 1919–1935*. Paris-La Haye: Mouton, 1968.

Conker, Orhan. *Turk-Rus Savaşlari*. Ankara: Sümer Basimevi, 1942.

Connolly, Violet. *Beyond the Urals*. London: 1967.

Conquest, Robert. *The Great Terror: Stalin's Purge of the Thirties*. New York: Macmillan, 1968.

Critchlow, James. "Signs of Emerging Nationalism in the Moslem Soviet Republics." In *The Soviets in Asia*, edited by Norton T. Dodge. Mechanicsville, Md.: Cremona Foundation, 1972, pp. 18–29.

————. "Uzbeks and Russians." *Canadian Slavonic Papers* 17 (1975): 366–74.

Davis, Horrace B. *Nationalism and Socialism, Marxist and Labour Theories of Nationalism to 1917.* New York: Monthly Review Press, 1967.

Davletshin, T. *Cultural Life in the Tatar Autonomous Republic.* New York: Research Program on the USSR, 1953.

Davletshin, Tamurbek. *Sovetskii Tatarstan.* London: Our World Publishers, 1974.

Davydov, S.; Dinmuhammedov, A.; Mahmudov, S.; and Fattakhov, N. "Ozdorovit' tatarskuiu Leteraturu." *Revoliutsiia i Natsional'nostei* (1931): 101–6.

Degras, Jane, ed. *The Communist International, 1919–1943.* Oxford: Royal Institute of International Affairs–Oxford University Press, 1956.

Deiatel'nost' Partiinoi Organizatsii Tatarii po Osushchestvleniu leninskoi Idei Stroitel'stva sotsialisticheskogo Obshchestva. Kazan: University Press, 1971.

Der erste Kongress der K.I. Protokoll der Verhandlung in Moskau vom 2 bis zum 19 Maerz 1919. Hamburg: Verlag des K.I. (Hoym), 1921.

Der zweite Kongress der K.I. Protokoll der Verhandlung vom 19 Juli in Petrograd und vom 23 Juli bis 7 August in Moskau. Hamburg: Verlag des K.I. (Hoym), 1921.

Desiatiletie sovetskogo Tatarstana (1920–1930). Kazan: Tatizdat, 1930.

Desiat' let soitsialisticheskogo Stroitel'stva v Tatarstane (1920–1930)— Sbornik. Kazan: Tatizdat, 1930.

Devletshin, G. "Klassovaia bor'ba v bashkirskoi khudozhestvennoi Literature." *Literatura i Iskustvo* 2–3 (1930): 136–51.

Dimanshtein, S. "Bashkiriia v 1918–1920 gg." *Proletarskaia Revoliutsiia* 5 (1928): 138–57.

————. "Metody revoliutsionnoi i kommunisticheskoi propagandy na Vostoke." *Zhizn' Natsional'nostei,* 8 (14), 1922.

————. *Natsional'naia Politika VKP (b) v Tsifrakh.* Moscow: 1930.

————. *Revoliutsiia i natsional'nyi Vopros,* vol. 3. Moscow: Communisticheskaia Adademiia, 1930.

————, ed. *Itogi Razresheniia natsional'nogo Voprosa v SSSR.* Moscow: 1936.

Druhe, David N. *Soviet Russia and Indian Communism.* New York: Bookman, 1959.

Dubner, A. *Bakinskii Proletariat v gody Revoliutsii (1917–1920).* Baku: 1931.

Dulatov, Mir-Yakub. "Ahmed Baitursun." In *Trudy Obshchestva Izucheniia Kirgizskogo Kraia*. Kzyl-Orda: 1922, vol. 3.

Dunsterville, General L. C. *The Adventure of Dunsterforce*. London: 1920.

Durocq, G. "Le Bolchevisme en Perse." *Revue du Monde Musulman*, vol. 51, 1922.

Dutt, V. P. *China and the World: An Analysis of Communist China's Foreign Policy*. New York: F. Praeger, 1966.

Dvadtsat' let Tatarskoi ASSR. Kazan: Tatgosizdat, 1940.

Dvenadtsatyi S'ezd R.K.P. (b), 17–25 Aprelia 1923 goda—Stenograficheskii Otchet. Moscow: Institut Marksizma-Leninizma, 1968.

Efendiev-Samurskii, N. "Persidskie lesnye Brat'ia." *Zhizn' Natsional'nostei*, 30 (38), 1919.

————. "Vroz' itti, vmeste bit' " (O vozmozhnosti ispol'zovaniia torgovoi Burzhuazii, Natsionalistov i drugikh sotsial'nykh elementov Vostoka v bor'be s Imperializmom). *Zhizn' Natsional'nostei*, 26 (34)–27 (35), 1919.

Eidus, Khaim T. *Ocherki rabochego Dvizheniia v Stranakh Vostoka*. Moscow: 1922.

Elagin, V. "Natsionalisticheskie iliuzii Krymskikh Tatar revoliutsionnye Gody." *Novyi Vostok* 5 (1924): 190–216; (1924): 205–25.

Emirov, N. *Ustanovlenie sovetskoi Vlasti v Dagestane i Bor'ba s germano-turetskimi Interventami 1917–1919 gg*. Moscow: 1949.

Enbaev. "Natsional'naia Politika R.K.P. (b)." *Izvestia Tatarskogo Tsentral'nogo Ispolnitel'nogo Komiteta*, 25 June 1922.

Eudin, Xenia, and North, Robert. *Russia and the East: 1920–1927: A Documentary Survey*. Palo Alto: Stanford University Press, 1964.

Ezhov, N. *Voennaia Kazan' v 1917 godu*. 2d ed. Kazan: 1957.

Faizullin, G. "Motivy Raskhozhdeniia Sultan Galieva s Partiei." *Vestnik Instituta po Izucheniiu Istorii i Kul'tury SSSR* 12 (1945): 58–65.

Faseev, K. F. *Iz Istorii tatarskoi peredovoi obshchestvennoi Mysli-Vtoraia Polovina XIX-nachalo XX veka*. Kazan: Tatknigoizdat, 1955.

Fedorov, E. *Ocherki natsional'no-osvoboditel'nogo Dvizheniia v Srednei Azii*. Tashkent: Uzgiz, 1925.

Fischer, H. H. *The Communist Revolution: An Outline of Strategy and Tactics*. Stanford: Hoover Institute, 1955.

Fischer, L. *The Soviets in World Affairs: A History of the Relations between the Soviet Union and the Rest of the World, 1917–1929*. 2 vols. Princeton: Princeton University Press, 1927.

Gabidullin, Kh. *Tatarstan za sem let (1920–1927)*. Kazan: Tatizdat, 1927.

Gabidullin, R. M. *Tridtsat' let Tatarskoi ASSR*. Kazan: Tatknigoizdat, 1950.

Gainullin, M. H. "Gafur Kulakhmetov: 1881–1918." *Izvestiia Kazanskogo Filiala Akademii Nauk SSSR* 1 (1955): 53–67.

Gainullin, M., and Vasieva, Z. *Tatar Adabiaty XX djzoz* (Tatar Literature in the Twentieth Century). 2 vols. Kazan: 1954.

Galoian, G. *Rabochee Dvizhenie i Natsional' nyi Vopros v Zakavkaze*. Erevan: 1969.

Galuzo, P. G. *Turkestan-Koloniia*. Moscow: KUTVa, 1929.

Galuzo, P. G., and Bozhko, F., eds. *Vostanie 1916 goda v Srednei Azii-Sbornik Statei*. Moscow-Tashkent: 1932.

Gankin, O. H., and Fischer, H. H. *The Bolsheviks and the World War: The Origins of the Third International: Collection of Documents*. Stanford: Hoover Institute, 1940.

Ganuev, D. "Imperiia Uzun Khadzhi." *Novyi Vostok*, vols. 4–5, 1928.

Gasanov, G., and Sarkisov, N. "Sovetskaia Vlast' v Baku v 1918 godu." *Istorik Marksist* 5 (1938): 32–70.

Gasanov, S. M. *Osushchestvlenie v Dagestane leninskikh Idei nekapitalis-ticheskogo Razvitiia ranee ostalykh Stran i Naradov*. Makhatch-Kala: 1970.

Gasprinski, Ismail. *Russko-Musul'manskoe Soglashenie-Mysli, Zametki, Pazhelaniia*. Baghchesaray: 1896.

———. *Russkoe Musul'manstvo-Mysli, Zametki i Nabliudeniia Musul'-manina*. Simferopol: 1881.

Gaven, Iu. "Krymskie Tatary i Revoliutsiia," *Zhizn' Natsional' nostei*, 48 (56) and 49 (57), 1919.

Gimranov. *Iapazitsiege karshy-Faktlar häm Sanlar* (Against the Opposition: Facts and Data). Kazan: 1927.

Ginsburg, S. B. "Basmachestvo v Bukhare." *Novyi Vostok* 10–11 (1925): 175–202.

Gökgöl, Cengiz. *Komunist Rusya ve Müslümanlar*. Ankara: Yeni Matbaa, 1958.

Goloshchekin, Filip. *Partiinoe Stroetel'stvo v Kazakhstane*. Moscow: 1930.

Grachev, E. *Kazanskii Oktaibr'*. Kazan: Tatizdat, 1926.

Grassis, Karl. *K natsional' nomu Voprosu*. Kazan: 1918.

———. "K Tataro-Bashkirskomu Voprosu." *Zhizn' Natsional' nostei*, 5 (61), 1920.

Griffith, William E. *The Sino-Soviet Rift*. Cambridge: MIT Press, 1967.

Grishko, V. "The Establishment of a Soviet Volga Tatar State." *East Turkic Review* 1 (1958): 43–68.

Groshev, I. I., and Shaumian, S. S. *Osushchestvlenie Printsipov Internat-*

sionalizma v natsional' noi Politike KPSS. Moscow: Mysl, 1975.

Gumanenko, A. *Oktiabr' v starom gorode Samarkande*. Tashkent: 1933.

Gurewitz, Baruch. "National Communism in the Soviet Union, 1918–1928." Ph.D. dissertation, University of Rochester, 1973.

Ibragimov, Galimjan. *Tatar Madaniyetine nindi yol blän barajaq?* (Which Way Will Tatar Culture Go?). Kazan: 1927.

————. *Tatary v Revoliutsii 1905 goda*. Kazan: Kazan University Press, 1926.

————. *Ural häm Uralchylar*. Kazan: 1926.

Inoiatov, Kh. Sh. *Central Asia and Kazakhstan before and after the October Revolution (Reply to Falsifiers of History)*. Moscow: Progress Publishers, 1967.

————. *Leninskaia natsional' naia Politika v Deistvii-(Otvet Ideologam antikommunizma, izvrashchaiushchim istoricheskii Opyt Stroitel' stva Sotsializma v Respublikakh Srednei Azii i Kazakhstana)*. Tashkent: "Uzbekistan," 1973.

————. *Towards Freedom and Progress (The Triumph of Soviet Power in Central Asia*. Moscow: 1970.

Iranskii. "Cherez voennuiu Diktaturu k natsional'nomu Gosudarstvu." *Novyi Vostok* 5 (1924): 101.

Iskenderov, M. S. *Iz Istorii Bor' by Kommunisticheskoi Partii Azerbaidzhana za Pobedu sovetskoi Vlasti*. Baku: Azgosizdat, 1958.

Iskhaki, Gayaz. *Idel-Ural*. Paris: 1933.

Istoria kommunisticheskikh Organizatsii Srednei Azii. Tashkent: 1967.

Istoriia K.P. (b) U. 2 vols. Kiev: 1933.

Istoria partiinogo Stroitel' stva v Kazakhstane. Alma-Ata: 1936.

Istoria Uzbekskoi SSSR (1917–1937), vol. 3. Tashkent: Academy of Uzbekistan, Institute of History and Archeology, 1967.

Istoricheskii Opyt Stroitel' stva Sotsializma v Respublikakh Srednei Azii. Moscow: 1965.

Istpartotdel. *Atkivnye Bortsy za sovetskuiu Vlast' v Azerbaidzhane*. Baku: Azgosizdat, 1957.

Istpartotdel Tatarskogo Obkoma. *Tataria v Bor' be za proletarskuiu Revoliutsiiu, Fevral' –Octiabr' 1917*. Kazan: 1957.

"Iz Deiatel'nosti Narkomnatza—Tatarskii (Musul'manskii) Otdel Narkomnatza za tri goda ego Sushchestvovaniia." *Zhizn' Natsional' nostei*, 41 (97) and 42 (98), 1920.

Iz Materialov i Dokumentov po natsional' nomu Voprosu i Organizatsii. Vestnik Nauchnogo Obshchestva Tatarovedenia 3 (1925): 29–39.

Jaeschke, G. "Der Turanismus der Junatuerken." *Die Welt des Islams* 23 (1941): 1–54.

———. "Die Republik Aserbeidschan." *Die Welt des Islams* 23 (1941): 55–69.

James, C. L. R. *World Revolution, 1917–1936: The Rise and Fall of the Communist International.* London: 1937.

Jansky, H. "Die tuerkische Revolution and der russische Islam." *Der Islam* 18 (1929): 158–67.

Karabekir, Kâzim. *Istiklâl Harbimiz.* Istanbul: 1960.

Kasymov, G. "Kul'tura Mas'alasynda Soltangaliefchelek" (Sultangalievism in Cultural Affairs). In *Kontrrivolutsion Soltangaliefsheleke karshy.* Kazan: 1930, pp. 65–68.

———. *Ocherki po religioznomu i antireligioznomu Dvizheniiu sredi Tatar do i posle Revoliutsii.* Kazan: Tatizdat, 1932.

———. *Pantiurkskaia Kontrrevoliutsiia i ee Agentura-Sultangalievshchina.* Kazan: Tatizdat, 1931.

———. *Soltangaliefchelek ham anyng tarikhi Tamyrlary* (Sultangalievism and Its Historical Roots). Kazan: Tatizdat, 1930.

Kazanbiev, M. A. *Sozdanie i Ukreplenie natsional'noi Gosudarstvennosti Narodov Dagestana.* Makhatch-Kala: 1970.

Kazanly, H. "The Sultan-Galiev Movement after 1923." *East Turkic Review,* vol. 4, 1960.

Kazanskaia Bol'shevistskaia Organizatsiia v 1917 godu. Kazan: Tatgosizdat, 1933.

Kazemzadeh, Firuz. *The Struggle for Transcaucasia (1917–1921).* New York: 1951.

Kaziev, M. *Nariman Narimanov-Zhizn' i Deiatel'nost'.* Baku: Azgosizdat, 1970.

Keddie, Nikki R. *Sayyid Jamal ad-Din "Al-Afghani." A Political Biography.* Berkeley–Los Angeles: University of California Press, 1972.

Kenzhin, A. "Kirgizy i Oktiabr'skaia Revoliutsiia." *Zhizn' Natsional'nostei,* 24 (122), 1921.

Khairov, N. "Pobednyi Put' Latinizatsii v Tatarii." *Revoliutsiia i Natsional'nosti* 7 (1933): 66–70.

Khasanov, M. Kh. *Galimdzhan Ibragimov.* Kazan: 1969.

Khidoiatov, G. *Pravda protiv Lzhi.* Tashkent: 1964.

Khodorovskii, I. I. *Chto takoe Tatarskaia Sovetskaia Respublika.* Kazan: Tatizdat, 1920.

Khojaev, Fayzullah. *Desiat' let Bor'by i Stroitel'stva.* Samarkand-Tashkent: Uzgosizdat, 1927.

————. *Desiat' let pobed (K desiatiletiiu Sovetskogo Uzbekistana)*. Tashkent: Uzgosizdat, 1935.

————. *Istoriia Revoliutsii v Bukhare i Razmezhevenie Srednei Azii*. Tashkent: Uzgosizdat, 1932.

————. *K Istorii Revoliutsii v Bukhare*. Tashkent: Uzgosizdat, 1926.

————. "O Mladoburkhartsakh." *Istorik Marksist* 1 (1926): 123–41.

————. *O vazhneishykh Zadachakh nashego Stroitel'stva*. Tashkent: Uzgosizdat, 1934.

————. *Uzbekistan na Pod'eme*. Tashkent: Uzgosizdat, 1936.

Khojanov, S. *K desiatiletiiu sovetskoi Avtonomii Turkestana*. Tashkent: 1928.

Khudadov, V. N. "Sovremennyi Azerbaidzhan." *Novyi Vostok* 3 (1923): 167–89.

Kirimal, Edighe. *Der Nationale Kampf des Krimtuerken mit besonderer Beruecksichtigung der Jahre 1917–1918*. Emsdetten: 1952.

Kirimer [Cafer Seydahmet]. *Rus Inkilâbi*. Istanbul: Cumhuriyet Matbaasi, 1930.

Klimovich, L. I. *Islam*. Moscow: Nauka, 1965.

————. *Islam v Tsarskoi Rossii*. Moscow: Gosudarstvennoe Antireligioznoe Izdatel'stvo, 1936.

————. "Religiznoe Dvizhenie v Tatarskoi Respubliks." *Antireligioznik,* vol. 4, 1927.

————. *Sotsialisticheskoe Stroitel'stvo na Vostoke i Religiia*. Moscow: Moskovskii Rabochi, 1929.

Kobetskii, M. "Sultangalievshchina kak Apologiia Islama." *Antireligioznik,* vol. 1, 1930.

Köcherli, Feridun. *Näriman Närimanov-Häyaty, Fäalijati vä Dünyakörüshu*. Baku: Academy of Science of RSS of Azerbaidzhan, 1965.

Kohn, Hans. *A History of Nationalism in the East*. New York: Harcourt Brace & Co., 1929.

Kolarz, Walter. *Communism and Colonialism*. London: 1964.

Kommunisticheskaia Partiia Sovetskogo Soiuza v Rezoliutsiiakh i Resheniiakh S'ezdov, Konferentsii i Plenumov Ts.K.—1898–1960. 7th ed. 4 vols. Moscow: 1954–60.

Kontrrivolutsiyon Soltangäliefcheleke karshy (Against the Counterrevolutionary Sultangalievism). Kazan: 1930.

Korbut, M. R. "Natsional'noe Dvizhenie v Volzhsko-Kamskom Krae v 1917 godu-Natsional'nye S'ezdy v Period Vremennogo Pravitel'stva." *Revoliutsionnyi Vostok* 8 (1929): 168—210.

Kostiuk, Hrihory. *Stalinist Rule in Ukraine*. Munich: 1960.

Kuramysov, I. *Za leninskuiu natsional'nuiu Politiku v Kazakhstane*. Alma-Ata–Moscow: 1932.

Kurat, Akdes Nimet, and Temir, Ahmed. "Rulsya'da Türklük ve Islâmiyet." In *Türk Dünyasl El Kitabi*. Ankara: 1976, pp. 1295–1303.

Lacheraf, Mostefa. *L'Algerie, Nation et Societé*. Paris: F. Maspero, 1965.
Laqueur, Walter Z. *Communism and Nationalism in the Middle East*. New York: 1956.
————. *Soviet Union and the Middle East*. London: Routledge & Kegan Paul, 1959.
Laqueur, Walter Z., ed. *The Middle East in Transition: Studies in Contemporary History*. New York: F. Praeger, 1958.
Laroi, A. *L'Ideologie Arabe Contemporaine*. Paris: F. Maspero, 1967.
Lenczowski, George. *Russia and the West in Iran, 1918–1948: A Study in Great Power Rivalry*. Ithaca: Cornell University Press, 1949.
Letifov, A. L. *Voznikovenie i Razvitie sovetskoi natsional'noi Gosudarstvennosti Narodov Dagestana*. Makhatch-Kala: 1968.
Lewis, Robert; Rowland, Richard; and Clem, Ralph. "Modernization, Population Change and Nationality in Soviet Central Asia and Kazakhstan." *Canadian and Slavonic Papers* 17 (1975): 286–301.

McVey, Ruth T. *The Rise of Indonesian Communism*. Ithaca: Cornell University Press, 1965.
————. *The Development of the Indonesian Communist Party and its Relations with the Soviet Union and the Chinese People's Republic*. Cambridge: MIT Press, 1954.
Magerovski, D. A. *Soiuz Sovetskikh, Sotsialisticheskikh Respublik (Obzor i Materialy)*. Moscow: 1923.
Maier, A., ed. *Boevye Epizody-Basmachestvo v Bukhare*. Moscow-Tashkent: 1934.
Maiskii, Ivan. *Vneshnaia Politika RSFSR, 1917–1922*. Moscow: 1923.
Manatov, Sherif. "Bashkirskaia Avtonomnaia Respublika." *Zhizn' Natsional'nostei*, vol. 1, 1923, pp. 40–45.
Manzhara, D. I. *Revoliutsionnoe Dvizhenie v Srednei Azii, 1905–1920gg (Vospominaniia)*. Tashkent: Sredazpartizdat, 1934
Mariátegui, José-Carlos. *Siete ensayos de interpretación de la realidad peruana*. Lima: Biblioteca Amauta, 1958. French translation by Roland Mignot, with a preface by Robert Paris. *Sept Essais d'Interpretation de la Réalité Peruvienne*. Paris: F. Maspero, 1968.
Masani, Minoo R. *The Communist Party of India*. New York: Macmillan Co., 1954.
Mehnert, Klaus. *Stalin vs. Marx: The Stalinist Historical Doctrine*. London: 1952.

Mel'nikov, G. N. *Oktiabr' v Kazakhstane.* Alma-Ata: 1930.

Memmi, Albert. *The Colonizer and the Colonized.* New York: Orion Press, 1965.

Mende, Gerhardt von. *Der nationale Kampf des Russlantuerkan.* Berlin: Weidman, 1936.

Mindlin, Z. "Kirgizy i Revoliutsia." *Novyi Vostok* 5 (1924): 217–29.

Mintz, Jeanne S. *Mohammed, Marx and Marhaen: The Roots of Indonesian Socialism.* New York: F. Praeger, 1965.

Mirza Bala, and Mehmet Zade. *Milli Azerbaycan Hareketi.* Berlin: 1938.

Mordzhinskaia, E. D. *Leninizm i sovremennaia ideologicheskaia Bor'ba.* Moscow: 1970.

Mostovenko, P. "O bol'shikh Oshibkakh v maloi Bashkirii." *Proletarskaia Revoliutsiia* 5 (1928): 103–37.

Mukhariamov, M. K. *Iz Istorii inostrannoi Interventsii i grazhdanskoi Voiny v Tatarii.* Kazan: Tatizdat, 1954.

———. *Oktiabr' i natsional'nyi Vopros v Tatarii-Oktiabr' 1917–Iul' 1918.* Kazan: Tatknigoizdat, 1958.

Mukhsinov, Z. "Dom tatarskoi Kul'tury." In *Ocherki Izucheniia Mestnogo Kraia.* Kazan: 1930.

Murtazin, M. L. *Bashkiriia i bashkirskie Voiska v Grazhdanskuiu Voinu.* Leningrad: 1927.

Nafigov, G. N. *Mullanur Vakhitov-Istoricheskii-biografıcheskii ocherk.* Kazan: 1960.

Nafigov, R. "Deiatel'nost' Tsentral'nogo Musul'manskogo Komissariata pri Narodnom Komissariate po delam Natsional'nostei v 1918 g." *Sovetskoe Vostokovedenie,* vol. 5, 1958.

Narimanov, Nariman. "Nasha Politika v Turkestane." *Zhizn' Natsional'nostei,* 9 (66), 1920.

Narodnyi Kommissariat po natsional'nym Delam. *Politika sovetskoi Vlasti po natsional'nomu Voprosu za tri goda, 1917–1920.* Moscow: Gosizdat, 1920.

Natsional'nyi Vopros i Sovetskaia Rossiia. Moscow: Narkomnatz, 1921.

Nemchenko, M. *Natsional'noe Razmezhevanie v Srednei Azii.* Moscow: 1925.

Nollau, Gunther, and Wiehe, Hans Jurgen. *Russia's South Flank: Soviet Operations in Iran, Turkey and Afghanistan.* New York: 1963.

Nove, A., and Newth, G. A. *The Soviet Middle East: A Model for Development?* London: 1967.

Novoselov, K. *Protiv burzhuaznykh Fal'sifikatorov Istorii Srednei Azii.* Ashkhabad: 1962.

Obrazovanie Kazakhskoi ASSR. Alma-Ata: Academy of Science, 1957.
Obrazovanie SSSR—1917–1923. Moscow: 1939.
Ocherki Istorii Kommunisticheskoi Partii Azerbaidzhana. Baku: 1963.
Ocherki Istorii Kommunisticheskoi Partii Gruzii. Tbilisi: 1963.
Ocherki Istorii Kommunisticheskoi Partii Kazakhstana. Alma-Ata: 1963.
Ocherki Istorii Kommunisticheskoi Partii Ukrainy. Kiev: 1964.
Ocherki po Istorii Komsomola Tatarii. Kazan: Tatknigoizdat, 1960.
Olscha, R., and Cleinow, G. *Turkestan*. Leipzig: 1942.
O Obrazovanii Bashkirskoi Avtonomnoi Sovetskoi Sotsialisticheskoi Respubliki. Ufa: Bashkir Branch of the Academy of Science, 1959.
Ordzhonikidze, G. K. *Izbrannye Stat'i i Rechi, 1911–1937*. Moscow: 1939.
Otchet Narodnogo Komissariata po Delam Natsional'nostei za 1921 god. Moscow: Narkomnats, 1921.
Ottaway, David, and Ottaway, Marina. *Algeria: The Politics of a Socialist Revolution*. Berkeley–Los Angeles: University of California Press, 1970.

Pakdaman, Homa. *Djamal ed-Din Assad Abadi dit Afghani*. Paris: G. P. Maisonneuve, 1969.
"Panislamizm ik Pantiurkizm." *Novyi Vostok* 2 (1913): 556–71, 596–619.
Paris, Robert. "José-Carlos Mariátegui et le Modèle du 'Communisme Inca.'" *Annales* 5 (1966): 1065–72.
Park, Alexander G. *Bolshevism in Turkestan, 1917–1927*. New York: Columbia University Press, 1957.
Parsin, Mehmet. "Iashlar arasynda Soltangalicfchelkenen ioqynlysy" (The Influence of Sultangalievism on the Youth). In *Kontrrivolutsion Soltangaliefsheleke Karshy*. Kazan: 1930, pp. 73–76.
Pavlovich, M. "Kolonial'naia i Natsional'naia Politika na II Kongresse III Internatsionala." *Zhizn' Natsional'nostei*, 26 (83), 1920.
———. "S'ezd Narodov Vostoka v Baku i ego znachenie." *Zhizn' Natsional'nostei*, 33 (90): 1920.
———. "Voprosy natsional'noi i kolonial'noi Politiki i III Internatsional." *Zhizn' Natsional'nostei*, 32 (89), 34 (81), 36 (93), 40 (96), 1920.
Pervyi Vsesoiuznyi tiurkologicheskii S'ezd-Stenograficheskii Otchot. Baku: 1926.
Pesikina, E. I. *Narodnyi Komissariat po Delam Natsional'nostei i ego Deiatel'nost' v 1917–1918 gg*. Moscow: 1950.
Pierce, Richard. *Russian Central Asia, 1867–1917: A Study in Colonial Rule*. Berkeley-Los Angeles: University of California Press, 1960.
Pipes, Richard E. "The First Experiment in Soviet National Policy: The Bashkir Republic, 1917–1920." *Russian Review* 10 (1950): 303–19.

————. *The Formation of the Soviet Union, Communism and Nationalism, 1917–1923*. Cambridge: Harvard University Press, 1957.

————. "Muslims of Central Asia: Trends and Prospects." *Middle East Journal* 9 (1955): 147–62, 295–308.

Politika Sovetskoi Vlasti po natsional' nym Delam za tri goda, 1917-IX-1920. Moscow: Narkomnats, 1920.

Poppino, Rollie. *International Communism in Latin America.* London: 1964.

Premier Congres des Peuples de l'Orient, Bakou, 1920—Compte rendu Stenographique. Petrograd: 1921.

Prodokoly Tsentral' nogo Komiteta R.S.D.R.P.—August 1917–Fevral' 1918. Moscow: 1929.

Protiv Sultangalievshchiny i Velikoderzhavnosti, Sbornik. Kazan: 1929.

Quelquejay, Chantal. "Le Vaisisme à Kazan—Contribution à l'Etude des Confréries Musulmanes chez les Tatars de la Volga." *Die Welt des Islams* 6 (1959): 91–113.

Raevskii, A. *Angliiskaia Interventsiia i Musavatskoe Pravitel'stvo.* Baku: 1927.

Raimov, R. "K Istorii Obrazovaniia Bashkirskoi Avtonomnoi Sotsialisticheskoi Sovetskoi Respubliki," *Voprosy istorii* 4 (1948): 23–42.

————. *Obrazovanie Bashkirskoi Avtonomnoi Sotsialisticheskoi Sovetskoi Respubliki.* Moscow: Academy of Science, 1952.

Rakowska-Harmstone, Teresa. *Russia and Nationalism in Central Asia: The Case of Tadzhikistan.* Baltimore: Johns Hopkins University Press, 1966.

Ramiev, Ismail. *Vaqytly Tatar Matbygaty* (Tatar Periodical Press). Kazan: Gashur, 1926.

Rasul Zade, Mehmed Emin. *L'Azerbaidjan en Lutte pour l'Independence.* Paris: 1930.

————. *O Panturanizme v sviazi s Kavkazskoi Problemoi.* Paris: 1930.

Ratgauzer, L. A. *Revoliutsiia i Grazhdanskaia Voina v Baku.* Baku: 1927.

Ravich-Cherkasskii, ed. *Marksizm i natsional' Inyi Vopros—Sbornik statei.* Kharkov: Proletarii, 1923.

Razumov, M. *Leninskaia natsional' naia Politika v rekonstruktivnyi Period.* Kazan: Tatpartizdat, 1933.

Renner, Karl. *Das Selbstbestimmungsrecht des Nationen.* Leipzig: 1918.

Reshetar, J. S. *The Ukrainian Revolution, 1917–1920.* Princeton: 1952.

Reztsov, L. *Oktiabr' v Turkestane.* Tashkent: 1927.

Rodinson, Maxime. *Islam et Capitalisme.* Paris: Seuil, 1966.

————. *Marxisme et Monde Musulman*. Paris: Seuil, 1972.

————. "Problèmatique de L'Etude des Rapports entre l'Islam et le Communisme." *Correspondance d'Orient*. Brussels: 1961, vol. 5.

Rodolsky, R. *Friedrich Engels und das Probleme der "Geschichtlosen Völker."* Hannover: Archiv für Sozialgeschichte, 1964.

Rohrlich, Ayşe-Azade. "Which Way Will Tatar Culture Go? A Controversial Essay by Galimdzhan Ibragimov." *Cahiers du Monde Russe et Sovietique* 15 (1975): 363–71.

Roshal', M. G. "O politicheskom polozhenii v Tatarskoi Respublike v 1920 godu." *Istoricheskii Arkhiv*, vol. 2, 1961.

Roy, M. N. *Memoirs*. Bombay: Allied Publishers Private Ltd., 1964.

Rubinshtein, L. *V Bor' be za leninskuiu natsional' nuiu Politiku*. Kazan: 1930.

Ryskulov, Turar. "Iz Istorii revoliutsionnoi Bor'by v Kazakhstane." *Revoliutsiia i Natsional' nosti* 11 (1935): 36–45.

————. *Kazakhstan*. Moscow: 1927.

————. "Komintern i rabota na Vostoke." *Zhizn' Natsional' nostei*, 40 (96), 1920.

————. "Protiv izvrashcheniia Istorii Kazakhskogo Naroda i Kharaktera Oktiabria v Kazakhstane." *Revoliutsiia i Natsional' nostei* 6 (1936): 62–67.

————. *Revoliutsiia i korennoe Naselenie Turkestana*. Tashkent: 1925.

————. "Sovremennyi Kazakhstan." *Novyi Vostok* 12 (1926): 105–20.

Rywkin, Michael. "Religion, Modern Nationalism and Political Power in Soviet Central Asia." *Canadian Slavonic Papers* 17 (1975): 271–86.

Saadi, Abdurrahman. "Ibragim Galimdzhan i ego literaturnoe tvorchestvo." In *Vestnik Nauchnogo Obshchestva Tatarovedenia*. Kazan: 1928.

————. *Tatar Adabiyaty Tarikhi*. Kazan: 1926.

Safarov, Grigorii. *Kolonial' naia Revoliutsiia—Opyt Turkestana*. Moscow: Gosizdat, 1921.

Saidasheva, M. A. *Lenin i sotsialisticheskoe Stroitel' stvo v Tatarii, 1918–1923*. Moscow: 1969.

Said-Galiev, Sahibgiray. "Koran i Revoliutsiia." *Zhizn' Natsional' nostei*, 5 (61), 1920.

————. "Polozhenie o Tataro-Bashkirskoi Respublike." *Zhizn' Natsional' nostei*, 4 (61), 1920.

Saifi, Fatyh. *Tatar Dini* (The Tatar Religion). Kazan: 1924.

————. "Tatary do Fevral'skoi Revoliutsii." In *Ocherki Izucheniia Mestnogo Kraia*. Kazan: 1930, pp. 192–235.

Samurskii (Efendiev), Najmuddin. *Dagestan*. Moscow: Gosizdat, 1924.

————. *Grazhdanskaia Voina v Dagestane*. Makhatch-Kala: 1925.

―――. "Grazhdanskaia Voina v Dagestane." *Novyi Vostok* 3 (1923): 230–40.

―――. *Itogi i Perespektivy Sovetskoi Vlasti v Dagestane*. Makhatch-Kala: 1927.

―――. "Krasnyi Dagestan!" In *Dagestan*, edited by V. Stavskii. Moscow: 1936.

―――. "Oktiabr'skaia Revoliutsiia i dal'neishie etapy eia razvitiia v Dagestane." *Proletarskaia Revoliutsiia* 33 (1924): 83–104.

Sarkisov, N. *Bor'ba za Vlast'*. Baku: 1930.

Schram, Stuart, and Carrère d'Encausse, Helène. *Le Marxisme et l'Asie*. Paris: A. Colin, Collection U., 1965.

Sef, S. E. *Bor'ba za Oktiabr' v Zakavkaze*. Tiflis: 1932.

―――. *Kak Bol'sheviki prishli k vlasti v 1917–18 gg v Bakinskom raione*. Baku: 1927.

Setton-Watson, Hugh. *The Pattern of Communist Revolution: A Historical Analysis*. London: Methuen, 1953.

Seydamet, J. *La Crimée*. Lausanne: 1921.

Shapiro, Leonard. *The Communist Party of the Soviet Union*. London: 1960.

Shaumian, S. *Bakinskaia Kommuna*. Baku: 1927.

Shorish, Mobin. "Soviet Developmental Strategies in Central Asia." *Canadian Slavonic Papers* 17 (1975): 404–17.

Skalov, G. "Sotsial'naia priroda Basmachestva v Turkestane." *Zhizn' Natsional'nostei*, vols. 3–4, 1923, pp. 51–62.

Soloveichik, D. "Revoliutsionnaia Bukhara." *Novyi Vostok* 2 (1922): 272–88.

Spuler, Bertold. "Die Wolga-Tataren une Baschkiren unter russischer Herrschaft." *Der Islam* 29 (1949): 142–216.

―――. *Idel-Ural*. Berlin: 1942.

Stalin, Iosif. *Marxism and the National Question* (English translation). New York: 1942.

The Stalinist Terror in the Thirties, compiled by Borys Levytsky. Stanford: Hoover Institute, 1974.

Stavrovskii, A. P. *Zakavkaz posle Oktiabria*. Moscow-Leningrad, 1925.

Stenograficheskii Otchet Deviatoi Oblastnoi Konferentsii Tatarskoi Organizatsii R.K.P.(b). Kazan: 1924.

Stenograficheskii Otchet Zasedanii Dvenadtsatoi Oblastnoi Partiinoi Konferentsii. Kazan: 1927.

Sullivant, Robert S. *Soviet Politics and the Ukraine, 1917–1957*. New York: 1962.

Sultan-Galiev, Mir-Said. "Batum i Armeniia." *Zhizn' Natsional'nostei*, 18 (70), 1920.

———. "K Obiavleniu Azerbaidzhanskoi Sovetskoi Respubliki." *Zhizn' Natsional' nostei,* 18 (70), 1920.

———. "Metody antireligioznoi Propagandy sredi Musul'man." *Zhizn' Natsional' nostei,* 29 (127) and 30 (128), 1921; and in pamphlet (Moscow: 1922).

———. "Mustafa Subhi i ego rabota." *Zhizn' Natsional' nostei,* 14 (112), 1921.

———. "O periodicheskoi Literature na tiurkskikh iazykakh." *Zhizn' Natsional' nostei,* 23 (121), 1921.

———. "Otnositel'no periodicheskoi Literatury na tiurkskikh narechiiakh." *Zhizn' Natsional' nostei,* 14 (71) and 15 (72), 1920.

———. "Polozhenie Turtsii v posledee vremia." *Zhizn' Natsional' nostei,* 14 (71)–15 (72), 1920.

———. "Sotsial'naia Revoliutsiia i Vostok." *Zhizn' Natsional' nostei,* 28 (46), 39 (47), and 42 (50), 1919.

———. "Tatarskaia Avtonomnaia Respublika." *Zhizn' Natsional' nostei,* 1 January 1923.

———. "Tatary i Oktiabr'skaia Revoliutsiia." *Zhizn' Natsional' nostei,* 21 (122), 1921.

———. "Vosem'desiat vliatel'nykh Printsev, Sultanov i Potentatov." *Zhizn' Natsional' nostei,* 39 (95), 1920.

Svechnikov, M. *Bor'ba Krasnoi Armii na Severnom Kavkaze—Sentiabr' 1918–Aprel' 1919.* Moscow-Leningrad: 1926.

Syromolotov, F. "Lenin i Stalin v Sozdanii Tataro-Bashkirskoi Respubliki." *Revoliutsiia i Natsional' nosti* 8:15–24.

Takho-Godi, A. A. *Revoliutsiia i Kontrrevoliutsiia v Dagestane.* Makhatch-Kala: Daggosizdat, 1927.

Tarasov, A. "Kontrrevoliutsionnaia Avantiura Tatarskoi Burzhuazii (1918 god)." *Istorik Marksist* 7 (1940): 93–100.

———. *Razgrom Kontrrevoliutsionnoi Avantiury Tatarskoi Burzhuazii v hachale 1918 goda.* Kazan: 1940.

Tatarskaia Sotsialisticheskaia Sovetskaia Respublika za piat' let, 1920–25/ VI-1925. Kazan: 1925.

Temir, Ahmet. "Türklük ve Sovyet Rusya." In *Türk Dünyasï El Kitabi.* Ankara: Türk Kültürü Arastirma Enstitusu, 1976, pp. 1304–16.

Tipeev, Sh. *Iz Istorii natsional'nogo Dvizheniia v Sovetskoi Bashkirii.* Ufa: Bashgiz, 1929.

———. *Millät, Milli Kul'tura* (The Nation and the National Culture). Moscow: 1929.

———. *Ocherki po Istorii Bashkirii.* Ufa: Bashgiz, 1930.

Todorskii, A. *Krasnaia Armiia v Gorakh-Deistviia v Dagestane*. Moscow: 1924.

Toran, Ahmed Zeki Velidi. *Bügünkü Türkili (Türkistan) ve yakïn Tarihi*. Istanbul: Göven Basimevi, 1942–47.

Tokarzhevskii, E. A. *Iz Istorii inostrannoi Interventsii i grazhdanskoi Voiny v Azerbaidzhane*. Baku: 1957.

Tucker, Robert C., and Cohn, Stephen F., eds. *The Great Purge Trial: Transcript of the Moscow Trial of Anti-Soviet Bloc of Rightists and Trotsky-ites, March 1938*. New York: Universal Library, 1965.

Tunaya, Tarik Zafer. *Türkiye'de Siyasî Partiler: 1859–1952*. Istanbul: 1952.

Tunçay, Mete. *Türkiye'de Sol Akïmlar: 1908–1925*. Ankara: 1967.

Tuzmukhamedov, R. A. *Otvet Klevetnikam*. Moscow: 1969.

Ukhanov, A. S. *Sotsialisticheskoe Nastuplenie i Religiia*. Kazan: 1932.

Ulam, Adam. *The Bolsheviks*. New York: 1965.

———. *Titoism and the Cominform*. Cambridge: Harvard University Press, 1952.

Uralov, Alexander [A. Avtorkhanov]. *The Reign of Stalin*. London: 1953.

Uzbekistan i Strany Vostoka. Tashkent: 1975.

Vakhabov, M. *Tashkent v period trekh Revoliutsii*. Tashkent: Uzgosizdat, 1957.

Validov, Jemaleddin. *Ocherki Istorii Obrazovannosti i Literatury Tatar do Revoliutsii 1917 goda*. Moscow: 1923.

Van Ness, Peter. *Revolution and Chinese Foreign Policy: Peking's Support for Wars of National Liberation*. Berkeley–Los Angeles: University of California Press, 1970.

Vasilevskii, K. "Fazy basmacheskogo Dvizheniia v Srednei Asii." *Novyi Vostok* 29 (1930): 126–41.

Verner, I. "Nasha politika v Krymu." *Zhizn' Natsional'nostei*, 10 October 1921.

VKP (b). Tatarskii Oblastnoi Komitet. *V.K.P. (b)-nyng XV-nie Tatarstan Ölke Konfirensiase Otchoty*. Kazan: 1930.

Wheeler, Geoffrey. *The Modern History of Central Asia*. New York–London: F. Praeger, 1964.

———. *The Peoples of Soviet Central Asia*. London: 1966.

———. *Racial Problems in Soviet Central Asia*. New York: 1962.

Wimbush, S. Enders, and Wixman, Ronald. "The Mesketian Turks: A New Voice in Soviet Central Asia." *Canadian Slavonic Papers* 17 (1975): 320–41.

Wolfe, B. D. "The Influence of Early Military Decisions upon the National Structure of the Soviet Union." *American Slavic and East European Review*. 9 (1960): 169–79.

Wurm, Stefan. *Turkic Peoples of the USSR: Their Historical Background, Their Languages and the Development of Soviet Linguistic Policy*. London-Oxford: Central Asian Research Center, 1954.

Yamak, Labib Z. *The Syrian Social National Party: An Ideological Analysis*. Cambridge: Harvard University Press, 1966.

Zabih, Sepehr. *The Communist Movement in Iran*. Berkeley–Los Angeles: University of California Press, 1966.

Zagoria, Donald S. *The Sino-Soviet Conflict, 1956–1961*. Princeton: Princeton University Press, 1962.

Za piat' let—Sbornik. Kazan: 1925.

Za Vlast' Sovetov. Kazan: Tatknigoizdat, 1957.

Zorin, A. N. *Revoliutsionnoe Dvizhenie v Kirgizii (Severnaia Chast') Frunze*. Kirgosizdat: 1931.

Index

Vaisi, 6, 32, 223
Verdi Khan, Khoda, 80, 81
Vernyi. *See* Alma-Ata
Volga Tatars, 11; as "historical"
nation, 4; organizational independence of, 59–62; proletariat
of, 11; as revolutionaries, 43,
55–56, 65

White counterrevolutionary forces:
attitude toward Muslims, 23–24;
inept leadership of, 26; typology
of Muslim support for, 31
Wrangel, Petr Nikolaevich, Baron,
25

Yamashev, Husein, 11, 210

Yeni Dünyä, 78
Yevsektsiia, 15
Young Bukharians, 26, 33, 87,
92, 223–24
Young Turks, 14

Zeki Validov, Ahmed, 24–26, 32,
83, 87, 210–11; and Basmachi,
76; and ERK, 166–67
Zhamdosov, 93
Zhizn' Natsional'nostei, 39, 67;
Dimanshtein in, 75; al-Harizi in,
55; *Social Revolution and the
East*, 52; *Thesis Concerning the
Task of the Proletarian Revolu-
tion in the East*, 54
Zinoviev, Grigorii Evseevich, 8, 57